$ 1 00

Doing Multicultural Education
for Achievement and Equity

Doing Multicultural Education for Achievement and Equity

CARL A. GRANT AND CHRISTINE E. SLEETER

Routledge
Taylor & Francis Group
New York   London

Routledge
Taylor & Francis Group
270 Madison Avenue
New York, NY 10016

Routledge
Taylor & Francis Group
2 Park Square
Milton Park, Abingdon
Oxon OX14 4RN

Printed in the United States of America on acid-free paper
10 9 8 7 6 5 4 3 2 1

International Standard Book Number-10: 0-415-95184-4 (Softcover) 0-415-95183-6 (Hardcover)
International Standard Book Number-13: 978-0-415-95184-5 (Softcover) 978-0-415-95183-8 (Hardcover)

Library of Congress Cataloging-in-Publication Data

Grant, Carl A.
    Doing multicultural education for achievement and equity / Carl A. Grant, Christine Sleeter.
        p. cm.
    ISBN-13: 978-0-415-95183-8 (hb)
    ISBN-13: 978-0-415-95184-5 (pb)
    1. Multicultural education--United States. 2. Educational equalization--United States. 3. Student teachers--Training of--United States. I. Sleeter, Christine E., 1948- II. Title.

LC1099.3.G717 2006
370.117--dc22   2006027419

Visit the Taylor & Francis Web site at
http://www.taylorandfrancis.com

and the Routledge Web site at
http://www.routledge-ny.com

Contents

Preface

No matter where you teach one day, you will have a diversity of students in your classroom. Your students may be racially or ethnically diverse, and very possibly will include immigrants in the process of learning English. Your students will also most likely be both male and female, from diverse social class backgrounds, and varying religious affiliations and academic abilities. They will also probably come from communities that have varying degrees of social power, and varying historical experiences with schools. While some communities have been well served by schools over the years, with other communities the relationships have been much more tenuous. Even if you want to believe that kids are just kids, and that background differences do not matter, you will still interpret your students and their backgrounds, and your interpretations will inform your teaching.

Regardless of your students' backgrounds, identities, or community histories, you can be sure that all of them will depend on you to teach them well, help them achieve, and nurture their growth. This is a huge responsibility and an exciting challenge. The larger society will also have expectations of you, although those expectations will not necessarily be consistent. Is your main responsibility toward society fulfilled by helping students do well on tests, preparing your students to help the United States compete internationally, developing engaged citizens, or breathing life into ideals of equality, freedom, and justice? And what might these ideals and responsibilities actually mean on a day-to-day basis in the classroom? What does it look like to ground teaching in larger ideals, as well as in the aspirations of your students and their communities?

The purpose of *Doing Multicultural Education for Achievement and Equity* is to help you examine these questions. This book aims to help you connect what you bring to the teaching profession, with a vision of high-quality teaching and student achievement, and the quest for equity in school and society. The ideas and concepts we present in this book are grounded in research-based evidence; the suggestions and experiences we recommend build on each other.

Doing Multicultural Education for Achievement and Equity provides a history and rationale for education that is multicultural both in school and the greater society. We see multicultural education as a process of education reform that is rooted in an ethic of human rights. Multicultural education conceptualizes students, their diverse communities, and their cultural backgrounds mainly in terms of their strengths and their use as springboards for learning. Multicultural education examines social institutions, including schools, through a lens of power, questioning who benefits most from policies and taken-for-granted practices, valuing policies and practices that affirm equity and fairness. While no single formula defines equity, fairness, human rights, and cultural strengths, there are developed bodies of thought and conceptual frameworks in which we plan to engage you, as we prod you to think through what teaching might look like in your future classroom.

The book employs self-help and interactive activities to help teacher candidates examine and develop a personal and teaching self. These interactive activities take into account teacher candidates' apprehensions and miseducation about problems and issues surrounding education and social justice in a multicultural society, including the belief that racial and class inequities were solved during their mothers' and grandmothers' generations.

How to Use This Book

Doing Multicultural Education for Achievement and Equity is organized into two parts. The first three chapters examine what we call the teacher–student–society triangle. We start in chapter 1 with you, the prospective teacher. In chapter 2 we consider students, and particularly the idea of student-centered teaching. Chapter 3 steps back to situate schools within a broader societal and institutional context, examining implications of that context for the work of schools.

Chapters 4 through 8 delve into various dimensions of classroom teaching. In chapter 4, we lay a foundation of caring relationships. In chapter 5, we examine building instruction for achievement on diverse students' assets, and doing so in a caring context. Chapter 6 explores curriculum as it relates to diversity, equity, and student learning, offering strategies for designing curriculum plans or modifying those you are expected to follow. Chapter 7 examines testing and assessment of learning in the context of diversity and equity. Finally, chapter 8 takes social ideals beyond the walls of the classroom, exploring their implications for the work of teacher-activists and students as citizens. Because the chapters build on each other, we recommend that you start with chapter 1 and read through the book in a consecutive order, rather than skipping around.

The book is conceptualized and designed to have various ways of talking "with" you. It is organized around 17 Building Blocks, or broad skill areas, that "fantastic teachers" share. These 17 broad skills anchor ideas and connect discussions of multicultural education and achievement across the eight chapters, translating thinking and investigations into implications for your work as a teacher. We use fictional students as a tool for exploring complexities of issues (e.g., race, gender, achievement) and allow them to rephrase issues in ways that teacher candidates commonly articulate them. Because you may be further along with some concepts (e.g., gender) than others (e.g., sexuality), we purposely use a *tone* in this book that is user friendly, respectful, and informal, while at the same time honest and direct. *Reflections* are used throughout the book — boxed pedagogical elements that engage readers with content material by asking questions and offering specific activities related to the text.

Each chapter begins with questions that the chapter will help you examine, followed by a *brief overview* of key concepts that underlie the content, and Building Blocks developed in that chapter. *Boxes* serve as a tool used to provide additional information on a topic being discussed. Figures and tables add to the user-friendly design of the book, and present the material in "manageable chunks." Finally, the end of each chapter offers a "Putting It Into Practice" feature that engages you in using concepts from the chapter in classroom practice.

Instructors may wonder how to connect this book with their course syllabus, other texts, or additional assignments. We recommend that instructors work with all 17 Building Blocks in this book. However, instructors need not feel that all Reflections are mandatory. We have drawn the interactive reflective activities largely from our own practice, but are aware that many instructors have excellent assignments and activities that accomplish similar goals. The Building Blocks can be thought of as the book's key intended learning outcomes; there can be multiple ways of attaining them.

Acknowledgments

We are grateful to the many people who encouraged and prodded us to take on this project. Catherine Bernard, our editor, was highly encouraging and supportive, offering valued critical comments for strengthening the book along the way. Associate editor Angela Chnapko also offered many helpful suggestions. We wish to thank the students in our classes at the University of Wisconsin–Madison and California State University, Monterey Bay, and classroom teachers and other colleagues whose questions about social and instructional issues and teaching challenges guided us as we wrote *Doing Multicultural Education for Achievement and Equity*. A special note of gratitude is offered to Elizabeth Day, Kim Wieczorek, and Kefferlyn Brown for their contributions to "Putting It Into Practice" activities. We acknowledge the helpful suggestions of Kim White, and of the anonymous reviewers. Great appreciation is extended to Karen Boyer for her editorial recommendations. A big thank you goes to Chris Kruger who lent her computer skills to this project.

one
Becoming a Fantastic Teacher

This chapter will help you answer the following questions:

- What kind of teacher do I want to be?
- Why do I want to become a teacher, and how might my reasons affect my professional development and willingness to stay in the teaching profession?
- How does my home and family culture influence my beliefs about teaching?
- How do media, peers, schooling, and religion influence me and my beliefs about teaching?
- Why do I need to develop a philosophy for good multicultural teaching?

When we (Carl and Christine) entered teaching, our goal was not just to be good or excellent teachers, but *fantastic* teachers! We wanted to be the kind of teachers whom students appreciated, who pushed students to achieve at their highest level, who made learning engaging, and who truly cared about and stood up for the best interests of their students. Most teachers and teacher candidates whom we meet have the same goals.

But what does it mean to be a fantastic teacher? In particular, what does this mean given the wide diversity of students in schools today, and how does one become a fantastic teacher?

Beginning in this chapter and throughout the book, we will engage you in examining what it means to teach in a diverse society, as well as discussing your personal and professional growth, especially your knowledge, skills, and attitudes, the foundation on which fantastic teaching is built. This book is organized around 17 Building Blocks for excellent teaching of diverse students. In this chapter, we will take up the first two building blocks:

Building Block 1: Critically Examining Yourself
Building Block 2: Developing a Philosophy for Good Multicultural Teaching

You will also, from time to time, be asked to share your thoughts with your classmates. The purpose of doing this is not to determine who is right, but rather to explore the reasoning behind your thinking and to become better acquainted with the experiences and viewpoints of others.

This chapter has three sections. The first section asks you to reflect on the kind of teacher you wish to become and the reasons you wish to teach. The second section prompts you to examine socializing forces that influence you and your perspectives. The third section discusses developing a philosophy for good multicultural teaching. Finally, we present a teacher-candidate challenge to help you put into practice ideas you have learned in the chapter. Let's begin the first section with your conception of yourself as a fantastic teacher.

Fantastic Me!

As you experience your professional preparation, many people will communicate to you their image of a fantastic teacher. Through publicly stated declarations, ways and means of operating, and course content and expectations, your teacher education program is informing you of its vision of the qualities you and your classmates should develop in order to become fantastic teachers. Many of the various people you interact with throughout your training will have an opinion of what makes a teacher fantastic. Your professors and the classroom teachers you work with during your field experiences will offer cogent insights about teaching skills and attitudes. Articles and books on teaching will cause you to rethink some of your ideas. The students in grades kindergarten through high school, whom you will meet during your fieldwork and student teaching, will have a lot to say about the qualities and attitudes of a fantastic teacher. Further, students will tell you, both verbally and through their actions, if your lessons are fun and engaging, and whether you have a caring and pleasant attitude. Your students' parents and community members might even share their opinions on what makes a teacher fantastic. Your classmates will also surely have something to say about qualities of a fantastic teacher based on their experiences with school. If you listen closely to classmates who come from racial, social class, or language backgrounds different from your own, you might hear various qualities emphasized that you hadn't previously considered.

However, of all the helpful informants, the most significant one is you. It is *you* and what *you* bring — the knowledge, skills, and attitudes you already possess, as well as how you think about and act on "becoming" a teacher — that will influence the kind of teacher you become. Your attention to professional growth and self-discovery is critical at this time in our nation's history. Today, teachers are asked to do much of the work of closing not one, but two sets of achievement gaps. The first set exists between demographic groups within the United States. This includes average achievement gaps between middle-class and lower-class students, and between White and Asian-American students, and African-American, Latino, and Native-American students. The second achievement gap exists (on the average) between U.S. students and students in some Asian and European countries. The Program for International Student Assessment reports that the United States ranked 24th out of 29 nations in math literacy (Cavanagh & Robelen, 2004). And, according to the Organization for Economic Cooperation and Development (2004), the United States, which once had the largest percentage of students graduating from college, is now second (38%) behind Canada (43.5%). Closing both sets of achievement gaps will require that all American students — regardless of race, ethnicity, social class, income, language, or geographic location — be taught in high-quality schools by fantastic teachers who will encourage and help them to achieve. Failure to do so will further exacerbate racial and social class divisions in the United States.

Teachers alone cannot make up for unequally distributed educational resources such as adequate school buildings and teaching resources, or life concerns such as hunger and disease due to poverty, or insecure lives due to parental joblessness and unaffordable housing. However, teachers matter significantly to the quality of education children receive, regardless of their background. According to the National Commission on Teaching and America's Future (1996), "What teachers know and do is the most important influence on what students learn" (p. 6). Haycock (2001) points to research showing that students of all backgrounds learn most from teachers who know their subject matter well, hold high expectations, and are able to engage students. Referring to a study in Boston, Haycock remarks that, "In one academic year, the top third of teachers produced as much as six times the learning growth as the bottom third of teachers" (p. 10).

You will probably hear quite a bit about federal requirements that all classrooms be staffed by "highly qualified" teachers. At an abstract level, probably no one would disagree with this idea. But what does it mean in reality? In brief, federal policy requires that schools staff classrooms with teachers who have earned a teaching certificate, and that they are assigned to teach subject matter for which they have state-approved degrees. This requirement is intended to address the problem of schools — particularly in low-income communities — hiring teachers with emergency credentials (i.e., not having completed teacher certification), and assigning teachers to teach subject matter outside their area of expertise, particularly at the secondary level.

We fully support the value of teachers having a deep knowledge of the subject matter they have been hired to teach. Indeed, it's almost impossible to delve into ideas or concepts, and to make them meaningful for young people, without knowing them very well oneself. But this conception of "highly qualified teachers" sets a fairly low bar, because it does not consider professional knowledge and teaching skill that enable teachers to connect subject matter with students.

This book will engage you with our vision of what fantastic teachers do, reflected in the book's 17 Building Blocks. In our view, fantastic teachers do the following:

- Critically analyze themselves (Building Block 1) in order to develop a philosophy for good multicultural teaching (Building Block 2), and to set professional learning goals for themselves (Building Block 5);
- Become well acquainted with students (Building Block 3) in order to construct student-centered teaching that prompts student learning;
- Discern fact from fantasy regarding societal and educational gaps (Building Block 4) in order to work toward significant equity goals;
- Build relationships in caring classrooms through conflict resolution (Building Block 6), addressing prejudice and stereotyping (Building Block 7), and focusing on cooperative learning (Building Block 8);
- Facilitate high achievement by making students' interests and background a focal point in teaching (Building Block 9), using students' learning styles when planning instruction (Building Block 10), making students' language a valuable learning resource (Building Block 11), and connecting with parents and the community (Building Block 12);
- Plan curriculum in a way that develops concepts from multicultural perspectives (Building Block 13), and uses quality multicultural teaching resources (Building Block 14);
- Use authentic assessment as a tool to evaluate student learning (Building Block 15); and
- Take action in the classroom and beyond by developing students' critical consciousness (Building Block 16) and building democratic participation (Building Block 17).

Several authors highlight the journey one makes in becoming a teacher. Carl Rogers (1961), the noted psychologist, argues in *On Becoming a Person* that human beings *become* through a process of personal growth and self-discovery. Parker Palmer (1998), in *The Courage to Teach,* observes, "[Seldom,] if ever do we ask the "*who*" question — who is the self that teaches?" (p. 4). He encourages teachers to ask questions such as these: "How does the quality of my selfhood form — or deform — the way I relate to my students, my subject, my colleagues, my world?" and "How can educational institutions sustain and deepen the selfhood from which good teaching comes?" (p. 4).

Building Block 1: Critically Examining Yourself

Let's start the self-discovery with your vision of a fantastic teacher. In Reflection 1.1, use words or pictures to describe your vision of the teacher you want to become.

Reflection 1.1
My vision of myself as a fantastic teacher

Discuss your vision both with a classmate and with an experienced teacher. Keep your vision and the discussion in mind as we proceed through this chapter. We will ask you to revisit what you wrote or drew toward the end of the chapter.

The remainder of this chapter will engage you in some critical reflection about experiences and beliefs that you bring to your teacher training, and particularly those that may impact on how you view diverse students and diversity issues related to schooling. We will begin by examining what has drawn you to the teaching profession, looking at some of the implications of those reasons for your professional development. We will then examine socialization factors that impact your beliefs, and implications for professional development. Following that, you will begin to work on a philosophy of education, which will become an ongoing guide to decisions you make regarding the daily work of teaching. After meeting some fictitious student colleagues, who will join you as you move through this book, you will have an opportunity to try out your creative thinking as you apply your beginning philosophy of education to a teacher-candidate challenge.

Exploring Reasons You Want to Teach

When asked why they want to teach, many teacher candidates reply: "I want to teach because I love kids," and "I want to teach because I want to help students academically and socially." These are powerful statements that have implications for teaching. "Love" suggests a very strong emotion, and implies a personal declaration: that you will be there for all students. Your declaration would be akin to the one made by Pedro Noguera (2003) who stated, "I fundamentally believe that educating all children, even those who are poor and non-white, is an achievable goal, *if* we truly value all children. Of course, that is the real question: Does American society truly value all of its children?" (p. 25).

The second reason teacher candidates give for wanting to teach, "to help students," also implies responsibility. "Help," according to *Webster's Dictionary* (1989), means "to give assistance or support to" (p. 450). This implies knowing what kind of assistance or support is beneficial to one's students — what temporary aid enables each one to move forward in his or her learning.

You may have an additional word or phrase that represents another reason for wanting to teach. In Reflection 1.2, list reasons for wanting to become a teacher, and describe what they mean to you.

The most frequently cited reasons given by teacher candidates for why they want to become teachers imply what the person hopes to *gain* from a teaching career. For example, if you want to teach because you love children, it is likely that you are focusing on what you anticipate getting from being with children, namely, the satisfaction of giving and receiving love. Similarly, you might be seeking personal satisfaction when you see students learn and grow due to your help.

But *love* and *help* do not necessarily last, and will not, in and of themselves, sustain a commitment to doing the hard work involved in teaching. The emotion or commitment may dissipate, and the desire to help may wane. Over one third of teachers leave the profession within the first five years. Surprisingly, for a group of people who enter the profession because of their commitment and passion, they leave at a higher rate than individuals in any other profession (Ingersoll, 2001).

Let us explore more fully what you hope to gain from teaching in relationship to why new teachers often leave the profession, and then we will return to what you wrote in Reflection 1.2. The teaching profession has always experienced its share of job turnover. In past decades teaching was seen as a stepping-stone profession. Teachers would teach for a few years until they earned enough money to go to law, medical, or business school. Or, a wife might teach to put her husband though graduate school and go on to other work when that goal was accomplished. Today, according to Ingersoll and Smith (2003), 39% of those who leave the profession do so to raise their children or because of family moves.

But half of the teachers leave due to dissatisfaction deriving from lack of support from school administration, lack of teacher influence over the decision-making process, student discipline problems, lack of student motivation, and lack of intrinsic rewards. Note how these reasons for leaving parallel reasons teacher candidates often give for wanting to enter the teaching profession. Early in their careers, teachers who anticipate giving and receiving love may find themselves having difficulty forming relationships with some, even many, of their students, particularly while they are simultaneously attempting to establish classroom rules and disciplinary processes. Teachers who anticipate finding satisfaction watching students learn as a result of their help may become frustrated when they find that in reality they do not know how to help the students they have, or feel they are being pressured into using curricular packages or test preparation strategies that conflict with their beliefs about teaching and learning. Although we don't want to scare you, it is important to note patterns in teacher attrition early on so that you can reflect on ways to sustain your desire to teach throughout your development and career.

Much dissatisfaction with teaching can be curtailed if teachers have a greater understanding of life in different schools, their teaching self, and how their students' identities and their own identity — including identities rooted in race, ethnicity, class, gender, sexual orientation, religion, or disability — influence teaching and classroom life. These understandings are reflected in reasons why teachers stay in teaching, especially those who stay in challenging and demanding schools. For example, Sonia Nieto (2003) worked with a group of seven urban teachers in Boston to think through what keeps teachers going. Several factors emerged.

Box 1.1

When teachers leave their school, not only does it affect the class the teacher has been working with, it also affects the esprit de corps and teaching rhythm of the entire school, and the quality of the school's performance. By this we mean that it can take months, if not years, for a school and its teachers to establish solid connections between home and school, and for the school and community to develop a trusting relationship. Whereas the hope is to establish good long-term relations between institutions — home and school — the lynch pin to good relationships are the people involved and the trust they forge with one another over the years.

High turnover also impedes teachers from getting to know one another, which in turn interferes with the professional growth that takes place when they work as a team, and lessens the rewards students reap because of these quality relationships. For example, when the same first-grade teachers work with the same kindergarten teachers over a period of years, they develop an understanding of what the students have learned and how the students are taught. Also, it is easier for teachers who know one another to pass on information about students' interests and other details that will be helpful to their learning.

Those who remained in the teaching profession had been involved in movements for justice, such as civil rights or bilingual education. Their experience in working for a better world had helped to convince them that education was central to improving life, and gave them sustenance to persist. The teachers expressed love for their students, which meant "a combination of trust, confidence, and faith in students and a deep admiration for their strengths." Love also meant affirming the identities of their students, particularly those from nonmainstream backgrounds. The teachers maintained a sense of hope and possibility, even when things got rough. At the same time, they felt a deep sense of anger toward the injustices many of their students had to experience, such as poverty, racism, and school policies that punish rather than support students. Anger and hope were flip sides of each other: Teachers saw much about the lives of young people that was harmful, but hoped that they could make a difference, supported by their involvement in social movements that had demonstrated the possibility of social change. It is important to emphasize that the teachers believed in their students, including those from impoverished and even desperate circumstances, attributing students' problems to injustices that could be addressed. They were committed to democracy and to the potential for helping young people learn to advocate for themselves, believing that ordinary people have ability to shape the future, and they invested in the long-term work entailed in that belief. Finally, the teachers were nourished by the intellectual work that can accompany teaching. They went into the teaching profession because they were intellectually alive, and thrived on conversations and explorations into real problems that they were able to have with colleagues.

Let us now revisit your reasons for wanting to enter the teaching profession. In Reflection 1.3, explore your reasons in terms of what you believe will and will not sustain you. In other words, will love and wanting to help students sustain you when you need to be tough with students? When students are from backgrounds different from your own? When you feel intimidated by some of your students? When students' parents express care in ways that are different from the way you are accustomed to?

As Nieto's teachers illustrated, it is important to weave through your reasons for going into teaching an appreciation of the diversity of students, and a willingness to learn to

Reflection 1.3
What will sustain me?

Reason for entering teaching	will sustain me if...	won't sustain me if...
Loving children...		
Wanting to help students...		
Another reason I want to teach includes...		

build equity in the context of diversity. By equity, we mean distributing the personal and professional tools and supports for learning in such a way that all of one's students benefit. Doing this does not necessarily mean treating all students the same. Darling-Hammond, Wise, and Klein (1997) tell us:

> If all children are to be effectively taught, teachers must be prepared to address the substantial diversity in experiences children bring with them to school — the wide range of language, cultures, exceptionalities, learning styles, talents, and intelligences that in turn require an equally rich and varied repertoire of teaching strategies. In addition, teaching for universal learning demands a highly-developed ability to discover what children know and can do, as well as how they think and how they learn, and to match learning and performance opportunities to the needs of individual children. (p. 2)

We believe that Darling-Hammond et al.'s observation provides an excellent characterization of *love* and *help*.

In Reflection 1.4, compare and contrast their statement with your statement (Reflection 1.2) on *love* and *help*. As you reflect on differences between your initial statement and the one by Darling-Hammond et al., can you identify some things you might need to learn in order to sustain your motivation to persist in teaching? Since teaching is a difficult and demanding profession — particularly in schools in poor communities or serving very diverse populations — it is important to immerse yourself in its challenges from the beginning, and seek help in learning to navigate those challenges while keeping students' learning as your main goal. Subsequent chapters in this book are designed to help you confront and reflect on many of those challenges.

Reflection 1.4
Love and help reexamined

Similarities between the statements   Differences between the statements

---

Your World: The Identity and Culture You Bring

The sense you make of students and the work of teaching is filtered through your cultural lenses: the beliefs, assumptions, and experiences you bring to the classroom. It is impossible, in fact, to understand other people without first understanding yourself and how your perspective shapes how you interpret others.

You may not think of yourself as having cultural lenses, or be able to describe yourself in terms of culture. According to Goodenough (1976), culture consists of "the concepts, beliefs, and principles of action and organization that … could be attributed successfully to the members of that society" (p. 5). By this, he was referring to all of the knowledge and principles that guide behavior, shared by members of a community. Similarly, Nussbaum (1997) described culture as "intelligent attempts to make a viable existence for human beings in the midst of the very considerable limitations that are endemic to human life" (p. 138). All of us learn behavior patterns, beliefs, language, and ways of making sense of the world in the context of webs of human relationships in which we participate and with which we identify.

Teacher candidates, like everyone, acquire culture while growing up within several significant socializing contexts, which include the family, media and advertisements, peers/friends, school, and religion, illustrated in Figure 1.1.

In the middle of Figure 1.1 are socially significant forms of human difference: race/ethnicity, sexuality, social class background, religion, and (dis)ability. These are obviously not the only forms of human difference, nor always the most significant forms, but they are generally significant enough that they form the basis for this book. These forms of difference act on people through social relations and webs of power in the larger society, and through the identities people internalize in the context of others who are similar to themselves. But socialization does not take place in the abstract in

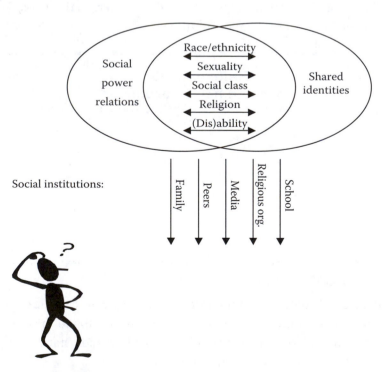

FIGURE 1.1 Teachers and students' socializing forces

relationship to these forms of difference, but rather through core social institutions, which include family, peers, religion, media, and school.

Let's begin by exploring the identity and culture you bring to teaching from your family. Reflection 1.5 asks you to consider one dimension of family life — how decisions are made — then reflect on its implications for the work of a teacher. For example, did one person make the most important decisions? Did the family discuss options and vote? Did children participate in decision making, or were decisions made mainly by adults? Were community elders consulted regarding significant decisions?

To what extent do patterns you learned in the family suggest what you believe are the best kinds of decision-making patterns in the classroom? It is important to reflect on this question because, while you may not encounter conflicts of expectations when your students come from homes similar to your own, such conflicts may arise when your students are from a background that is different from your own. For example, depending on how you grew up, you might assume that everyone should vote on major decisions, but find yourself in a context in which the students do not expect to participate in decision making, and therefore resist your efforts to involve them. You then need to decide whether to teach them a new pattern, or adapt your expectations to fit what is comfortable for them.

Now that you have an idea of how to think about the culture of your family upbringing and its relationship to schooling, complete Reflection 1.6 on the next page to help you recall and describe your home and family culture.

Compare the description of your home and family culture with a classmate's experience. In what ways were they similar, in what ways different? What implications do the ways of living you learned at home have for your expectations of classroom life? What are your assumptions about family life? What has been your preparation for understanding family patterns that differ from those you grew up with?

Reflection 1.5
Family decision-making patterns

Write a description of the way in which decisions were usually made within your family, regarding matters affecting the family as a whole. Give an example.

How might your experiences with this pattern of decision making affect your beliefs about the ways that decisions should be made in other settings, including classrooms?

Now let's consider the schools you attended. You have spent at least 15 years in school, so you already know quite a bit about what schooling is like. But that knowledge can get in the way of considering new ideas. Reflection 1.7 asks you to write a description of schools in which you were a student, reflecting on who was in the school, relationships among students and teachers in the school, and the way teaching and learning were constructed there.

Throughout this book as well as your teacher education program, you will probably be challenged to think about teaching somewhat differently from how you have experienced it. Further, you will be challenged to consider school experiences of people who are different from yourself, and who have experienced schooling differently from you. Reflecting on your own experiences will help you realize why some approaches to teaching "make sense" to you and others do not, and help you identify new experiences that can broaden your understanding. You may feel that this is an interesting challenge, or you may find it intimidating. Recently when one of us asked new teachers to reflect on their school experiences, one teacher who had grown up in a White middle-class town was concerned that her experiences were too limited to share with classmates. It is helpful to realize that everyone brings useful experiences to teacher education, and everyone's experiences include riches as well as limitations.

The self-study in Reflection 1.8 will help you to assess additional dimensions of your prior socialization.

Reflection 1.7
Your school experiences

For each school you attended, write a description that addresses the following:

1. What was the racial/ethnic and social class composition of the student body? To what extent did the school facilitate you becoming familiar with people who differ from yourself racially, ethnically, and by social class?

2. Were there students with disabilities in your classes? To what extent did you get to know them? To what extent did you get to know the points of view held by people with disabilities *about* ability/disability matters, including school matters?

3. What kinds of children or youth were designated as "smart" or high achievers? What kinds were designated as low achievers? In what ways were they designated (for example, by being grouped in classrooms)?

4. Describe a typical day of instruction in the classroom. To what extent might you have learned to view that typical day as "normal" teaching?

Reflection 1.8
A quick self-study

Read the following 15 statements and put a check beside any item(s) that you agree with.

_____ 1. The community where my family lived when I was growing up was made up mostly of people who looked like me and who were of the same socioeconomic class.

_____ 2. When I am able to splurge on a magazine or two, they are fashion or beauty magazines.

_____ 3. If I had or would have had a teacher who was gay, I would have had no problem with that.

_____ 4. My desire to be slim and trim is as much for beauty and sex appeal as it is for my good health and physical fitness.

_____ 5. My pre/K–12 education was in schools that had only a limited amount (1–10%) of racial desegregation.

_____ 6. While growing up, I was actively encouraged to become fluent in two languages.

_____ 7. While I was growing up, I interacted with people and in communities different from the community and neighborhood in which I lived and grew up.

_____ 8. I have had a quality friendship with a person from a different religious group.

_____ 9. When I was in middle and high school, and continuing now into college, much of the time I was (am) brand conscious (e.g., Gap, Nike) when selecting clothes and other items.

_____ 10. When I have a personal problem (not involving money) I discuss it with my friends before my family members.

_____ 11. I have had more than one teacher from a racial group different from my own.

_____ 12. The curriculum in the schools I attended was rich with the history and contribution of White women and women of color.

_____ 13. In school and socially when I hear someone make negative comments about gays, lesbians, or transgendered people I take issue with their statements.

_____ 14. Most of the books and articles that I read for pleasure are about White, native English-speaking, heterosexual people.

_____ 15. My parents would disapprove if my special friend (e.g., boyfriend, girlfriend, partner) is of a racial and religious group different from our own.

What is your assessment of how your socializing forces are influencing you?

not at all _____ somewhat _____ a great deal _____

If you checked "not at all," ask yourself if you have ever attributed someone else's behavior or values to the way the person grew up. You may not be aware of it, but most likely other people have made the same attribution about you.

If you checked "somewhat" or "a great deal," you may wish to see if there are patterns to your responses. How are your responses influenced by your multiple identities that connect to your race, ethnicity, primary language, social class background, gender, sexuality, and religion? For example: question 1 addresses the race, ethnicity, and social class of families; question 2 addresses media/advertisements; question 3 addresses school and sexuality.

In addition, if you are concluding that this assessment is also informing you about your multicultural educational knowledge, particularly your perspectives and beliefs about multiple forms of human differences, you are correct. Family, community, peers, and media are influenced by identities that relate to race, ethnicity, language, gender, social class, sexuality, (dis)ability, and religion. By this we mean that access, opportunity, equal treatment, and inclusion are often strongly affected by one's identity and by forms of discrimination connected with identity and personal characteristics. For example, in the United States your family's access to the neighborhood where you grew up and your opportunity to attend the high school you did were very much based on race and socioeconomic status.

Drawing on your experiences in the various contexts we have been considering, you have shaped a personal identity or sense of who you are. Identity can be understood as a narrative a person constructs about herself or himself, in relationship to other people and to social situations. The narrative we construct about ourselves describes the kind of person we are, and the kinds of people affiliated with us. For example, your friends affect not only your beliefs and values, but also the way you understand the kind of person you are, and are not. You might see yourself as a "surfer," a "computer geek," an athlete, or someone who likes to have a lot of fun, these being identities you share with friends. The people you interact with and the beliefs you hold are reinforced by your sense of who you are, and the "kind" of people who are like you.

Multicultural teaching can be challenging when it forces you to step outside your comfort zone, and to act in ways that may differ from who you see yourself as being. For example, a teacher who grew up in a family that has worked to become middle class, and identifies as middle class, may find it very difficult to be asked to interact respectfully with people who are poor, because they represent what the now-middle-class family deliberately left behind: "They" are not "us."

Many heterosexual teachers find it very difficult to respect people who are gay, and wonder why gay people seem to be obsessed with sex. Beneath this difficulty often lies fear that if one affirms homosexuality, other heterosexual people will think one is gay. Thus, rather than risk one's own identity and other people's understanding of that identity, many heterosexual people avoid learning about gay issues and perspectives.

```
┌─────────────────────────────────────────────────────────────┐
│                        Reflection 1.9                        │
│                      Affiliation groups                      │
│  1.                                                          │
│                                                              │
│  2.                                                          │
│                                                              │
│  3.                                                          │
│                                                              │
│  4.                                                          │
│                                                              │
│  5.                                                          │
└─────────────────────────────────────────────────────────────┘
```

For Reflection 1.9, list five groups or "kinds" of people you affiliate with. Then reflect on how you think about people who are not part of this affiliation group, and how your thoughts or feelings might affect your ability to see school or social issues from the point of view of members of groups who are outside your affiliation or reference group.

Now, let's consider how a person's socializing forces and multiple identities might influence his or her thoughts on some big issues in today's society such as marriage, abortion, and terrorism. Table 1.1 illustrates connections between these socializing forces and three issues: marriage, abortion, and bilingualism.

For Reflection 1.10, on the next page, apply the kind of analysis shown in Table 1.1 to your beliefs about an issue related to teaching, schooling, or working with young people.

These last few reflections have enabled you to look at the sources of your beliefs and perspectives, and factors that are likely to reinforce them. We have also asked you to consider how your beliefs might affect your thinking about teaching, learning, students, and their parents. You may be feeling that some of our questions are personal and have no relationship to schooling. But consider the fact that in school, other people's children will surround you for six or eight hours per day, and their parents will be entrusting you with the responsibility of helping their children learn and grow. Teaching by its very nature is highly interpersonal. Teachers who know themselves well are in a much better position than teachers who do not know themselves well, to treat students and their families with respect and fairness. If you know why you react to different people the way you do, you have some control over your reactions and can learn to modify them, question them, or grow beyond your present boundaries. If you do not know why you react as you do, interpersonal differences can lead to frustration and conflict.

Now that you have taken a beginning look at yourself and the contexts in which your beliefs and assumptions about diversity and schooling have formed, we will shift toward starting to develop your philosophy for good multicultural teaching. We have chosen philosophy as the first building block of multicultural teaching because whatever you

TABLE 1.1 Connection between socializing forces and beliefs

Marriage	Abortion	Bilingualism
Family plays a major role in whom one marries and how one understands what marriage is	Family values influence your attitude about abortion	Family provides the unit and primary relationships through which language is first learned
Media and ads influence the protocol and the decorations of a wedding, as well as beliefs about marriage itself	Media provide debates and commentary that may influence what you come to believe	Media show which language has most power, status, and prestige, and may also show stereotyped images of speakers of other languages.
Peer support influences how one thinks about whether to marry, and prospective partner	Discussions with peers may formalize ideas about abortion	Peers reinforce which language(s) have most value
The amount of schooling you have will probably influence whom you marry	Pro and con discussion in school may help form an opinion on abortion	School teaches which language(s) have value by using language; also models extent to which sophisticated thinking occurs in which languages
Your religion may influence your beliefs about who can marry, what marriage is, and the type of wedding you plan	Your religion may influence your beliefs about abortion	Your religion may offer a way to think about the value of diverse languages

---

Reflection 1.10
Connection between your socializing forces and your beliefs

Select an issue related to schooling, teaching, or working with young people, and jot down some main points that describe how you think about that issue:

Describe how each of the following impacts on your beliefs:
Family:

Media:

Peers:

Schooling:

Religion:

do in the classroom will be filtered through your beliefs. By making them explicit, you can begin to identify areas in which to grow, assumptions and beliefs you might rethink, and commitments that you hold strongly.

Building Block 2: Developing a Philosophy for Good Multicultural Teaching

Ask the next fantastic teacher you meet: "What is your educational philosophy?" Also ask, "Has your philosophy changed over the years you have been teaching?" Initially, the teacher may be surprised by the question, because these questions are not often asked of teachers once they have finished college and have taken their first teaching position. More than likely, the teacher will spell out her or his philosophy, because good teachers have developed one. As you listen, you will notice that the teacher's philosophy is not static. It is alive and vibrant, and reflects constant growth, development, and refinement.

Many teachers begin developing and using their philosophy early in their teaching careers once they learn that "philosophy" is not something left to old men with long beards. Philosophy is, as some explain, a "love of wisdom" (Robinson & Groves, 1999). But also, it is an activity, a way of thinking logically about big and little questions that concern humankind (Duck, 1981). Philosophy can be a hunt for knowledge about questions as profound as: "What is the meaning of life?"; "What is truth?"; "What is knowledge?"; "What is happiness?"; "What is causality and reality?"; "What is art and beauty?"; "What is right and what is wrong?" (Robinson & Groves, 1999).

Philosophy is also a hunt for how we ground answers to questions that deal with daily behavior and activities: "Why do I do as I do?"; "Why do I believe as I do?"; and "How should I raise my kids?" In addition, philosophy is an analytical tool to help professionals such as scientists, politicians, and teachers to examine ethical problems and issues that are challenging them. Furthermore, philosophy guides one's thinking about what one believes "should" happen based on assumptions about human nature and society. For teachers, an educational philosophy serves as a tool that clarifies what a "fantastic teacher" is, what it means to achieve, and what all of this has to do with diversity.

Garforth (1964) suggests four ways that philosophy will help you become a good teacher. First, philosophy brings new interpretations to old problems, and helps in analyzing, refining, and modifying existing concepts and procedures. For example, feminist philosophy brought new and different interpretations and syntheses to issues in history, psychology, economics, and other disciplines by thinking these issues through from the vantage point of women rather than men. As feminist scholar Dale Spender (1982) explained, "Our problem had not been perceived as a problem; it was the recognition that we simply did not exist within the disciplines that women's studies was born: once we had come to accept that we were not included in the knowledge made by men, we also accepted that if we want knowledge, from the perspective of women's existence, we would have to make it ourselves" (p. 14).

In the 19th century, abolitionist and freed slave Sojourner Truth spoke the following line in her "Ain't I a Woman" speech: "Look at me! Look at my arm…! I have plowed, and planted, and gathered into barns, and no man could head me — and ain't I a woman?" Some would argue that Sojourner Truth was using a Black feminist philosophy to challenge the way White men and women perceived Black women.

In Reflection 1.11, discuss either Dale Spender's or Sojourner Truth's new interpretation of old ways of conducting business.

A second way that philosophy will help you become a good teacher, according to Garforth (1964), is that it acts as a clearinghouse not only for evaluating traditional knowledge, but also for analyzing and clarifying problems as yet unsolved — problems whose nature is still unclear and whose solution is not yet seen. A philosophy can help the scientist, the theologian, or the educator to see her or his way more clearly, to ask the right questions, and to avoid pursuing false trails or being misled into error by confused concepts or faulty arguments. In other words, with philosophy, teachers have a tool for assessing and responding to circumstances and events that occur throughout the school day, and a guide for setting up classroom processes that the students and teacher will follow throughout the school year. For example, although each school has discipline policies and procedures which are established by the school district and school, a teacher's philosophy will help to determine the day-to-day processes the teacher and students will use in implementing the school's broad policies. A teacher may decide to adopt a very teacher-centered model, or she or he may prefer a student-centered model in which students help set classroom rules and collaborate to solve discipline problems. The particular model of discipline the teacher chooses depends partially on her or his philosophy of education.

Third, philosophy offers a source of ethical guidance; it is useful in helping to make practical decisions about right and wrong, and what one ought to do. It can help to explain the meaning of terms like good and evil; it can point to alternative choices within a situation and suggest the possible consequences of one choice or another. Thus it helps to ensure that moral decisions are based on good evidence and sound reason-

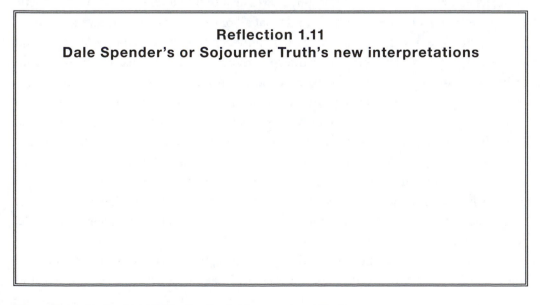

Reflection 1.11
Dale Spender's or Sojourner Truth's new interpretations

ing. What follows in Table 1.2 is an example of a discussion between two feminist high school teachers of health regarding their personal view about *Roe v. Wade*, which is being discussed by many female students. As you can see from the example, the two teachers used different priorities to define what feminist philosophy means and how abortion should be thought through.

A fourth way philosophy will help you become a good teacher is by helping you hone your reflective habits of mind. In this way you will develop the habit of asking why one policy or process is better than another, rather than simply accepting what you are told or assume to be true. Garforth (1964) states, "Philosophy induces valuable habits of mind, like tolerance, impartiality and suspension of judgment; it protects against precipitancy of both assent and dissent; it encourages a resolute aversion to all forms of intellectual shoddiness; it brings, too, a serenity which springs from insights into acceptance of the situation as it is" (p. 92). Philosophy may help one to take a more tolerant view of others' ideas because it helps to provide a process for suspending judgment and looking at more than one perspective. Also, philosophy provides a way of analyzing and critiquing what is being said, as well as guiding the construction of a response. In other words, philosophy helps a teacher to examine policies and procedures rationally and then determine how to meet both the needs of the students and the demands placed on teachers.

Finally, philosophy is the search for wisdom, truth, and knowledge regarding the universe or humankind. A philosophy of education asks questions related directly to education, such as: What is the nature of children? What is the nature of learning? Whose interests are being served? What knowledge and whose knowledge should schools teach? For example, as teachers work with students from diverse language backgrounds, they construct notions and contemplate questions about the nature of children and language. How does language relate to learning? Of what value to the student and society is fluency in more than one language? Teachers who ask such questions may come to believe

TABLE 1.2 Differences in philosophy

Teacher 1: I support much of the feminist philosophy. I believe in equal rights for women. However, I am not in agreement with feminists who believe in prochoice. I do not accept the reasoning of prochoice advocates because I believe that, based upon medical and religious evidence, the fetus is a "person." Also, I contend that because of my religious beliefs — not that I adhere to all of the Catholic Church's doctrine — abortion is not right because, if the fetus is a person, then aborting it entails killing a person. I am not saying that people who believe in abortion are evil and people who don't are good. It's just that I believe our society should support life.

Teacher 2: This is interesting. Your philosophy allows you to accept some feminist ideas, and reject others. You are using the tools of feminist philosophy — comparing, critiquing, and searching for alternative choices — to forge your own particular idea of feminist philosophy. Although I disagree with your stand on abortion, I see that you are using what you believe to be good evidence and sound reasoning. However, we differ because I believe medicine doesn't define what is or what is not a human being or who, other than the woman herself, should control a woman's body.

that not only are students with two languages at an advantage in certain learning and social opportunities, but that such students are also capable of maintaining and developing both languages as they do their schoolwork. As teachers contemplate these kinds of issues, they may ask whose interest is being served with the promotion of "English only." Such inquiry will probably lead teachers to be more successful with a wider diversity of children, especially those who are not achieving well in school.

Now that you have read more about the purpose of educational philosophy, we would like you to begin to reflect upon your own philosophy of education. Although it may seem early to begin doing so, we believe that it is important for you to consider your current knowledge, ideas, and beliefs. You already have a notion of the purpose of schooling and what fantastic teachers are like, otherwise, you wouldn't be pursing a career in teaching!

Reflection 1.12 provides an opportunity for you to work on your educational philosophy. It is important to realize that there is no one right answer for these questions. What matters is how deeply you consider the basis on which your answers rest, and their implications for teaching.

You now have the beginnings of an education philosophy. As you work through this book and your teacher education program, you will be asked to think more specifically about how you see the nature of young people, the learning process, and the most important matters to learn about and teach. You will also be challenged to consider these issues from multiple perspectives, and to develop cohesion in your own thinking. But you now have a start. Keep Reflection 1.12 handy to elaborate on or revise as you continue to learn.

Reflection 1.12

**Your philosophy of education:
How would you answer the following questions?
Provide a rationale for your answers.**

1. What is the main purpose of schools?

2. How does this purpose relate to or serve a diverse society?

3. How does this purpose relate to or serve a socially stratified society?

4. What are the implications of what you wrote above for the work of a teacher?

Your Vision of Your Teaching Self, Revisited

Earlier in this chapter you were asked to develop a vision of the kind of teacher you want to become. Since that time, you have engaged in multiple discussions and activities about familial, educational, and cultural influences on your beliefs. You have begun to develop an education philosophy. In Reflection 1.13, rewrite your vision statement, and then compare and contrast your first statement in Reflection 1.1 with the second statement. Have you made changes to what you wrote earlier? If so, what changes have you made and in what areas? Discuss your writings with a classmate. Also discuss any implications these changes have for what you want to learn as you prepare to become a teacher.

In the next section of this chapter, you meet Celia Mendez, Lisa Thompson, and Gilbert Roland. They are teacher candidates who will be with us through the remainder of the book. The chapter will then conclude with an activity making use of your beginning philosophy of education.

Reflection 1.13
My vision revisited

As a teacher I envision myself…

Meet Some Classmates

Very much like you, Celia, Lisa, and Gilbert will be reflecting on what they read, raising questions, making observations, agreeing and disagreeing with each other and with us. They are fictitious, but real in the sense that they are composites of our own students. We have included them in this book to provide another set of students — your peers — to engage with the issues in this book, which we hope will prompt you to think more deeply and help you to see issues from additional points of view. Our introduction will include a brief description along with some information from their applications to the teacher education program, and an interview.

Celia Mendez

Celia Mendez is 22 years old. She is of medium height, with skin the color of café latte, and shoulder-length brown hair. She is a little bit quiet when she is in a group. Her mother came to the United States from the state of Guanajuato in Mexico when she was 19, in search of work. She met Celia's father in Los Angeles, where he was working in a restaurant. Celia's father's family traces its roots in California back several generations.

Celia grew up in south central Los Angeles. She is slightly older than the traditional age for teacher education students, because she took a little longer to graduate due to poor advising and a need to work.

Interviewer: Celia, why do you want to become a teacher?

Celia: Well, I love being around children. I helped raise my three younger siblings. I used to like to play school with them as a way of getting them to behave. But I didn't think about teaching at first when I came to college, I just thought about doing what I needed to do to graduate. Then I started to think about how I could become the kind of teacher that is needed in my community. I remember my third-grade teacher, Señora Baca, who was my very favorite teacher. She let me really be me. It's hard to explain. She pushed me to learn, and she seemed to know who I was and what all I could do. Most of my other teachers were nice, but it's like they were trying to make me become someone else. They weren't from my same background, so they just didn't know who I was as Señora Baca did. I've realized now that I can be that person for other children. So that's why I want to become a teacher.

Interviewer: What do you think you'll need to learn to become an excellent teacher?

Celia: Oh, my, let me think [silence]. One of the things I want to know more about is why kids thrive more with some teachers than with others. I want to learn more about the kind of teaching where kids really thrive, like, what the teacher does. I want to learn how to set up a bilingual classroom. Señora Baca's was really the only one I've actually seen, and that was a long time ago! I love to read, and I want to learn about all of the literature that I can use with children. I also want to learn how to make schools better places for a variety of kids. Not just in my own classroom, but how to advocate for kids too. And how to get schools to relate better to parents. I know a lot of parents who care a great deal about how their children are doing, but they and the schools just don't relate. Take my parents, for example. They always cared about how I was doing in school. But my mother hadn't been to school in the United States, and her English isn't great, so she didn't really like to talk to teachers. My father, he was usually working, so he couldn't come to school for meetings. But they always asked me about my work and encouraged me at home. I'd like to know how to connect the school with them better. I know I have to take a lot of courses to become a teacher, I don't know what all is in those courses, but I imagine that it will help me.

Interviewer: What is the main strength you believe you bring to the teaching profession?

Celia: I'm a very patient person with children. I really am. I've been around children all my life, and I know how to be patient with them. [Pause] Do I have to talk about only one strength?

Interviewer: No, please continue!

Celia: My culture and my language is another. I don't know exactly how to use it in teaching yet, but I know that I bring a culture and language that the schools really need. For the longest time, especially in high school, I pretended like I didn't know any language except English because I was embarrassed for anyone to know where I come from. I thought it was bad, lower class, like. And you know, it's so weird, this college requires you to know another language and I already do! I never thought about knowing Spanish as being a strength, but when I got here I found out that I could almost pass the second language requirement! I couldn't quite pass it, I had to take a Spanish-for-Spanish-speakers class to learn to read and write better, but I found out that being bilingual is a strength! So my culture and my language somehow will be an asset in school. For instance, I know that I'll be able to talk with Spanish-speaking parents. A lot of them just don't have teachers they can talk directly to.

Interviewer: That's great! Is there anything else you'd like to say?

Celia: No. I wasn't always the best student in the world. Here especially, I've had to work hard. I wasn't very well prepared for college. So I know what it means to work hard in school. I think I can help kids who don't just get everything right away. I know what it's like. You can do it. They can, I can, I know how to push people to succeed.

Interviewer: Thank you, Celia, good luck!

Lisa Thompson

Lisa Thompson is tall and slender, with short, curly blond hair and hazel eyes. She has a bubbly, vivacious personality. She gets along well with almost anyone. She just turned 20. She grew up in a small, predominantly White town about 150 miles away from the university she is now attending. The town has experienced a gradual diversification in its ethnic and racial composition. Lisa always knew that she wanted to be a teacher. She is also a strong and enthusiastic tennis player, having played seriously since junior high. She maintained about a B+ average through high school and college.

Interviewer: Lisa, why do you want to become a teacher?

Lisa: That's what I always wanted to do. I can't see myself doing anything else. My mom is a teacher, and she has always liked it. She teaches fifth grade. She says that she likes it because there's always something new that comes along. It doesn't get boring. She likes working with most of the kids, and likes watching them grow and learn. I'm a lot like my mom, and I guess I always figured I'd follow in her footsteps.

Interviewer: Can you tell me a little bit about your mother's school, and if you see yourself teaching in the same kind of school, or the same general area?

Lisa: My mom teaches at the same elementary school where I went to school, except of course I didn't have her when I was in fifth grade. It's mostly a middle class, just average school. It's mostly all-White, although that's changing somewhat.

Last time I was home, Mom said that some of the more affluent parents were starting to send their kids to private schools since the school is getting more and more minority kids. They are starting an ESL program there now. Where do I want to teach? I'm not sure, but I guess I always pictured myself teaching somewhere like where I grew up. I don't plan to move into the city, it's too big and has too many problems. I don't plan to move back home, either, but I'll probably live somewhere kind of like home. I really like it here, this town is nice and has a lot going on, with the university and all.

Interviewer: What do you think you'll need to learn to become an excellent teacher?

Lisa: I know I need to get better in math. I'm taking calculus right now, although I won't be teaching calculus, thank goodness! Hmmm, what will I need to learn? That's a good question. Like, I know I'll need to learn how to get kids to do what I tell them to do. I'm a little bit worried about kids not behaving, and not doing what they are supposed to do. My mom says that classroom management will come, but I get worried about it. I really want to learn more about special education kids. I remember when I was in junior high and high school, there was this blind girl in our school. Well, almost blind, she could see a little bit. I didn't really know her, but she was in a couple of my classes. She seemed nice. Part of the day she went to a different school where they had the right materials for her, but part of the day she went to school with us. I also remember this retarded girl in our P.E. classes. I'd sometimes help her with things. Her name was Barbara. Anyway, I know there are a variety of different kinds of kids in classrooms, and I'd like to learn more about how to work with them.

Interviewer: What is the main strength you believe you bring to the teaching profession?

Lisa: I like people and I'm a good worker. I know my grades haven't been spectacular, but at least I'm consistent. I do a good job with things, and I'm pretty creative. Like, in my English class we were supposed to write a paper, and so I decided to write it like a play, you know, with dialogue and all. I was afraid my professor wouldn't like it, but he did. I like to make things fun, like that. If you give me a task to do, I'll get it done, but along the way I'll try to figure out how to have some fun with it. When I was a kid in school, I remember that I liked classes where teachers tried to make things fun. I know there's a lot of stuff in school that you just have to learn, and it can be a drag unless the teacher has fun with it. That's how I approach things. Sometimes people say I'm not serious enough, but if you are too serious as a teacher, you make things boring.

Interviewer: So true. Is there anything else you'd like to say?

Lisa: I think I'd also be a good role model for girls who like athletics. I play tennis here on the tennis team, and I jog regularly. Lots of girls are afraid to use their bodies. I know girls who are anorexic, and girls who are overweight. I've learned to take good care of my body, and to enjoy athletics. That's something I can offer as a teacher.

Interviewer: Thank you, Lisa, we'll get back to you!

Gilbert Roland

Gilbert Roland is of Korean and African-American descent. He is six feet, four inches, and the blending of the two races has made him uniquely handsome. He grew up in Chicago, where he earned excellent grades. His passion was history, any kind of history. He relished discovering different interpretations of contemporary and historical events. He also found math and science easy and fun. In high school he was in the honor and other advancement placement classes for science, math, and French. However, he is somewhat uncertain about his choice of profession, to become a middle school teacher. A counselor encouraged him to apply for admission to the program, but he isn't sure about all of this.

Interviewer: Gilbert, why do you want to become a teacher?

Gilbert: To be honest, I am still trying to make up my mind. I know I like kids. In high school, I was a part of a program where we would help middle school and elementary students who were having academic problems. Also, I enjoyed working with the kids at the Boys and Girls Club.

Interviewer: Do you have issues or concerns about teaching or the program that I could possible clarify?

Gilbert: Not really, everything seems to be pretty clear. Although, to me there does seem to be a great number of methods, classes, standards, and developing a portfolio, looks like a lot of busy work.

Interviewer: Yes, I hear you, but you will find that most of it will be helpful.

Gilbert: I hope so.

Interviewer: What do you think you'll need to learn to become an excellent teacher?

Gilbert: First you need to know your subject matter. And, I believe I know that. Next you need to know how to teach and to discipline. It is here that I believe I may need help.

Interviewer: What are the main strengths you believe you bring to the teaching profession?

Gilbert: I know the subject matter, and when I worked with middle school students when I was in high school, I was always understanding and supportive.

Interviewer: Is there any thing else you would like to say?

Gilbert: Hopefully, before long I will know if I really want to teach. Until then I will do all that is expected of me.

Interviewer Thanks for saying that. Anything else you'd like to know?

Gilbert: No, not now.

Interviewer: Thank you Gilbert, it was good to meet you and we will get back to you.

Putting It Into Practice

So far we have engaged in discussions and activities where you courageously examined your worldview, investigated a myriad of influences on yourself and your beliefs, and anxiously tried to make sense out of philosophy and its relationship to teaching. The teacher-candidate challenge below requires that you bring together this learning and actively apply it. It asks you to apply the theoretical ideas discussed in the chapter to a practical classroom lesson.

J. K. Rowling's books on Harry Potter are very popular. Children and adults from all walks of life are great fans. By the summer of 2000, the first three books in the Harry Potter series sold over 35 million copies in 35 different languages and earned approximately $480 million (http://www.hogwarts.esmaratweb.com/jkrowling.htm). There are currently six books in the series, and one additional book is slated for publication. The books chronicle the school experiences of Harry Potter from ages 11 to 17. Given the popularity of the books, they will probably be a part of the curriculum in many schools for years to come. Today, many teachers are finding ways to incorporate the Harry Potter stories into their curriculum. They argue that children's literature provides descriptions of society and life, and often represents the beliefs, values, and aspirations of a community of people.

In Reflection 1.12, you sketched your beliefs regarding the role of school in society and implications for teaching. Below, write your thoughts about how that sketch might guide your work with a work of children's literature.

Now select one of J. K. Rowling's books and prepare a lesson plan for using the book as "curriculum" to teach your students an integrated lesson of at least two of the following: mathematics, science, music, social studies, literacy, physical education, spelling, or art. Follow the guidance of your beginning philosophy of education. The purpose is to develop a critical awareness about any and all materials you use with students as well as materials you use for you own personal satisfaction. Such a critical awareness is essential to becoming a fantastic teacher.

Box 1.2 Harry Potter and Diversity

Race and racial construction are not specifically attended to in the Harry Potter series, and for many people this omission is cause for criticism.

Gender construction and the relationship between males and females are ripe topics to explore — particularly the roles assigned to the characters in the story, and the predominance of male characters.

Socioeconomic differences among the students are constructed to maintain a wedge and influence opportunities.

Disability appears within the silences and assumptions embedded within the text as a way of pointing out who is considered "normal."

You may choose the grade level or the age of the students, although for this exercise, we recommend fifth grade or higher. In Box 1.2 are some observations to prompt your thinking. A skeletal lesson plan format appears in Table 1.3. When you are finished, compare your ideas with those of your classmates. Look particularly for consistency between stated philosophical beliefs, learning objectives, and teaching procedures. Have you ever thought about Harry Potter as suggested above?

TABLE 1.3 Lesson plan format

Title of Plan: Literature Across the Disciplines, J. K. Rowling's ...

Subject Area: Interdisciplinary Subject Area

Grade level:

Time for Completion:

Objectives (what you want students to learn as a result of instruction)

1.

2.

3.

Suggested Procedures (how you will go about teaching to the objectives above)

1.

2.

3. and so on

Evaluation (how you will find out the extent to which students learned what you intended)

1.

2.

two
Students and Achievement

This chapter will help you answer the following questions:

- How do various conceptions of achievement differ from each other?
- What is deficit theorizing, and how do teachers fall into it?
- How can I influence achievement for students from all cultural groups?
- What is student-centered teaching and learning?
- How can a teacher get to know his or her students and their world?

You are probably aware that teachers today are under considerable pressure to raise students' achievement scores. Most states have legislation requiring schools to improve test scores every year, and this requirement is also built into federal legislation called the No Child Left Behind Act. In this chapter, we will explore various meanings of achievement in relationship to students.

We will begin by stepping back from test score conceptions of learning and achievement, to consider achievement more broadly within the context of young people's lives as a whole. Then the chapter will present **Building Block 3:** Becoming Acquainted With Your Students.

In order to work through this chapter, you will need access to the following:

- The Internet (for Reflections 2.1 and 2.5);
- Three adults to interview (for Reflection 2.2);
- One to three children or youth you can talk with, at least one of whom should be as different from you as feasible (for Reflections 2.6 and 2.8);
- A store that caters to young people (for Reflection 2.7).

Achievement

In the pages that follow, we explore various meanings of achievement in relationship to test score measures of academic achievement. We then consider how teachers make judgments about why some students achieve well while others do not, and what to do in response to students' achievement and behavior in the classroom. We lead this discussion toward a focus on students' perspectives, because starting with students and building teaching around them has the best potential for fostering productive learning.

Meanings of Achievement

Pick up a newspaper or listen to a conversation about achievements of young people today, and much of what you hear will refer to test scores. For example, the online version of the *San Francisco Chronicle* carried a story about achievement:

> The annual reports, which have come to be known as the Nation's Report Card, usually cover only a few test years at a time. But the new, long-term report sheds light on decades of achievement, showing progress not only for students of color, but among nearly all students. (Asimov, 2005, p. 13)

You can see how this story equated achievement with test scores. Similarly, you may have experienced your own achievements cataloged in terms of how well you did on tests in school.

Tests are a fact of life in today's world; we do not claim they are unimportant. Test scores can be a useful indicator of student learning, and as a teacher you won't be able to get away from them. However, achievement in a broader sense means a good deal more than test scores, so we urge you to think broadly about what it can mean for students. We say this because we have seen schools ignore important areas of student growth and learning in the press to raise test scores. In your own life, you were probably proud when you did well on tests, but also proud of a range of other achievements, including academic and intellectual achievements that tests did not capture.

Actually, teachers who place test scores within a broad consideration of achievement may be able to reach their students more effectively than teachers who do not do this, by connecting academic growth with varied dimensions of students' lives. So, we introduce this chapter with Reflection activities that probe into varied meanings of achievement.

Let's start with conceptions of achievement that you can find if you browse the Internet. For Reflection 2.1, go to a computer and see how many different conceptions of achievement you can find, before reading on.

When we tried this search, we found the following:

- Academy of Achievement (http://www.achievement.org): Interactive virtual museum about various historical figures who are well known and have shaped history.
- Junior Achievement (http://www.ja.org): Organization that helps young people to learn to become successful in business.
- Top Achievement: (http://www.topachievement.com): Software tools to help people learn strategies for goal setting.
- Achieve, Inc. (http://www.achieve.org): Organization of state governors and corporate leaders that helps states raise academic achievement in schools by improving accountability systems (including tests).

We found websites that describe various notions about what achievement means. Meanings included the following: making a difference to one's community or one's country; setting and attaining personal goals (such as developing athletic skill or learning to drive); making money; establishing a successful small business; and doing well on tests.

Now that you have considered various conceptions of achievement you have found on the Internet, let's expand the list you started in Reflection 2.1 by interviewing three people you know whose achievements you admire (see Box 2.1 for interview tips). The three people should be as different as possible by race, class, gender, disability, sexual orientation, and access to power and privilege. What kind of persons are these individuals, and what kind of skills (such as thinking skills, personal skills, academic skills communication skills, etc.) did each person need to develop in order to accomplish their achievements?

Box 2.1 Tips for Conducting Interviews

Several times throughout the book you will be asked to conduct interviews. Here are some tips that will help the experience go smoothly.

Reducing Nervousness

One good way to cut down on any nervousness is to practice asking your questions. First you may wish to practice by yourself, and then practice with a friend or classmate.

Arrangements

Call in advance to make an appointment.

Identify yourself by name and institution. Answer any questions or concerns by letting the interviewee know the purpose of the interview and course instructor.

Preparation

In most instances, we have suggested the interview questions. Nevertheless, you may want to change them or add follow-up questions.

Read the chapter material before you proceed with the interview. Don't just read the interview assignment and believe that you are prepared.

Have the interview questions readily available and a notepad for writing down the response you receive.

Bring along more than one pen or pencil.

The Interview

Record the time and place of interview and the name of the interviewee.

Don't launch directly into the interview, even if you only have a few minutes; take a minute for casual conversation, this will help to relax both you and the interviewee.

Focus on the person you are interviewing and be an attentive listener. Ask questions at a moderate pace and don't fidget about.

If a response is not clear, ask, "Can you say that another way?" or "Will you clarify that for me?"

If the interviewee is evasive, or you believe that you have "struck a nerve," proceed with caution or strike the question.

If by chance the interviewee wishes to go off the record, don't write down any information; just listen.

If the interviewee goes on and on, politely interrupt saying something like: "Good, now let me ask you this."

Try to limit the interview to no more than 30 minutes. However, it the interviewee wishes to continue, and you have the time, stay with it because you may collect valuable information.

After the Interview

Review your handwritten notes as soon as possible. Correct or clear up any shorthand notes or abbreviations. Don't trust that you will remember your shorthand or scribbling.

Look across the interview for common trends and patterns related to the responses and ideas connected to your questions.

Based on ideas from Black (2002) and Grant & Sleeter (1996).

Reflection 2.2
Interviews about achievement

Ask the individuals you select the following questions:

1. Describe what you consider your greatest achievements in life.

2. What kind of skills do you believe helped you accomplish your achievements (such as thinking skills, personal skills, academic skills, communication skills, etc.)?

3. What kind of achievements do you admire in persons you respect?

Now, return to the list of conceptions of achievement in Reflection 2.1. How would you revise or expand it? Compile the various conceptions from the websites and what you know about the three people you admired. Then use Reflection 2.3 to prioritize what you consider to be the first, second, and third most important conception of achievement.

Reflection 2.3
Prioritized conception of achievement

Based on the websites I reviewed and my recall of the achievements of three people I admired, I think the three most important conceptions of achievement are:

1.

2.

3.

Share your list with some classmates, and your reasoning behind your lists. How similar are they? What are some key differences? Does your classmates' reasoning cause you to rethink some of your own reasoning? Were you or your classmates' conceptions of achievement influenced along race or gender lines?

Thinking beyond test scores has direct implications for your work as a teacher. For example, one of us worked with a second-grade teacher, Juanita, who teaches in a low-income school. Her school was designated as a "low performing" school, and was under pressure to raise test scores. Juanita believes that her students should learn to read, write, and do math at grade level, and she views tests as an indicator of how well they are doing. However, she became concerned that an exclusive focus on raising test scores was making her classroom boring. She commented, "I enjoy teaching but I didn't find it fun. I did not find anything fun about it, it was all about paper and pencil, and I knew the kids were getting bored. I was getting bored myself, because I'm used to more interactive and engaging activities" (Sleeter, 2005, p. 130).

So, Juanita thought more broadly about achievement. Believing strongly that her students should be prepared for college, she asked some high school teachers what students must learn to do in order to succeed in high school and college. They told her that students should be able to create documents on a computer and do research. These ideas expanded achievement beyond test scores. So, Juanita reconstructed her curriculum to teach her second graders how to do Internet research, and how to create documents that included text, scanned photos, and clip art. She then created books with her students' papers.

Her ideas about achievement expanded from students mastering basic skills, to students becoming producers of knowledge, using higher-order thinking skills and technological tools. Her conception of achievement also focused on preparation for college. With that conception, she embedded reading, writing, and math skills in an environment that emphasized thinking and creating. In the process, her teaching became much more engaging to her students. Please don't think that Juanita's discussion with high school teachers about what students need to know to succeed in college was premature because she teaches second graders. The education and best-practices literature tells us that a good number of students, although physically present in school, have mentally tuned out school by fourth grade if they have become bored.

In addition, the sooner you can start pointing out to students their life opportunities the more comfortable they will become discussing preparation for professions and vocations. Can you recall the time when you first knew you would go to college, or knew you wanted to go? When this question was asked in a Teacher Education class at the University of Wisconsin–Madison, all of the 48 students said they had known since they were very young. And, a few said, "It was always an expectation, a forgone conclusion."

The acclaimed elementary teacher Ron Berger (2001) spent years cultivating his teaching around an expanded and ambitious vision of achievement. In a discussion of his vision in relationship to test scores, he commented,

Imagine if students and schools were judged instead on the quality of student work, thinking, and character. Imagine an expectation that an adult should be able to enter a school and expect that any child in that school older than seven or eight would be ready to greet him [or her] politely, give an articulate tour of a well-maintained, courteous school environment, and present his [or her] portfolio of academic accomplishments clearly and insightfully, and that the student's portfolio would contain original, high-quality work and document appropriate skills. (p. 102)

Berger went on to point out that if we assumed that this broader vision was how we were judging achievement, the energy that now goes into preparing students to take tests would be directed toward "building thoughtful students and good citizens" (p. 102).

Student Dialogue 2.1

Gilbert: This is somewhat of a different way for me to view achievement; a bit challenging, to say the least. Achievement to me, by and large, has always meant performing at a high level at school, on tests. Yes, I know doing well, let's say in gymnastics, or winning a trophy because you were a member of the championship swimming team at your middle school, or having perfect school attendance, are all forms of achievement. But *real* achievement is "kicking it" in the books.

Celia: So Gilbert, when I saw you last night at the poetry slam, you were applauding and stomping your feet in celebrating some of the performances. Are you saying that the winners of the Slam did not achieve?

Lisa: Yes, Gilbert, think about it. Do you think that entertainers and sport stars, especially those who, like, leave high school or college at an early age, would argue that achievement should be defined by scores on a test?

Celia: Yeah, they'll probably define achievement by the sizes of their contract, the location and size of their house, and the number of outside endorsements they've received!

What Influences Achievement?

Teachers constantly make judgments about what they believe influences their students' achievement. Whether students are doing well or poorly, teachers usually not only know how well they are doing, but also have theories about why they are achieving as they are. Teachers tend to express these theories in terms of what they believe motivates their students, or how much home support they believe students have. Such theories of student motivation, ability, and home support tend to guide the actions teachers take in the classroom, and the kinds of programs that schools offer students, such as programs for "gifted students," "college-bound students," or "remedial students."

Let us explore some processes that occur when interpreting reasons that lie behind students' achievement. Teachers make assumptions about what motivates or facilitates achievement based on what students do in the classroom — their performance, their behavior, how they respond to the teacher and classroom tasks, and so forth. Reflection 2.4 asks you to consider the relationship between classroom behavior and various factors that might underlie that behavior. The boxes on the left ask you to picture a student with various characteristics; boxes to the right ask you to describe the typical classroom behavior and effort of such a student, and to consider what a teacher might do in response.

Now examine the descriptions of students' probable behavior. How similar are they? How similar are your descriptions of their effort? How similar are your descriptions of what a teacher can do?

We have used this reflection several times in our classes, but have set it up a little differently from how we present it here. In our classes, we divide teacher candidates into four groups, then give each group only one of the students to reflect on, rather than all four, without telling the class that each group has something different. After groups write and discuss their answers to the questions, they report to the rest of the class. The reports start by describing very similar behavior, and usually similar effort. Teacher candidates usually describe their case student as restless, inattentive, and off-task, either exhibiting too little effort, or trying, but not effectively. Up to this point, the

---

Reflection 2.4
Interpreting classroom behavior

Picture a student who:	Describe classroom behavior of such students.	How much effort do students invest in this case?	What should a teacher do?
Is bored, unchallenged, considers the work too easy.			
Is in the process of learning English, and is not yet fluent in English.			
Sees little point in what is being taught, even though he or she is capable of doing the work.			
Is frustrated because the work is too difficult, requiring skills or background student lacks.			

class believes they are all describing the same student. When they report their recommendations for what a teacher can do, however, they not only disagree with each other, but at first are baffled by what other groups are saying. Their recommendations range from offering more challenging work, to making the work easier; from figuring out what the student finds interesting, to referring the student to a program such as special education or bilingual education. We then show the class the four different cases they were responding to, and discuss the implications of the fact that their recommendations were based not on students' classroom behavior, but on presumed *reasons* for that behavior.

In the classroom, teachers make judgments about students' learning potential and motivation based on their class work, effort, behavior, and other visible factors. Judgments are also made at the school level. For example, secondary schools commonly divide students into different tracks based on assumptions that students with different learning potentials require different preparation for different futures.

But, as this reflection activity illustrates, the same classroom behavior can be due to a wide variety of reasons; how you respond to it may be appropriate or totally inappropriate. Although it might seem evident that you would know why students respond as they do, and which response is best, there is considerable evidence that teachers often misread their students.

This misreading of students' classroom behavior often takes place through lenses that are coded by race, ethnicity, language, and social class, without teachers being aware of those lenses. We as teachers then respond to students based on our interpretations of them, and students in turn respond to us, our interpretations of them, and how we are treating them. This then can become continuous, leading some students to drop out, either mentally or physically, unless the cycle is broken by the teacher.

Student Dialogue 2.2

Gilbert: Reading this section affirms some things that I had always thought were going on — that teachers saw me in interesting and complex ways. For some, my Asian-ness made them think that I would be good in science and math; and my Blackness caused them to wonder about my family. I was often asked if I lived with both my mother and father, or whether I was from a single parent home. In addition, until they got to know me, guys would wonder, since I'm reasonably tall at six-four, and since I'm half-Black, if I could play basketball.

Celia: You know Gilbert, I hate to admit it, but I wondered similar things about you when we first met. It is for certain that if I would have had to choose a science partner, I would have chosen you over Lisa. No offense Lisa. I just figured because of who you are, that you wouldn't be good in science and math.

Gilbert: Are you talking about the Asian side of me or the Black side of me, or both?

Celia: Oh, I am sorry Gilbert. I didn't mean to offend you.

Gilbert: No offense, I was just having fun at your expense.

Lisa: I'm offended that you would pick Gilbert over me. It shows that those stereotypes are really working you. I want you to know that I was a B+ science
student, in the science honor classes in high school.

There is an old saying, "Don't judge a book by its cover." Similarly, don't judge a person by the color of his or her skin, or assume that gender foretells the person's skill and
ability to perform in certain occupations or professions. A few years ago, Carl boarded a
plane for a flight. Several males, already on board, were in a discussion about the woman
pilot they had seen enter the cockpit. Their comments centered on the assumption that
she was the copilot, and they were pleased that the other pilot was a male. However, as
the plane was taxiing, a female voice announced that she was the pilot, and that the first
officer (let us say) Jane Smith, was in charge of this leg of the flight. The men all stared
at one another and frowned; Carl chuckled to himself.

Our point here is that ideas about what some people can or cannot do — which still
exist in the 21st century — are based upon beliefs that teachers will want to interrogate.
In addition, we wish to remind teacher candidates that the ideas that are used to make
judgments about students and others do not remain static. Terms and labels that are used
to stereotype become more sophisticated and nuanced without really changing meanings. For example, in the 1960s, educators used the term *culturally disadvantaged* or
deficient to refer to poor students and students of color; in the 1970s they used the term
inner city or *culturally different*; in the 1980s the term shifted to *urban student*; in the
1990s they used the terms *culturally diverse* and *at-risk* student; and now in the 2000s,
educators continue to use the term *at-risk*, along with code words such as "from a single
parent home." All of these terms label poor African-American and Latino students.
Although *culturally diverse* may sound better than *culturally deficient*, educators are
nevertheless speaking about the same students. Only the code word(s) has changed.

Teachers commonly see students who are White or Asian as more teachable than
students who are Black or Latino/a, and students of middle- or upper-class backgrounds
as more teachable than those from lower-class backgrounds, even when they exhibit the
same behavior in the classroom. Teachers have been found to attribute Asian immigrant
students' academic difficulties to their inability to speak English, but academic difficulties of African-American students are attributed to family background, and particularly the teacher's beliefs about the extent to which parents value education (Baron, Tom
& Cooper, 1985; Codjoe, 2001; Cooper & Moore, 1995; Hauser-Cram, Sirin, & Stipek,
2003; Irvine & York, 1993; Pang & Sablan, 1998; Tettegah, 1996; Warren, 2002).

Consider the following statement by a teacher: "I am frustrated when I enter the
classroom during the day and I know that these pupils, who are seated in front of me,
arrived to school without energy, without motivation, and they live in really sub-human
conditions" (Shields, Bishop, & Mazawi, 2005, p. 1).

This statement illustrates what it means to "pathologize" students, or attribute their
difficulties in school not to what happens in school, but to their lives outside school.
Another term for this is *deficit theorizing*, or explaining their achievement in terms

of perceived deficits they bring to school. If students can't learn because of their home environments, why expend energy trying to figure out how to engage them?

You may have noticed that the above discussion did not turn directly to the students or their parents to ask what works for them in school and what doesn't. When we engage in deficit theorizing, we assume there is little we can do to help students achieve, and we usually do not ask the students or their parents for advice, particularly if we assume them to be too poorly educated (and perhaps too apathetic) to know. Actually, it is a fallacy of becoming professionally prepared to teach to assume that you will (or should) have all of the answers to run a classroom well. Well-prepared professionals appreciate the limitations of their own knowledge, and value asking and listening, and admit it when they do not know something. Schultz (2003) explains the importance of becoming a listener and a learner as a part of becoming a teacher:

> Listening closely to students implies becoming deeply engaged in understanding what a person has to say through words, gesture, and action. Listening is fundamentally about being in relationship to another and through this relationship supporting change or transformation. By listening to others, the listener is called on to respond. (p. 9)

In this book, we will steer you toward starting instruction by listening to and engaging with students, not as objects of teaching to whom something is done, but rather as active agents of learning.

Student-Centered Teaching

A sizable body of research supports student-centered teaching. The American Psychological Association put forth a set of *Learner-Centered Psychological Principles* in 1993, based on a synthesis of research on conditions that best support high levels of achievement. The principles are shown in Table 2.1. According to McCombs (2003):

> Putting learners first is at the heart of learner-centered teaching. The focus is shifted from "what teachers teach" to "what students learn." Learner-centered teachers understand that they must find ways to know their individual students and provide a safe and nurturing context before the job of teaching can begin. Learner-centered teachers also understand that not only is learning a natural lifelong process, but motivation to learn also comes naturally when the learning context is supportive. (p. 96)

Because students and contexts differ, there is no formula for learner-centered instruction. Learner-centered instruction requires that teachers get to know their students and invite students' input into the teaching–learning process so that learning can build on what students know. In fact, according to McCombs (2003), "students' perceptions of their teachers' learner-centered classroom practices are the most significant predictors of student motivation and achievement" (p. 96). This means that teachers, and particularly their receptiveness to students' feelings and ideas, have a lot to do with student motivation. What counts most in motivating students to achieve are *"students'* perceptions that teachers encourage positive interpersonal relationships and honor student voices" (McCombs, 2003, p. 96).

TABLE 2.1 The APA Learner-Centered Psychological Principles
COGNITIVE AND METACOGNITIVE FACTORS

1. Nature of the learning process: The learning of complex subject matter is most effective when it is an intentional process of constructing meaning from information and experience.

2. Goals of the learning process: The successful learner, over time and with support and instructional guidance, can create meaningful, coherent representations of knowledge.

3. Construction of knowledge: The successful learner can link new information with existing knowledge in meaningful ways.

4. Strategic thinking: The successful learner can create and use a repertoire of thinking and reasoning strategies to achieve complex learning goals.

5. Thinking about thinking: Higher-order strategies for selecting and monitoring mental operations facilitate creative and critical thinking.

6. Context of learning: Learning is influenced by environmental factors, including culture, technology, and instructional practices.

MOTIVATIONAL AND AFFECTIVE FACTORS

7. Motivational and emotional influences on learning: What and how much is learned is influenced by the learner's motivation. Motivation to learn, in turn, is influenced by the individual's emotional states, beliefs, interests and goals, and habits of thinking.

8. Intrinsic motivation to learn: The learner's creativity, higher order thinking, and natural curiosity all contribute to motivation to learn. Intrinsic motivation is stimulated by tasks of optimal novelty and difficulty, relevant to personal interests, and providing for personal choice and control.

9. Effects of motivation on effort: Acquisition of complex knowledge and skills requires extended learner effort and guided practice. Without learners' motivation to learn, the willingness to exert this effort is unlikely without coercion.

DEVELOPMENTAL AND SOCIAL FACTORS

10. Developmental influence on learning: As individuals develop, they encounter different opportunities and experience different constraints for learning. Learning is most effective when differential development within and across physical, intellectual, emotional, and social domains is taken into account.

11. Social influences on learning: Learning is influenced by social interactions, interpersonal relations, and communication with others.

INDIVIDUAL DIFFERENCES FACTORS

12. Individual differences in learning: Learners have different strategies, approaches, and capabilities for learning that are a function of prior experience and heredity.

13. Learning and diversity: Learning is most effective when differences in learners' linguistic, cultural, and social backgrounds are taken into account.

14. Standards and assessment: Setting appropriately high and challenging standards and assessing the learner and learning progress--including diagnostic, process, and outcome assessment--are integral parts of the learning process.

From McCombs, 2003.

Student-centered teaching means becoming familiar with one's students, including their membership in wider sociocultural communities, and inviting students to frame education in relationship to their concerns. Using culturally relevant, learner-centered teaching, it is possible to ignite substantially higher levels of achievement than one usually sees.

For example, in 2003, a Social Justice Education Project began in Tucson, Arizona with high school Chicano students who were failing high school and considering dropping out. It was "launched as a research study investigating if and how students of color experience inequities in the educational process. It quickly evolved into an effective alternative method of teaching 'under-performing' students" (VisionMark, 2005). Three Latino educators, including a high school teacher, the director of the Tucson Unified School District's Mexican American/Raza Studies Department, and an assistant professor from the University of Arizona, collaborated to develop a social studies curriculum that met state standards, taught racial and economic inequalities from a Chicano perspective, and involved students in reading college-level material and doing community research, in which they developed "advanced, graduate-level skills in research, writing, and critical thinking" (VisionMark, 2005). By 2005, students who completed this program were graduating from high school and seeing themselves as capable learners, and over half were attending college. According to the project's codirector Julio Cammarota, "Student involvement is the missing element needed for effective school change or reform processes. The quality of educational and life experiences for students of color will not significantly change until students become central voices in developing educational policy and practices" (VisionMark, 2005).

Building Block 3: Becoming Acquainted With Your Students

Because student involvement and student voice are so central to students' learning, when considering how to do multicultural education for academic achievement, this is where we begin. The best teachers shape their work around their students, and in order to do that, they make it a habit to become acquainted with their students, not just at the beginning of the school year, but throughout the year. Schultz (2003) describes this practice as taking a listening stance toward students. By "listening," she means that teachers form relationships with students, and through those relationships, attend carefully to the individual students in their classrooms, the tenor of students as a group, and the wider context of students' lives. Her notion of listening involves not just listening to what students say, but also "hearing" their voices represented in their class work, their body language, their whispers, and even their silences. It means tuning in to students, not from a distance but through building relationships with them, and using a listening relationship as "the starting place for teaching" (p. 8). Throughout this book, you will have various opportunities to listen to students, using different kinds of tools: interviewing them, talking with them, and inviting them to be your "tour guide" of their neighborhood.

Schultz (2003) developed a framework for listening to students, beginning with individual students, and moving outward. Becoming acquainted with individual students involves considering how they experience school, the questions they ask, intellectual capabilities they bring, and points of view they hold. Listening to the rhythm and balance of the classroom involves attending to the dynamics of the group, and relationships among the people in a classroom. Listening to the social, cultural, and community contexts of students' lives involves considering relationships between students' lives outside school, and what happens in the classroom for the purpose of connecting these dimensions of students' lives to prompt genuine learning and growth. Finally, when teachers listen for silences, they are concerned about what is not being discussed as much as what is being discussed. In other words, whose perspectives are being blocked from the classroom, whose voices are not being heard? Most likely, you are not yet working in a classroom as a full-time teacher. We anticipate that you are stepping into the ocean of teaching, but not yet swimming or in a position to swim. Therefore, we begin with students, not by guiding you in attending to particular students (which you likely do not have), but rather tuning into students' worlds outside school.

Student Dialogue 2.3

Lisa: This student-centered teaching sounds great, but who really does it? Have you ever seen it in action? It's not really an idea used in the teacher education program to teach us "how to teach."

Gilbert: Right, it wasn't used in my high school, nor have I encountered it in college. So what are Grant and Sleeter talking about?

Celia: I think you two are missing the point. You seem to be thinking that student-centered teaching is about tailoring your teaching to every student. While it would be super to be able to individualize instruction, I understand student-centered teaching as meaning starting with the needs and questions of the students in class, and not with the subject matter.

We readily admit that student-centered instruction is demanding, especially so in the beginning. Learning about who the students *really* are is a challenge; learning what they are about — their hopes, dreams, failures, and thoughts about school takes time; and learning how and where they plan to make it (achieve) requires gaining their trust. That said, we can tell you that the alternative is worse — that is, teaching a subject without considering the background of the students. Subject-centered teaching may push students down a path that leads to dropping out, poor test scores, and poor overall academic achievement.

Diversity of Students

There is no generic student. Good teachers work at getting to know every new group of students. As Schultz (2003) points out, despite attempts to increase student achievement by handing teachers standardized texts, teaching materials, and teaching procedures, "many teachers hold on to the goal of beginning with the particularities of the children in their classrooms" (p. 37).

One way of considering the diversity of students is to examine demographic data that describes them. Nationally, the "average" classroom would fit the following portrait: Of its 30 students (15 girls and 15 boys), 17 are White, five are African American, six are Latino (3 Mexican American, 1 Puerto Rican, 1 Central American, and 1 Cuban American), one is second-generation Asian American, and one is American Indian. The primary language of six students is not English. Two of the African-American students, three Latino students, and two White students come from families who live below the poverty line, while another four White students are from upper-income homes. The composition of students' families varies widely. Only two students come from families in which the father but not the mother works outside the home, nine are from single-parent families (5 of which live below the poverty line), and both parents of 18 students hold or have recently held jobs, at least part time. One student lives with her grandparents, rather than her parents. One family is going through a divorce right now, and some students live in blended families (National Center for Education Statistics, 2005). Further, as Eck (2001) has noted, today's students are living in a country where the majority of its inhabitants are Christian, but which has become the world's most religiously diverse nation.

But teachers do not work with broad composites of student profiles. Teachers work with specific students in specific schools and communities. You can begin to explore the demographics of your local area by using online tools to locate students within the communities and histories that shape them. Reflection 2.5 asks you to explore statistics that are available from the National Center on Education Statistics, using a search tool in the Common Core of Data.

Reflection 2.5
School district data

Go to either: http://nces.ed.gov/ccd/districtsearch to explore a school district or community, or to http://nces.ed.gov/ccd/schoolsearch/ to explore a specific school. Find out what kind of data are available, then write a description of the demographics of students.

Name of school district or school:

Description based on data:

These data actually tell you very little about specific students in the school or school district, but they suggest some questions you might want to ask. For example, if students in a particular school are mainly White, but there is a small proportion of Asian students (many of whom speak another language at home), might most of the Asian families be newcomers into the area? If so, where are they from? How might their children experience the school, the newcomer process, and the other students? Are there also White families who are newcomers, but who, because they blend in visibly, are not perceived as new? Do teachers and other students have ideas about who belongs in the school and who does not, and if so, how are these ideas acted out?

Asking such questions should not presume answers. Indeed, some questions may turn out to be fairly meaningless in a given context while other, much more salient, questions emerge. But we encourage teacher candidates to enter classrooms primed to listen in relationship to the diversity of students who are there.

Discovering the Students' World

In chapter 1, you explored your world. The same strong socializing influences that shape your world also shape your students' world, including family, media and advertisements, peers, religious institutions, and school, as depicted in Figure 1.1. These socializing forces form an interlocking system. However, for every individual student, the shape these forces take varies, influenced by the diverse identities of students, the people around them, and by students' location in systems of unequal power based on race, ethnicity, language, class, sexuality and gender, social class, and ability.

There is a range of ways in which teachers can take into account students' world forces. For example, consider the extent to which the curriculum affirms and builds on, or ignores, a student's world. For Reflection 2.6, consider the relationship between a young person's world, the curriculum in her or his classroom, and the teacher. You will see five columns: one labeled "Socializing Forces," two labeled "Curriculum," and two labeled "Teacher." Each double column has a plus (+) and a minus (-). The plus indicates ways in which the student's world forces are reflected or affirmed by the curriculum and by the teacher; the minus indicates ways in which they are ignored or contradicted.

Select a student or young person of any age to interview. Ask the young person to describe a typical day in school. Then ask her or him for any relationships between what is being taught (curriculum) and what the student has learned in the family; what he or she sees in the media; and so forth. Similarly, ask for any relationships between the kind of people the student's teachers are, and the kind of people his or her family members are, and so forth. In the boxes, write examples, based on what the student says.

After filling in the chart in Reflection 2.6, ask the young person when, and to what extent, the examples he or she described matter. It is quite possible that the youngster will not have thought about this before. Sometimes teachers and students become too used to there being a minimal connection between classroom instruction and the students' world, and resulting student apathy.

For example, several years ago one of us asked a group of elementary teachers to examine the extent to which their language arts curriculum related to students' lives outside school. They realized that there was virtually no relationship. But more surprisingly, they had not even thought about this, and had simply assumed that students' disinterest in reading was due to their home environments rather than their lack of interest in the language arts curriculum.

Gaps between students' world and classroom instruction may be large or small, relatively unimportant or hugely significant. Igoa (1995) presents portraits of immigrant children, illustrating how profound such gaps can be. For example, she offers the case of a Vietnamese refugee student whose family had fled Saigon in 1975, and came to the United States. Although the teachers were aware that she was a recent immigrant, they were simply unaware of a myriad of experiences that made schooling difficult for this student. The girl often arrived late to school, for example, as she learned to adjust to American schedules, but her tardiness was treated as a rule infraction. Igoa comments,

> Perhaps if the teacher had known that Dung had just experienced the horrors of war, the teacher might have supported her more and her tardiness would have diminished. Neither parents nor teacher knew the struggle she was undergoing during this period of adjustment to the new country. (p. 95)

Igoa goes on to explain that many immigrant children experience a "cultural split" when they need to become one person at school but a different person at home. She explains, "A cultural split is a wound, because part of oneself is lost to the other part" (p. 107).

A teacher can't know whether gaps between the worlds of students and the world of the classroom are large or small, unimportant or profoundly important, without carefully listening to students. Each socializing force individually or collectively conveys messages to students and teachers which can influence their thoughts about equity and achievement. A series of *New York Times* articles on the plight of African-American men concluded that their life chances and opportunities are more dire than what is presented in common employment and education statistics (Eckholm, 2006, p. 2). One of the articles was used to provide discussion points in both a middle school class and a preservice teacher education class. In the middle school class, where there were several African-American boys, this article generated more robust participation from them than the teacher had heretofore experienced. They commented about such things as how African-American men are portrayed in movies, and how they hear put-downs about home life and family, especially their fathers. But, they don't know how to respond because the teacher or faculty member(s) whom they overhear saying such things are the "boss." In the preservice class, the teacher candidates looked upon the material as pointing out to them the need to look more closely at the general and prevailing assumptions as to why African-American males face difficulty in society. One teacher candidate asked, "You know, I have always wondered why the Black kids wear their pants hanging down so low. Was it their idea, or did they get it from the media, or somewhere else? I still don't know, but I do know the White want-to-be's [White kids who act Black] were socialized from the media, their Black friends, and their White want-to-be friends."

Insights From Marketing Research

Marketing research gives teachers insights into the world of students and ideas about how to make the curriculum and instruction engaging. Market researchers study the habits, likes, and dislikes of young people in order to figure out how to draw them in. In classrooms, young people are a captive audience. Stores, however, cannot assume them to be a captive audience, and need to figure out why young people might want to be there and participate. To do this, market researchers attend to differences between boys and girls (indeed, one can argue that they help to manufacture some of those differences), one age group in comparison to the next age group, and physical characteristics of students (e.g., Siegel, Coffey, & Livingston 2001; Zollo, 1999). Although one can question the commercial motives involved in marketing to children and youth, we nevertheless find helpful insights.

Siegel et al. (2001) argue that there are four essential motivators that drive the choices students make, especially those between the ages of 8 and 12. They are *power, freedom, fun,* and *belonging* (pp. 43–44). *Power* is concerned with control, participation, and being able to make one's own decisions. *Freedom* is about "safe" independence. A kid gets on a bike or scooter and journeys some distance from home, but tries not to stray too far from home. Also, freedom includes taking advantage of opportunities to be out of sight and range of the family, but staying connected via cell phone, e-mail, or pager. *Fun* is a state of mind and activity that deals with anything other than work, sadness, or fear. Also, fun occurs through situations like grossing out adults and playing word games. *Belonging* involves being accepted by the groups you admire and respect.

Stores make use of these ideas in ways that teachers can learn from. Stores that pay attention to such details as the height of clothes racks, cashier counters, and mirrors, along with the type of continuous music playing in the background, will have greater appeal than stores that are not as deliberate in their marketing strategy (Zollo, 1999). For example, a four-foot girl who stands taller than the cashier counter feels in control (*power*) when she pays for her purchases. She has *freedom* or a feeling of independence because she is not shopping in a store that is designed for, and caters to, adults. In addition, she is having *fun*, because shopping is made especially for her age group, while the adults who may be with her are grossed out by the interior design and music. Finally, because of the power, independence, and fun she is having and the location where it is taking place — a "store designed with her in mind" — she has *a sense of belonging*.

In order to examine how merchandisers have used this framework from market research, visit a store that caters to a particular age group or ethnic group of young people. Using Reflection 2.7 as a guide, observe the design and set-up of the store.

After the visit, reflect on strategies the store used to cater to specific communities of young people. What implications does this exploration have for constructing a classroom environment, curriculum, and program of instruction?

Reflection 2.7
Design and setup of store

The store gives the students a sense of power by _____

The store gives the students a sense of freedom by _____

The store makes shopping fun by _____

The store gives the students a sense of belonging by _____

Whose values does the store promote?

The store uses media and advertisement in the following ways:

Would any of your peers or classmates not feel comfortable in the store? If so, why not?

Does the store market more to students from urban, suburban, or rural schools?

Does the store deal with or recognize religion in any way?

Does the store cater to students whose first language is not English?

How does the store address the differences in race, class, gender, and socioeconomic demographics in the client population?

As much as possible, as later chapters in this book discuss, students should participate in curriculum, instruction, and assessment decisions, thereby sharing *power* with the teacher. The activities should provide opportunities for students to learn curriculum concepts in different ways, especially ways that the students suggest, thereby giving them *freedom* and making the activity *fun*, with the teacher maintaining oversight and responsibility. Activities should allow for students to invest the concepts being studied with activities and procedures that take into account their age group, thereby giving them a *sense of belonging*. And all of the learning should make certain that attention to the multiple identities students bring is not marginalized or muted.

But it is important to dialogue with young people, rather than making assumptions about what interests or works for them. To explore how a young person thinks about implications of market researchers, identify a young person who is different from you in as many of the following factors as possible: race or ethnicity, primary language, social class background, religion, disability, sexual orientation, and gender. Tell her or him that you are learning to become a fantastic teacher, and need her or his help. Reflection 2.8 offers some questions you can ask.

After completing this interview, reflect on ways in which you are more similar to the student than you expected. What surprises emerged? What implications would the interview have for your work as a teacher, if this student were in your classroom?

Discuss what your student told you with some classmates. Do any patterns emerge when you combine your interview with those of your classmates?

We believe that with a bit of imagination, classrooms can be set up with much of the same appeal to students. Remember, a classroom should give all students (girls and boys equally) a sense of power, provide freedom and fun, and encourage a sense of belonging. Paying attention to the demographic characteristics of students is necessary in order for you as their teacher to provide them with the four essential motivators that drive their choices. There is a fine line, however, between paying attention to such characteristics

---

Reflection 2.8
What a student says

1. Kids usually don't have too much power. Can you describe a situation or activity in which you've felt like you have a sense of power?

2. Often kids don't feel like they have very much freedom. Can you describe a situation or activity that gives you some freedom?

3. What kinds of activities are fun for you out of school? In school?

4. Where or when do you feel like you have a sense of belonging?

5. If I were your teacher, what are the two most important things I could do or learn in order to be a really fantastic teacher?

---

and using them stereotypically. We use demographic characteristics to alert us to the diversity of a class, then listen carefully to students themselves to figure out what their diversity might mean.

In Reflection 2.9, list under each heading — curriculum, instruction, and classroom environment — ideas for providing power, freedom, fun, and a sense of belonging in the classroom to the students you and your classmates interviewed.

Once you complete the chart, discuss your ideas with classmates. How much difference did it make to talk with some students before doing this? How much difference did it make to select students who differ from yourself? What did you learn by doing this?

Student Dialogue 2.4

Lisa: You know, completing Reflection 2.9 got me thinking. I understand the ideas of "fun," "belonging," and especially "freedom," because I have been hearing and learning about it during all of my time in school. You know, we learned about "freedom" when we studied the Revolutionary War of 1775 and the signing of the Declaration of Independence in 1776. Freedom is an idea that students are very familiar with. But I've always had a hard time really understanding discussions about "power."

Celia: Why?

Lisa: Well, it doesn't get much attention in school. Not like "freedom" does.

Gilbert: Good point. You study wars the United States has been in, and the textbooks describe them as being all about freedom. They usually don't say a whole lot about power.

Lisa: But in classrooms, a lot of what happens is about power. I've been worried about controlling kids, but that's all about teacher power.

Celia: So you're asking where kid power fits in, right? That's a really good question, and I hadn't thought about it either.

It is important to understand that power operates both invisibly and visibly, and that schools and most institutions are full of power relations. According to Roper-Huilman (1998), power "passes through as it is exercised by persons and structures at all levels in the social system" (p. 23). Teachers and students have power they can opt to exercise in certain ways, and which is present within all relations, for example, teacher-student, student-student. Thus, by understanding the flow of power in a classroom and school, teachers are better able to get to know their students. They can better interpret their attitudes and behaviors.

Putting It Into Practice

At the fictional State University, all teacher candidates are required during their junior year to work in a program that puts them in contact with students outside of the regular school day. One purpose of the program is to help teacher candidates get to know their students outside of the school structure. Program assignments include volunteering at the community center, being a tutor-teacher at an after-school class, and working with any number of sport and art/music after-school programs.

When Glenda, a student at State U, received her assignment to work in the after-school tutoring program at Marshall Middle School, she was upset. Marshall, she knew from the media, was a school on the south side of town under fire because of low test scores. The school population was mostly students of color and 80% of the students were eligible for free or reduced cost lunch. Glenda had requested a school on the west side, not too far from the university. She was angry that her request was not honored, and wanted to voice her concern to Professor King, the coordinator of the program, but was reluctant to do so. She though her question would be interpreted as not wanting to work with the students at the school. "The race and multicultural thing is everywhere in this program," she said to herself.

When Glenda arrived at Marshall to get the particulars of her assignment, things in her estimation went from bad to worse. She was assigned to work with six-sixth grade boys: three African American, two Vietnamese, and one Salvadoran. Each of the boys' reading and math scores were at least two years below grade level. The school provided her with some "supposedly" high interest math and reading material, along with some chapter reading books.

The materials brought a frown to the boys' faces along with a loud moan, as Glenda placed the materials on her desk. The boys were very unhappy and went completely off-task as they talked among themselves and ignored Glenda. That night, Glenda fretted as she tossed and turned in the bed asking herself, "What should I do? What can I do?"

If you were Glenda, what would you do? Write a plan of action on the next page. Here is what Glenda did. Glenda decided that she would bring cookies and soda, and reward students whenever they completed an assignment. The cookie and soda routine worked for about two days, and then lost its effectiveness. When that happened, Glenda felt as if she was right back where she started, or even deeper in trouble.

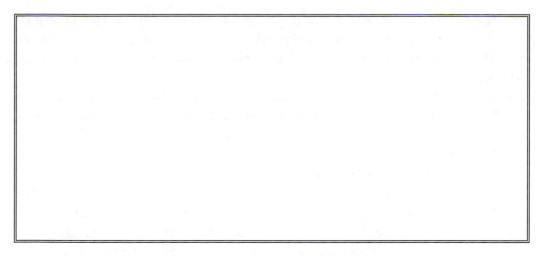

In the university seminar that accompanied the after-school experience, Professor King had assigned *Doing Multicultural Education for Achievement and Equity*. Glenda had blown the text off as one written by two liberals, for people who wanted to teach in urban areas. She kept her head down when Professor King led discussions on the book, and she criticized its focus on multicultural education when the class broke into small-group discussion. She told her classmates during the small-group discussion that the book was taking time away from studying more important concerns that teacher candidates needed to know about, for example, classroom management.

As the days went by, Glenda became increasingly desperate. She was looking for any port in the storm. In addition, in spite of herself, she found she was becoming a bit attached to the students. They, in their own way, were charming. She decided to try a new tack, one she borrowed from *Doing Multicultural Education for Equity and Achievement*. At the next class, Glenda informed the students that they were not going to do workbooks or read chapter books, instead they were going to talk to get to know one another. She suggested that they divide into two groups and each group should come up with three questions that they wanted to ask her and three questions they wanted to ask the students in the other group. In addition, she said she would come up with three questions.

Manuel, the Salvadoran student, said: "We all know each other, so can we ask you six questions?" Glenda said, "That's a deal, if I can ask you six questions too." Everyone laughed and the students moved into their groups. Glenda noticed a good deal of laughter in the two groups, but also a seriousness that was not usually present in the small-group work. Each group had appointed a note taker without being told, and all of the students were participating.

Glenda was surprised by the students' questions. They were serious, not idle curiosity. The students asked: "Where did you grow up?" "What kind a work do your parents do?" "What kind of people lived in your town?" "Why do you want to become a teacher?" "Did you think the university is too big?" "Do you play sports?" After Glenda answered the six questions, She said, "Now it's my turn." Glenda asked them to tell her about things they do outside of school. "What things do you and others — not members in your family — say you do well?" "Who do you admire and why?" "If you had the responsibility for planning this after-school time what would you plan, and how would you plan it?" And, finally Glenda asked, "What would help you to become more academically successful in school?"

Once again, Glenda was surprised about the seriousness of the responses. All of the kids had responsibilities at home, much like she had when she was in middle school (e.g., caring for a younger sibling, participating in house-cleaning chores). Every boy stated that he performed well in some sport, but also mentioned other achievements. For instance, Danny, one of the Vietnamese students, was a good salesperson for his family, who sold produce, which they grew themselves, at the local farmers' market. One African-American boy mentioned how well he did caring for and hanging out with his 90-year-old great grandfather. Manuel mentioned how well he was learning English, and that his family counted on him to do the accounting and translation at the monthly bill-paying time.

Glenda was particularly surprised at the responses to her question about who they admired and why. They did not have real heroes. All had a sport or music celebrity they admired, but no real hero. John, one of the African-American kids, called out Rev. Martin Luther King Jr.'s name, and all the students said, "Yeah, but we don't really know that much about him."

When Glenda looked at her watch, she realized that they had gone way past the 90 minutes scheduled for the program. However, the students had not complained, nor had anyone made a move toward the door as they normally did. She said to them, "I know we are over time but will you take a minute and answer one more question?" She carefully combined her last two questions together and asked: "What could your regular teacher do and what can I do to help you have more success in school?" Danny looked at Glenda and said, "Continue doing what we did this afternoon." Manuel said, "Yeah, this was fun." John responded. "Not only fun, but I learned that maybe, if that university is not too big for you, it will not be too big for me."

The news commentator Paul Harvey is noted for telling you the first part of a story and then reporting on the second part of the story. The second part of this story is that Glenda has applied to teach in Chicago.

Do you see Glenda's actions as a radical departure from the teacher–student structure? Some may say that, although Glenda "stepped outside of the box" (in her own mind), what she did was not unusual. It was, instead, what fantastic teachers do to connect with their students. Unusual or fantastic, or neither, count the number of times over the past month you have stepped outside of the box or stepped up to help a student. Are you pleased with your results? Identify two students whom you could help have greater academic achievements if you stepped up. Figure out how you can step up, then do it!

three
The Quest for Equity in School and Society

The chapter will help you to answer the following questions:

- When and why did multicultural education get started in the United States?
- How much progress toward equity have we made in the United States since the mid-1950s?
- What are some illusions of progress about equity in schools, and why do such illusions persist?
- How do institutional and personal constraints influence teachers' teaching?
- How can fantastic teachers work toward equity in their classrooms and schools?

At a general level, most people favor equity. But what does that mean? Secada (1989) points out that equity, which has to do with distribution of society's resources, includes two important but different considerations: (1) how one makes decisions about the distribution of such resources as quality instructional materials, good teaching, housing, or medical care; and (2) how one decides what constitutes the most fair or desirable distribution. Equity does not necessarily mean the same thing as equality. The latter word refers to elements that can be counted or measured, such as test scores, funding formulas, or numbers of books in the library. Further, equality often suggests treating everyone in exactly the same way, or distributing resources uniformly across the population. Equity, on the other hand, refers to judgments about what is most desirable and just, and draws attention to ways in which resources or opportunities might need to be distributed unequally if groups that start with unequal advantages are to succeed.

School reform movements, as products of their political and cultural contexts, have historically vacillated between emphasizing "excellence" and "equity." As Tyack and Cuban (1995) pointed out, "conservative political climates favored a rhetoric of competition and quality, while liberal eras such as the 1930s and 1960s stressed an ideology of access and equality" (pp. 44–45). At the same time, there have always been many who maintain that excellence and equity cannot be advanced as competing goals. Mario Fantini (1986), for example, argued passionately that, "Quality in the public schools is achieved when *all learners succeed*, not only those considered most able" (p. 50; emphasis in original).

You will hear much about efforts to close achievement gaps. As you work through this chapter, we will prompt you to discern fact from fantasy regarding what it means to close them. No Child Left Behind, passed by Congress and signed into law in 2001, has been put forth as advancing both equity and excellence. The law specifies that states receiving federal funding must

> Implement statewide accountability systems covering all public schools and students. These systems must be based on challenging State standards in reading and mathematics, annual testing for all students in grades 3–8, and annual statewide progress objectives ensuring that all groups of students reach proficiency within 12 years. (U.S. Department of Education, 2001)

By school year 2013 to 2014, all students are to score at or above the proficiency level established by their state. Schools that fail to meet targets not only receive negative publicity and sanctions, but ultimately may be shut down. Concern for equity is reflected in the requirement that student achievement data be disaggregated by "poverty, race, ethnicity, disability, and limited English proficiency to ensure that no group is left behind," as well as provision of choices for parents and students.

This chapter addresses equity both in and out of schools, in relationship to gaps in student learning and achievement, access to high-quality education, disparities in the number and location of supportive caring classrooms and educational resources, disparities in access to economic resources, and so forth. The chapter situates schools in a broader social context, since schools reflect and contribute to societal demands and structures. Not a day goes by when teachers are not influenced by state and national events, policies, and practices.

The chapter begins by considering the rise of multicultural education, its history, and its efforts to close achievement gaps. This consideration is followed by an examination of illusions of progress in society and school, focusing on persistent inequitable patterns in school practices that need to be changed. Two building blocks are presented, along with background and context that will help you to see "the gaps" and determine how you wish to close them.

Building Block 4: Discerning Fact From Fantasy Regarding Societal and Educational Gaps

Building Block 5: Setting Professional Learning Goals for Yourself

In order to work through this chapter, you will need access to the following:

- An educator who taught school during the 1960s or 1970s (for Reflection 3.2);
- The Internet (for Reflections 3.2 and 3.3);
- A high school which has a good record of sending students to college (for Reflection 3.5);
- A teacher who has taught in a local school for several years, a community newspaper, local supermarket (for Reflection 3.7);
- Two students and a teacher you can interview (for Reflection 3.10);
- A gay, lesbian, or bisexual parent/caregiver who has a child in school (if you can locate a person who is "out") (for Reflection 3.11).

The Rise of Multicultural Education

You probably hear the terms *multiculturalism* and *multicultural education* fairly often, but in the mid-1970s, very few people, other than scholars and a few media people, used these terms. *Multiculturalism* became an increasingly popular term of artists and writers in the 1980s; and *multicultural education* gained popularity as a concept that offered a different point of view on educational policies and practices in the late 1970s and early 1980s. The three events or issues often credited for the rise of multicultural education are: (1) the Civil Rights movement; (2) community activism challenging biased curriculum materials; and (3) racist assumptions about learning potential. Since we discuss the third issue in chapter 5, we will focus on the first two here.

Student Dialogue 3.1

Celia: Oh dear, here comes the history part of the book!

Gilbert: What's wrong with history?

Celia: It's usually boring. It's usually about old-time things and dead people. I want to know more about what's happening now.

Lisa: Me too. Like, most of this equity stuff was taken care of back in the old days when my parents were young. I don't know why we have to hear about history when we are trying to learn to teach.

Gilbert: I happen to be a history buff, and can tell you that what's happening today rests on history. You can't understand today without knowing how things got the way they are. And, no offense, Lisa, but equity issues weren't all solved "back in the old days."

Lisa: Well, some of them were. We're here together in the same university, same program, and same opportunities. From what I hear, that wouldn't have happened back when my folks were kids.

Celia: OK, I get it. Working toward equity is a process, not a single happening. To see where we are now, it can be useful to turn the clock back for a few minutes to see where we've been.

The Civil Rights Movement

Multicultural education grew out of the 1960s Civil Rights movements led predominately by African Americans in order to eliminate racism in social institutions, and in everyday social policies and personal practices. Numerous events set off the movement, but two are often mentioned. The first is the landmark Supreme Court decision *Brown v. the Board of Education of Topeka* (1954), which struck down the "separate but equal" clause of *Plessey v. Ferguson*, a Supreme Court decision in 1896 that upheld racial segregation of public facilities. The second event, just over one year after *Brown,* was launched when Rosa Parks (who is popularly referred to as the "Mother of the Civil Rights Movement") refused to give up her seat on a bus in Montgomery, Alabama to a white man. Four days later, on December 5, 1955, the Reverend Martin Luther King Jr. urged the Black community to boycott the buses. The Montgomery Bus Boycott, which illustrated the power of passive resistance, ended racial segregation on buses in Montgomery, and is often heralded as the premiere event that initiated the Civil Rights movement and culminated in the Civil Rights Act of 1964.

During the 1960s, civil rights workers often risked their safety and even their lives. Many times the actions between the civil rights marchers and their racist opponents became heated, confrontational, and sometimes violent. This had been true of earlier confrontations, such as the race riot in Atlanta, Georgia in 1906, when several Black citizens were killed and the city came to a standstill for several days, or the "Silent Protest Parade" that Blacks held in New York City in 1917, to protest lynchings in the South (Ploski & Williams, 1989). However, during the 1960s, U.S. citizens could see and feel the anguish of the Civil Rights movement each night as they watched the television news. There, they could see violation of the Constitutional and civil rights of U.S. citizens who lived in the South and in other parts of the North and West. They could see many citizens physically, verbally, and emotionally abused because of the color of their skin and because some Whites feared that accepting people of color as equal would cost them institutional and personal power — White privilege. As the U.S. public watched, racists cursed, and in some cases even, National Guard troops prevented little Black boys and girls from entering public schools. David K. Shipler (1997), writing about this time in *A Country of Strangers: Blacks and Whites in America*, states:

> Americans of my generation, who were youngsters when the civil rights movement began in the 1950s grew up on awful, indelible images. I am haunted

still by the cute little white girls who twisted their faces into screams of hatred as black children were escorted into schools. I saw for the first time that the faces of pristine innocence could be merely a mask. (p. 4)

Many Americans of all racial and social class backgrounds were becoming increasingly dismayed, frustrated, and angry about the blatant racism they saw, which began to push them toward wanting to do the right thing. Their moral and ethical compass received much needed corrections with the assassinations of President John Kennedy, Robert Kennedy, and Martin Luther King Jr. King's death, especially, motivated many U.S. citizens to think deeply about social justice and civil rights in the United States, and caused some to say, "Enough is enough!"

Along with the violence that was occurring in parts of the South, people across the United States were seeing and reading about racism and de facto segregation of students of color in many Northern schools. Many questioned their own role in sustaining racist attitudes and behaviors. For example, some Whites engaged in "White flight"— they would move out of their neighborhoods if African American families moved in. Carl recalls:

I remember a police car parked across from my home the first day my family moved into what had been an all-White neighborhood. My mother and father had purchased this home on Chicago's Southside. By the end of the same week, I watched as over one-third of the White families moved out. On the school playground, my younger brother and I were ignored when we tried to play basketball with the other kids. By the end of the second week every White family had moved not only from the block where we lived, but also the surrounding blocks.

For Reflection 3.1, try to personalize the feelings of people ostracized because of the color of their skin. Think of a time when you have been ostracized, and write about how you felt.

Share your feelings with a classmate. What do your reactions suggest about how people deal with ostracism? Your reactions and those of a classmate may include internalizing negative feelings about yourself, striking back, or feeling frustrated without knowing what to do. The Civil Rights movement became an organized and constructive way of fighting back and trying to rectify unjust situations.

African-American actions spawned additional movements by historically disenfranchised groups. During the late 1960s, Mexican Americans organized to press for equal

---

Reflection 3.1
Putting yourself in the shoes of someone ostracized

Have you ever been humiliated, ostracized, or made to feel invisible? If so, describe how you felt and how you reacted to ostracism. If not, write how you think the author felt when he and his younger brother were ignored on the playground. What would you have done if you were the author?

---

opportunity in schooling, as well as decent wages and living conditions. A key organization for students was Movimiento Estudiantil Chicano de Aztlan (MEChA), founded in California. American Indians organized to protest the constant breaking of treaties the U.S. government had made with Indian nations, and institutions such as boarding schools that were designed to strip Indians of their culture and language. The National Organization for Women (NOW) was founded in 1966 "to take action" to bring about equality for all women (http://www.now.org/history.html). *Ms. Magazine*, founded in 1977, featured women as multidimensional human beings and activists who were working to remove social barriers based on sex.

Immigrant groups also advocated for equal opportunity in schools. In 1974, the United States Supreme Court was asked to rule on the question of whether linguistic minority children have a right under the Fourteenth Amendment to special programs designed to help them overcome language barriers to learning. In *Lau v. Nichols*, Chinese children in San Francisco public schools argued that they were not provided an equal opportunity to study and learn by not being given supplemental language instruction. The Supreme Court granted the students' request for additional and better language education, which affirmed that language minority students have the right to instruction in the English language, and the right to learn content in a language they understand while in the process of learning English.

Disability rights advocates joined the Civil Rights movement's emphasis on historically marginalized groups claiming voice and a right to organize on behalf of their own needs. Linton (1998) explained that although people commonly think of a disability as a medical or psychological condition, disability scholars and activists use it as a marker of identity that signals shared sociopolitical issues that need to be addressed, such as providing ramps, reading material that is accessible for people with low vision, and so forth.

Teachers, parents, and others of a wide variety of backgrounds brought the Civil Rights movement into schools and classrooms. They demanded changes in teacher preparation programs and urged staff development programs to retrain the current teaching force. They called for a new and different curriculum that would address diversity, and demanded more teachers and principals of color (Kravetz, 1983; Parkay, 1983). As Charles Silberman (1970) put it in *Crisis in the Classroom: The Remaking of American Education*:

> The public schools are failing dismally in what has always been regarded as one of their primary tasks … to be "the great equalizer of the condition of men" (sic), facilitating the movement of the poor and disadvantaged into the mainstream of American economic and social life. Far from being "the great equalizer," the schools help perpetuate the differences in condition, or at the very least, do little to reduce them. (p. 57)

Similarly, Forrest W. Parkay (1983) in *White Teacher, Black School* explains, "Spurred to self-examination by increasingly militant minorities in the late 1960s, educators begin to realize that ghetto schools, reflecting the subtle, yet powerful, biases of the larger society, had in effect 'institutionalized' failure" (p. ix). Parkay went on to address the need for new programs to meet the challenges that teachers, students, and society in general were facing. He argued that many new education programs were needed to meet the demands of minority group parents, school officials, and frustrated teachers, "all of whom realized that traditional teacher education programs were not adequately preparing teachers to practice in the inner city" (p. xvi).

Such demands led to the development of multicultural education. James Banks (1975), in the preface of *Teaching Strategies for Ethnic Studies*, one of the early multicultural education books, argued for the need for such program and text material:

> In recent years, vigorous attempts have been made in school districts throughout the nation to eliminate the "great lie of silence" that has haunted the American public school for decades. These efforts have resulted from the belated realization by educators that students attain only a partial education when they learn little about American ethnic groups and the role of race and ethnicity in American life. (p. xi)

Banks developed this book to provide "strategies, concepts, and resources needed to teach comparative ethnic studies and to integrate ethnic content into the regular curriculum" (p. xi).

In order to get a first-hand perspective about the influence of the Civil Rights movement on education, complete Reflection 3.2, which either involves interviewing an older person about his or her work in schools during that time, or visiting a Civil Rights movement website.

Reflection 3.2
Civil rights movement and education

Interview an educator who worked in schools during the 1960s and 1970s. Ask him or her about changes in education that came about because of the Civil Rights movement. If you are unable to locate an educator to interview, visit the Civil Rights movement on a website, such as the Public Broadcasting Station's extensive collection "Eyes on the Prize" (http://pbsvideodb.pbs.org/resources/eyes).

The Civil Rights movement challenged exclusion in a wide range of social institutions, from housing to jobs to schools. Within schools, parents and students organized against practices that were exclusionary and symbols of exclusion and inequity. One of these was instructional materials, which we consider next.

Biased Instructional Materials

Multicultural education grew through the activism of parents, community members, and teachers (supported by several studies of textbooks and materials), who took a stand against textbooks and other instructional materials that were filled with race and gender bias. Until the 1970s, textbooks were all-White, contained racial and ethnic stereotypes, and were noted for omitting the history and culture of people of color and other nonmainstream groups (Kane, 1970; Klineberg, 1963; Michigan Department of Public Instruction, 1963). Upon analyzing a popular 1976 basal reading series, Butterfield and her colleagues (Butterfield, Demos, Grant, Moy, & Perez, 1979), for instance, stated:

> Even though there is less bias in books from the late seventies when compared to the books of the sixties and early seventies, bias that can negatively affect young readers is still present. If one believes that children are entitled to develop to their maximum potential without the crippling effect of stereotyping, then children have the right to bias-free material which publishers and educators have the responsibility to provide. (p. 388)

In addition to racial bias, textbooks had a great deal of gender bias. Women on Words and Images (1975) claimed that textbooks featured two and one-half to three times as many males as females, and portrayed males in almost six times as many occupational roles. Textbooks rarely featured women working outside of the home; women were assigned roles of mother and wife only.

Many parents, community members, and teachers denounced and refused to purchase all-White, middle-class, sexist textbooks, and demanded that publishers remove the stereotypes and provide more inclusive representation of the history and contributions of different ethnic, racial, and gender groups that live in the United States. Faced with the loss of major sales, which would amount to millions of dollars, textbook publishers grudgingly began to make some changes. For example, publishers included more people of color, especially African Americans, in the stories. They expanded the roles of women. Also they gradually stopped producing separate editions of textbooks with the same title and for the same grade level, for the North and the South.

In 1990, we analyzed 47 textbooks that were popular in grades 1 through 8, with copyright dates between 1980 and 1988, for social studies, reading and language arts, science, and mathematics (Sleeter & Grant, 1991). We found Whites consistently received the most attention, were shown in the widest variety of roles, and dominated the story line and lists of accomplishments. Blacks were the next most included racial group, but were shown in a more limited range of roles with only a sketchy account of Black history. Asian Americans and Latinos appeared mainly as figures on the landscape with virtually no history or contemporary ethnic experience, and Native Americans were locked in the past and almost invisible. The texts addressed gender mainly by taking out sexist language and most overt sex stereotypes, and depicting more females in nontraditional roles. Social studies books were the least equitable, with some depicting 80% of the people as male and 20% as female. Males also predominated in most reading and literature books, where many books showed both sexes in largely stereotypic gender roles, although to avoid controversy, some texts replaced stories about people with stories about animals. Gay or lesbian people were absent. Although a growing number of books for children and adolescents address sexual orientation, textbook publishers have avoided referring to people who are not heterosexual because of backlash when schools have attempted to do so. People with disabilities appeared only occasionally. Textbooks were written as if everyone were middle class, with only occasional depictions of people who live above or below the middle-class level. The concepts of racism, conquest, sexism, and social class were not discussed at all.

What are educators saying about textbooks today? Reflection 3.3 invites you to find out for yourself.

We will return to textbooks in chapter 6, where we work more with curriculum content. Textbooks are part and parcel of deeper patterns of exclusion; they were so during the Civil Rights movement, and they still are today.

Student Dialogue 3.2

Celia: Sometimes people say that it shouldn't matter who is in textbooks, because everyone should be learning what's important. Do you ever hear that?

Lisa: My mom says that. She thinks we should be worrying more about kids learning what they need to know. Like, schools should be teaching science, math, and writing better. Worrying about whose pictures are in the textbooks seems extra.

Celia: It's complicated. I agree that schools should teach everyone better. But I'll also have to say that by the time I was in junior high, I reacted to not seeing people like myself in the curriculum. I know a lot of kids from my neighborhood who just tuned out of school because they felt like school was for someone else.

Gilbert: It is complicated, all right. To me, the pictures in texts are symbolic of whose point of view the curriculum represents. I don't care so much about the pictures, but I care a lot about the point of view. Lisa, what would be a feminist point of view on science, for example?

Lisa: Gee, let me think. I know that women's work has traditionally involved care giving. So science from a feminist perspective might start with what people know about nature through caregiving work, like babysitting, say. It might involve applying science to caring for people.

Celia: That's an interesting idea. We could then look at, say, a middle-school science text and see to what extent it tries to work with what students know based on caregiving work at home —in addition, that is, to counting the number of women scientists in the book. I know I get more interested in material that takes my experiences into account than material that doesn't.

Lisa: So bias in textbooks is a lot deeper than I had originally thought. I can't wait to talk to my mom about these new ideas!

Bias in textbooks, in the context of the Civil Rights movement, was one major factor that prompted the development of multicultural education. It must be remembered that the larger issue for educators was challenging the various forms of inequity and exclusion in schools. The students' comments above suggest a link between whose points of view structure curriculum, and who finds that curriculum engaging. In many other ways that we will consider throughout this book — including expectations for learning, tracking, and grouping, working with parents and community, and working with diverse languages — schools can include diverse students and educate them well, or perpetuate exclusion and inequitable achievement.

What has happened to the inequitable attitudes and behaviors of yesteryear? Do we still need to argue for new education programs that better meet the needs of all students in a society that promotes equity and equality? The days of separate lunch counters and water fountains are in our past (Colored only — White only). Segregation of students based upon race and disability is no longer legal or officially sanctioned, although it is still a de facto reality. Education programs which have as their purpose taking into account diverse needs of students, as well as education standards within programs that champion student diversity and social justice, are found in most colleges and universities. Nevertheless, a goal of these programs — training and promoting teachers who practice from a multicultural and social justice perspective — has yet to be achieved.

Building Block 4: Discerning Fact From Fantasy Regarding Societal and Educational Gaps

As you look around, is it hard to imagine that some of what we addressed above — the injustices and inequities — still go on today? What if things look good on the surface, but when you scratch just below the surface, the image changes? We call this phenomenon an "illusion of progress." Building Block 4 guides you in looking below the surface so that you can become an effective advocate for young people, and so you can understand what it means to do multicultural education today.

In schools, illusions of social progress abound. For example, many would argue that racial segregation is a thing of the distant past. This argument is supported by observations in the school cafeteria and on the playground, where students of diverse ethnic groups often have friendly interactions. In addition, student groups composed of a single ethnic group are not feared or perceived by another group as planning to harm them. Gender segregation rarely exists in the form of so-called boy classes (auto shop) and so-called girl classes (e.g., home economics). Home economics has been renamed "Family and Consumer Studies," and is popular with both sexes. Students in wheelchairs participate in many school activities, and not only attend proms, but also dance in their chairs with nondisabled students. The cheering squad, band, and sports teams often reflect the diversity of the student body. Moreover, a person of color may be the president of the student council, a class officer may be gay or lesbian, or an Arab-American student maybe a member of the homecoming court.

Teachers and school administrators inform students that they have access to all courses and activities. School officials support and coordinate events that recognize the contributions of people of color and women. In addition, teachers welcome students with disabilities and bilingual students into their classes. Many do not tolerate sexist behavior and gay and lesbian bashing; and virtually all teachers try to treat students who receive free or reduced lunches the same as students who pay for their lunch. Further, many teachers examine their curriculum materials for bias, and willingly attend workshops to learn strategies for teaching language minority students. Such descriptions suggest equity and fairness in the pursuit of academic excellence for all students is the natural order of business in classrooms, schools, and the general society.

However, to the discerning observer, descriptions such as these present illusions of progress. Let's take social class, for example. Is the United States becoming more equitable, less equitable, or staying the same? A Gallup Poll in the spring of 1998 found that even though the proportion of those who described themselves as poor had increased since 1988, the proportion who believed that poverty is diminishing had also increased. It found further that only 39% agree that there is actually a division between "haves" and "have-nots" in America (Duffy, 1998). People like to believe that we are equal, but outside of the college classroom, when was the last time you heard a discussion about social class? Of course, someone may talk about "welfare moms" or "poor kids," but

---

Reflection 3.4
Social class quiz

What percent of U.S. wealth ownership is held by the bottom 50% of the population?
2.8%_____ 22.5% _____ 7.5%_____

What percent of U.S. wealth ownership is held by the next 40% (from 51 to 90%)?
60.3%_____ 25.2%_____ 27.4%_____

What percent of U.S. wealth ownership is held by the next 5% (from 90 to 94%)?
8.3%_____ 12.1%_____ 16.7%_____

What percent of U.S. wealth ownership is held by the next 4% (from 95 to 98%)?
40%_____ 25% _____ 6.9%_____

What percent of U.S. wealth ownership is held by the top 1% of the population?
25.5% _____ 32.7% _____ 15.6%_____

---

in-depth discussions about class stratification in U.S. society do not often take place. Test your knowledge about U.S. social class stratification in Reflection 3.4 on the previous page.

Answers appear at the end of this chapter. How close did you come? Would you be surprised to learn that, from the late 1970s to the late 1990s, the poorest fifth of the population saw a 6% decrease in income (adjusting for inflation), while the wealthiest fifth enjoyed a 55% increase (Economic Policy Institute, 2000)?

Let's take racial integration as another example. Yes, there is racial integration in many schools. But generally speaking, due partly to widespread housing segregation, racial segregation among schools has returned to pre-Civil Rights levels. Kozol (2005) states:

> One of the most disheartening experiences of those who grew up in the years when Martin Luther King and Thurgood Marshall were alive is to visit public schools today that bear their names, or names of other honored leaders of integration struggles that produced the temporary progress that took place in the three decades after *Brown* and find how many of these schools are bastions of contemporary segregation. (p. 1)

It is important for teachers to hone their ability to distinguish fact from fantasy in the quest for equity in order to direct their efforts most effectively. If one simply takes as given the notion that continuous progress is the order of the day, then one is unlikely to see reasons for doing anything other than established practice. On the other hand, if one believes that U.S. society and its schools are hopelessly inequitable, one is likely to feel powerless to make an impact. Neither stance prompts teacher candidates to learn to address deep-seated school or society equity issues.

However, teachers can make a difference working in their classrooms and joining collective efforts to advocate for young people. Teachers, for example, are central to closing achievement gaps among various groups of students. To get beyond believing either that progress toward equity is automatic, or that such progress is impossible, we will engage you in looking at issues in relationship to what sociologists refer to as "institutional structure" and "personal agency."

Institutional Structure and Personal Agency

Institutional structures are socially organized patterns of relationships. For purposes of considering equity, the concept refers specifically to divisions of people into categories used to allocate resources, rules, and treatment — whether by law, routine procedures, or simply de facto. For example, schoolchildren are divided by age into different grade levels, then taught according to shared assumptions about what children at various ages need and are able to do. "Grade levels" have become firm structures defining children, curriculum, testing, and so forth. Institutional structures are not necessarily inequitable or limiting, but as we will show later in this chapter, they can be.

Personal agency refers to the capability people have of acting as they desire, within or even regardless of institutional structures (Giddens, 1984). For example, a third-grade teacher is expected to teach a "third-grade curriculum." However, third-grade teachers interpret what that means in quite different ways, and as a result each third-grade teacher will work in a different way with children and materials, and differ too in her or his expectations for third graders.

Often teacher candidates who haven't thought about these matters assume people have complete "free will." Making that assumption leads teacher candidates not to see the institutional constraints people face. For example, many teacher candidates assume that families who are struggling aren't trying hard enough, or youth who are not completing their homework don't care about education. A flip-side assumption — equally problematic — is that people's problems result solely from institutional pressures, and that no one — including teachers — can do anything about the problems.

Learning to discern fact from fantasy regarding equity entails learning to recognize inequities that exist, situating them within relevant institutionalized patterns, and at the same time seeing possibilities for students, teachers, and other adults to work toward equity. Institutional structures have a good deal of power, but people have created them. Through our everyday actions, we re-create institutional structures, and have the capability to disrupt them. In that respect, we can make changes where needed.

Student Dialogue 3.3

Gilbert: I generally come down on the side of what they are calling here "personal agency." I'm quite aware of discrimination, but I think people bring a lot on themselves.

Celia: Can you give an example of what you mean?

Gilbert: You're not going to like this, I bet. But let's take women's professional sports. I know that women have made huge inroads into sports, especially after Title IX in 1972, which I believe prohibited sex discrimination in education institutions receiving federal funds.

Lisa: Right. I hear that's why I was able to get really involved in athletics. What's your point?

Gilbert: Well, a lot of people don't like the fact that men's sports, especially football and basketball, get so much more attention and money than women's sports. But let's face it, as a group, women don't put as much into honing their athletic skills as men do, and — now let me finish — women don't spend the time watching women's sports that men spend watching sports, and watching sports generates money.

Lisa: Excuse me, Gilbert, but are you aware of all the ways that women's sports continue to get marginalized? Women's sports often don't get the prime schedules, facilities, coaches …

Celia: OK, Gilbert, I think you are dead wrong. But I can see where our argument is over the importance of institutional structure versus personal agency. That, I get.

Reflection 3.5 will help you to see behind illusions of progress by investigating who gets access to what kind of education. For this reflection, go to a high school that has a record for sending a majority of its students to college or to outstanding technical vocational schools. As best you can, gather data on the composition of students in different kinds of classes, as indicated, paying attention to their race/ethnicity, social class background, or gender. The school may be homogeneous by one of these factors, but very likely not by all three.

What did you discover? The chances are that you'll need to ask about the social class backgrounds of students, which may not be apparent visually. Compare your observations with two classmates who have completed Reflection 3.5. Are there patterns common to these investigations?

Much education literature reports that a disproportionate number of African-American, Latino/a, American Indian, and low-income students are not in the advanced classes (Lucas, 1999; Oakes, 2005). Why is this so? Do barriers continue to prevent good and caring teachers and other members of society from helping and supporting students of color and students from low-income families from gaining the preparation necessary for the academically advanced classes? The answer is "Yes." Business as usual — encompassing institutional and personal constraints — is difficult to disrupt.

Institutionalized barriers keep disproportionate numbers of students from some racial and social class groups out of the advanced classes. Barriers may include requiring an overly high grade point average for admission to advanced placement, not preparing such students for advanced study from elementary school onward, and assigning such students the least experienced teachers. Personal constraints include teachers' beliefs that low-income students, or students from single-parent homes, do not have the knowledge or commitment it takes to be successful at a high academic level, leading teachers not to counsel such students in that direction or expend extra effort making sure students learn. For example, if a student is poor, a person of color, or comes from a single-parent home, some teachers mouth the equal opportunity and equity discourse, but personally believe that this so-called "at-risk" student does not have the disposition or academic ability to be successful in school and mainstream society.

Let us now examine inequity issues in the broader society, then look at how these are reflected in and reproduced through schooling.

Illusions of Progress in the Broader Society

To begin, let's examine the distribution of some major societal indicators of living the "good life": wages and jobs; home ownership and good housing; and quality of health care. Use Reflection 3.6 for a quick mental survey of where you believe the United States has made progress over the past few decades and where it has not, with respect to equitable distribution of these social resources.

Reflection 3.6
Progress or illusions of progress?

For each of the following, describe the progress you believe the United States has made in equalizing distribution across race, gender, and ability, and areas in which you believe progress has not been made.
Earnings:

Access to jobs:

Home ownership:

Access to quality health care:

As you read below, check your descriptions against the data we present. Let's begin by looking at earnings and access to jobs.

Earnings and Jobs   When you were growing up, was the amount of money your caregivers/parents earned monthly or yearly discussed with immediate family members? Teacher candidates in our classes say, No, they did not really discover their parents' annual earnings until they were applying for college loans or scholarships. On the other hand, most teacher candidates have a fairly good understanding of the nature of their parents/caregivers' jobs. In addition, they are informed in various ways while growing up of the status (high or low) of their parents/caregivers' jobs. Fundamental to both points is that parents/caregivers want their children to get good jobs making at least a decent amount of money, so that they can support themselves. A respected job which pays good money is a major status symbol in the United States, in addition to being what many regard as a fundamental human right.

Who gets decent-paying jobs, and are there enough to go around? Further, will a visit to most major corporations and societal institutions in the Untied States reveal a good deal of diversity throughout, including at the middle and upper management levels? Of course, one will probably find a few African Americans or Latino/as and some White women in management positions, but will they hold such positions in proportion to their representation in the population? Perhaps equally important, who has jobs and who does not? In which jobs in our two-tier (service and technology) job market will you find some groups of people much more than other groups of people?

Here is what the U.S. Census and other reliable sources report. Being White and male today still has measurable economic and employment advantages, including better access to jobs. In 2005, only about 4.4% of Whites were unemployed, while the unemployment rate for Latinos was 6.6%, and for African Americans, 10.4% (U.S. Department of Labor, 2005). White high school graduates earn about 20% more than African-American and Latino/a high school graduates, and about 40% more at the professional degree level (U.S. Bureau of the Census, 2000; p. 158, Table 252). Many Native American tribes experience devastating poverty and unemployment; 32% of Native Americans lived in poverty nationwide in 2001, with unemployment rates that were typically 2.5 times the U.S. average (U.S. Department of Health and Human Services, 2001).

Women participate in the labor market in ever-growing numbers, and are making substantial inroads into some high-paying, traditionally male fields including law, medicine, and engineering. But earnings of full-time working women are only about 76% of the earnings of full-time working men. This wage gap has fluctuated since the mid-1970s, hovering in the mid-70% range throughout the 1990s and 2000s. In addition, contrary to the thinking of some of our teacher candidates, education does not close the gender gap in earnings. For example, in 2001, the average male with a bachelor's degree earned $56,264, while the average female with a bachelor's degree earned $40,768 (U.S. Department of Labor, 2002). Despite the movement of women into many traditionally male occupations, women are still concentrated mainly in low-paying "pink collar" ghettos such as clerical and childcare work.

As more women become heads of households, this persistent wage gap contributes to poverty among children. In 2004, about 28% of single-parent female-headed households were living in poverty, compared to only 13% of single-parent male-headed households (U.S. Bureau of the Census, 2005). This situation heavily affects children: In divorce proceedings, women are given custody of children much more frequently than are men, and often must attempt to support the family on a low-wage budget.

Assistive technology for people who are disabled has greatly increased in recent years, with motorized shopping carts and wheelchairs, and text-telephones. In addition, federal and state legislation such as the Individuals with Disabilities Education Improvement Act (IDEIA) demands inclusive classrooms. Yet at the same time, most disabled adults are either unemployed or employed part-time, and their earnings are often below the poverty level. In 1998, only one third of disabled high school graduates were employed, a slight increase over 25 years earlier (U.S. Department of Labor, 1998). Unemployment and poverty are particularly severe among disabled people of color, who face double discrimination in the job market.

In sum, since the mid-1980s there has been an illusion that equity exists in the job market. But in fact wage gaps are widening at an ever-increasing rate. Between the mid-1970s and the mid-1990s, average hourly earnings in the United States fell from $12.06 to $10.83 as manufacturing jobs were exported and U.S. workers were laid off (Sklar, 1995). From 2001 to 2003 alone, 11.4 million workers were displaced (U.S. Department of Labor, 2004). Low-paying service work, particularly part-time work, replaced full-time technical and semiprofessional work that had paid considerably more. Temporary work is the fastest growing segment of the labor market. Often working part-time, temporary workers are less likely to have benefits (such as health insurance or vacation time) than are permanent, full-time workers, and most states exclude them from labor law protections and unemployment insurance. At the same time, corporate profits and upper management salaries have risen sharply (Leondar-Wright, 2004).

Food and Housing Family earnings directly affect children's access to food. Roughly 13 million U.S. children live in households that experience hunger or the risk of hunger. Almost 3 million of these children regularly eat too little, sometimes going an entire day without food. City officials attribute the growing inability to pay for food to the increase of low-paying jobs, soaring housing costs, and unemployment (Headley & Lowe, 2000). Churches and charities strain to meet nutrition needs of U.S. hungry people (Bread for the World, 2002). At issue, too, is housing. Several very touching television commercials feature first-time home ownership. As you watch TV, you have probably seen them. In those that we have seen, usually a poor person or person of color receives the key to his or her first home. Intended or not, the commercials imply that with hard work and self-sacrifice, home ownership can be a reality for industrious people who adhere to the work ethic. The commercials also convey to viewers that home ownership is a dominant feature of the "American dream." For many in society, especially those who are trapped in poverty, the commercial is a (hopeful) illusion of the good life.

It is true that home ownership among all racial groups has gradually risen, from 65% of the total U.S. population in 1996 to 69% in 2004. Home ownership is highest among Whites (73% in 2004), as compared to African Americans (49%), Asians (60%), American Indians (56%), and Latinos (48%) (Infoplease, 2006). But, according to Habitat for Humanity (2005), over 30 million U.S. families today lack access to affordable housing. On any given night, about 600,000 people in the United States are homeless. Sixty percent of homeless women and 41% of homeless men have children (Burt et al., 1999), and large numbers are people with disabilities, many of whom were formerly living in institutions. Many more families have inadequate housing, often living in overcrowded quarters due to increasingly insufficient affordable housing.

You can look at how people manage their budgets, given these expenses and inequities in earnings. Reflection 3.7 asks you and a classmate to identify a local school, and explore what difficulties students' parents are dealing with.

Reflection 3.7
A good job makes a difference

Along with a classmate speak to a teacher who has worked in the school for several years about the students' parents' occupations. From this information make an educated guess about the parents' annual income. Ask someone who pays taxes approximately how much to subtract for federal and state taxes. Then divide by 12 to get a monthly income estimate. Write it here:

Review a community newspaper or check with the local real estate company about the cost of housing or apartment rental. Write a monthly figure here:

Next, do your grocery shopping at the neighborhood supermarket in order to ascertain the price paid for food. Write a monthly estimate here:

See if you can find out what people normally pay per month for utilities, including heat, water, telephone, etc. Write a monthly estimate here:

Budget in: an occasional movie, the monthly cost of cable television, having a meal out twice a month at a neighborhood restaurant for a family of four.

Tabulate the expenses:

Discuss with your classmates whether the parents earn enough money for the students to attend school without financial concerns. Now let's add the cost and quality of health care to the mix.

Health Care   Readers of this book may have very good health insurance and receive excellent medical care. The hospital or doctor's offices that you attend may be first rate: no huge lines and no sitting around all day waiting to see a doctor. The nurses, doctors, and other medical personnel may even know you personally, and even if they don't, they probably treat you with courtesy and care. And you would not want it any other way. However, you are fooling yourself if you think that such treatment is routine for everyone.

The reality is that there are significant gaps in health insurance, which affect access to and quality of health care. About 16% of Americans lack health insurance, and over 8 million children lack health insurance (U.S. Bureau of the Census, 2006). Although Medicaid is the main source of health insurance for poor people in the United States, as recently as 2000, about one third did not even have this form of insurance (U.S. Bureau of the Census, 2001). During the early 2000s, while 89% of White Americans were covered by health insurance, 82% of Asian Americans, 80% of African Americans, 67% of Latino Americans, and 71% of American Indians and Alaska Natives were similarly insured (U.S. Bureau of the Census, 2005). Further, even when income, health insurance, and medical conditions are similar, Whites get better and more thorough health care (Pugh, 2002), and they enjoy a longer life expectancy than people of color. In 1998, life expectancy of the Black male at birth was 67.8 compared to 74.6 years for the White male (U.S. Bureau of the Census, 2000, p. 84, Table 116), and life expectancy of Native Americans was 2.5 years less than that of other groups of color (U.S. Department of Health and Human Services, 2001). Because the United States has no federal law protecting the rights of gays, lesbians, and bisexual people, and many states still have laws outlawing "homosexual conduct," more often than not, gay or lesbian domestic partners lack health insurance.

Financial concerns of parents do not preclude them from wanting their children to do well in school. In fact, families are probably hoping that when their children grow up they will have it better than their parents, and view schools as the route by which that can take place.

Student Dialogue 3.4

Lisa: This is so depressing! I'm feeling guilty for being White and growing up in a middle class home, and I'm feeling terrible about all of these problems!

Celia: It can be depressing when you look at it. But why are you feeling guilty, Lisa?

Lisa: Well, it looks like White people get all of these advantages. I don't feel advantaged, but then I read this material. I'm not rich, so maybe I shouldn't blame myself.

Gilbert: Lisa, you didn't create all of this. You were born into it. All of us were. I think the question is what can we do now? We are planning to be teachers, so it seems like at least we have to help the kids we teach and not be part of what hurts them.

Celia: Someone at our college recently said that we are the future. Sometimes I think about that. We aren't the past so much as we are the future. And the kids we teach are the future's future. We didn't get born into a terrible country by any means, but it is a country that has some huge problems.

Gilbert: There have always been problems.

Celia: And all kinds of people who have worked on them — people like us.

Lisa: Maybe we can make things better. Maybe the kids we teach can make things even better after us.

The students above are speaking to the idea of agency, or the ability of people to change how institutions work and who has access to what. Agency is a bit different from personal responsibility, a term that refers to the ability of individuals to manage their own lives and take advantage of resources that are available to them. *Agency* refers not only to managing one's own life, but also the ability to set in motion actions that can transform the world around us. For example, not everyone can take personal responsibility for providing adequate health care for their families if adequate health care and health insurance are too expensive for many people. Agency refers not only to doing what one can within the constraints of what is available, but also working to change the rules in order to reduce institutional inequities — in this case, advocating for broader access to health care.

Illusions of Progress in Schools

To set the stage for connecting societal disparities to gaps in access to quality education, complete Reflection 3.8. It asks you two thinking questions about the school in which you may be doing a field placement. Also, note the comments of Gilbert, Lisa, and Celia, and bear in mind that their comments are constructed out of their life experiences and the knowledge they are gaining from reading this material.

**Reflection 3.8
School issues**

1. Imagine that the school where you are currently doing your field placement needs computers. The parents plan to have a fund-raiser because the school budget is tight and students would have to wait several years to receive computers. Each computer will cost the school approximately $1,000. Estimate how many new computers the school will receive from this fund-raising activity. Write a short report, being as specific as possible on why you estimate as you do.
2. How many of your students do you think will be going on to college, and why do you think so? How much influence do you believe that you have to affect their decision about going to college, and their choice of college? Write a short report, being specific as possible on why you believe as you do.

Student Dialogue 3.5

Gilbert: Now here's a problem. My school isn't going to end up with many computers if the parents have to buy them. Computers should be bought by the school district, and every student should have access to one! The parents in my school just don't have that much money.

Lisa: The parents would buy their child a computer if they really cared how their children were doing in school. That's what my parents did. Or, get a used one, at least.

Celia: Lisa, not everyone's parents can afford a computer. If my high school hadn't gotten some financial help from the local businesses to buy computers, I wouldn't have learned to use one until I came to college!

Lisa: Well, I just want to teach in a place like where I grew up, so I'm not sure I need to consider these issues. I really don't want to teach in a poor school or a school with a lot of minority students. (pause) Gilbert, I see you rolling your eyes at me. No offense, but the more we have to discuss these multicultural issues, the more I begin to question not only if I can become a successful teacher, but also the choice I have made to teach.

Celia: Lisa, you can learn.

Gilbert: Lisa, listen. When I was a kid, I was stuck with whoever was there to teach me, whether they wanted to teach me or not. Schools need you. The kids need you, as long as you are willing to learn.

Celia: Most people, including my teachers, thought I wasn't going to college. They thought that the best thing for me was to prepare for a job after high school. But I wanted to go to college and my parents wanted me to go too. Maybe we could talk with our students about college life, and see where the discussion goes. My music teacher, Mr. Jasper, who's White and middle class, by the way, did that. And here I am!

Gilbert: And just think, Lisa, some day some kid who struggled against the "isms" of the world …

Celia: Including the school system …

Gilbert: Yeah, exactly. Some day that kid will be sitting in a college classroom talking about how her favorite teacher, Ms. Lisa Thompson, inspired her to learn to become somebody.

Lisa: I'd like that.

Celia: Me, too!

Gilbert: Me, three!

Schools work reasonably well for some students, but not so well for others. To become a fantastic teacher you will need to disrupt some silences. In other words, you may have to think of clever ways to introduce topics that are not receiving much attention, but need to be talked about, and then acted on, in order to create access for all students to a full range of educational opportunities. Fantastic teachers become aware of and support the aspirations communities have for their children, even if many in the community lack the know-how for achieving those aspirations. Fantastic teachers learn the folkways of the community in order to establish rapport and build upon the backgrounds and interests of the children. Also, they learn to identify wellsprings (human and material resources) for learning and growth in whatever community their students are from. In addition, fantastic teachers are politically astute. They are able to see the political and economic constraints communities are bounded by and work to help kids recognize and free themselves from the restrictions to success that society imposes on them.

Many constraints, including physical facilities and working conditions, affect the quality of teaching, and work against teacher candidates becoming fantastic teachers (Corcoran, Walker, White, 1988; Earthman & Lemaster, 1996; Olsen 2003; U. S. Department of Education, 1998). Since the mid-1990s, the federal government has been active in publishing or sponsoring reports on the condition of schools and how such conditions constrain teachers' effectiveness and quality of work. The reports observed that poor-quality schools often serve students who are most in need of fantastic teachers and teaching. One report compares characteristics of schools in poor condition with schools in good condition, claiming that the same subgroup of schools (inner-city schools, schools in the western United States, large schools, and those with high minority or high poverty concentrations) consistently emerge as those with the most problems (U. S. General Accounting Office, 1996). A second GAO report claims that in 1999 close to 22% of the nation's schools were overcrowded; operating at 25% over capacity. Additionally, the most overcrowded schools report the poorest physical conditions (45% reported at least one type of building in less than adequate condition; 59% reported at least one building feature in less than adequate condition; and 46% reported at least one unsatisfactory environmental condition). The GAO report further notes that schools facing overcrowding tend to differ by percentage of minority enrollment and geographic region from those that are not overcrowded (U.S. Department of Education, 2001).

Due to passage of the No Child Left Behind Act, today's high-stakes testing environment also affects teachers' quality of work life. Under high-stakes testing, test results are used (often exclusively) to allocate resources, and to determine promotion to the next grade, college entrance, school funding, scholarships, and so forth. Rewards or sanctions accrue to students, teachers, principals, and schools as a result of how well (or poorly) students perform on tests (Secada, 2003). It is debatable whether the changes that high-stakes testing programs bring to school and classroom practices are in the best interest of the teachers and students, especially from the standpoint of teachers. According to Abrams, Pedualla, and Madaus (2003), teachers believe that high-stakes state-mandated testing programs contradict teachers' views of effective educational practices. Teachers feel they are spending more time doing things like coaching for the test and placing greater emphasis on covering the material on the tests, and much less time on other curricular areas. Also, the "specific test preparation, activities, coaching and instruction geared toward the test can yield scores that are invalid" in that the scores do not hold up when students take other tests measuring the same content or skills (Abrams et al., 2003, p. 10). In addition, Abrams et al. report that teachers are stressed out and their morale is suffering, and they note that, "Increased levels of anxiety, stress, and fatigue are often seen among students participating in high stakes testing programs" (p. 20). State curriculum standards and high-stakes testing will be considered in subsequent chapters. Below, we turn to recurring institutionalized patterns that affect equity in education, beginning with classroom instruction.

Classroom Instruction   When you are in a class, what is the one word that best describes the kind of curriculum and teaching that makes you want the bell to ring? "Boring," right? Too much of classroom instruction is just plain boring. In a study we conducted in a junior high school, *boring* was the word students used most often to describe instruction (Grant & Sleeter, 1996). When students are bored, they tune out and often fidget. Many teachers interpret such behavior as a discipline problem. We recently talked with a retired reading specialist who had moved to the area and had signed up to substitute. She was called one day to substitute in a special education elementary classroom. There, because of the state's emphasis on phonics instruction and basic skills, the only teaching resources were workbooks that drilled children on isolated skills. She spent the day doing her best to make things interesting, but saw the children were obviously bored. Another teacher who was used to the skill drills, however, praised her ability to manage the children's behavior, commenting that they were usually more off-task. The retired reading specialist was aghast that a class of struggling readers was having to slog through workbooks every day without even a taste of literature, and that their behavior, which she saw as a direct result of boredom, was perceived as a result of their learning disabilities or as bad behavior.

In Reflection 3.9, briefly describe two classes in which you were bored. Explain why you were bored.

Reflection 3.9
What makes a class boring?

1. I was bored in my _____ class because_____

_____

2. I was bored in my _____ class because_____

_____

Most elementary classrooms have more variety in instruction than secondary classrooms, although several patterns are common. During reading instruction, many teachers work with one group and assign seatwork to the rest of the class. During math, social studies, science, or language arts, many teachers teach the whole class by using a textbook. The instruction may include chalk-and-talk, using questions that are provided in the teacher's edition of the text, along with assigning students pages in the textbook or using commercially published handouts, or workbooks. Some elementary teachers also individualize instruction, use learning centers, and use small group instruction.

At the secondary level, there is more uniformity in instruction. One researcher described instruction at the secondary level as "rows of tablet-arm chairs facing a teacher who is talking, asking, listening to student answers, and supervising the entire class for most of the period — a time that is occasionally punctuated by a student report, a panel, or a film" (Cuban, 1994, p. 222). Labs in science classes offer the main variation in academic courses; vocational, physical education, and art classes' offer more varied activities.

Since passage of the No Child Left Behind Act, instruction has become even more uniform, especially those in schools that are under the gun to improve. Elementary teachers in low-performing schools often have to teach directly from the textbook and teacher's manual. A good deal of drill and practice, and preparation for tests take place (Grant & Brown, 2006). Kozol (2005) points out that teachers have to contend with impersonal and mechanist practices mandated by the states, noting that, "Few teachers, of whatever age, can take it as an evidence of even minimal respect for their intelligence to be provided with a "teacher-proof" curriculum" (p. 28).

Does this all sound familiar? Repetitive patterns become boring if not interrupted. Review Reflection 3.9, and add suggestions for how you might change each class so they do not bore students.

Teacher Expectations   Teachers' expectations of students affect student access to high-quality teaching. You have considerable power to set your expectations high — or low. Teachers' expectations may serve as much of a constraint on learning as any of the institutional constraints we discussed. Many studies over the years have examined the correlation between a student's race and the expectation the teacher has for that student. These studies consistently find that teachers tend to view White and Asian students as more academically capable than African-American or Latino/a students (Irvine, 2003). But what matters is how expectations affect what you do. How teachers teach and interact with students communicates how much learning they expect, and students pick up on teachers' actions quite well. For example, how much time teachers spend actually teaching and having students take responsibility for learning as opposed to doing other things (playing games, students talking quietly among themselves), communicates to students how seriously a teacher takes his or her learning. How teachers talk with students — the depth and breadth of discussion, the extent to which it pushes them to learn — also communicates expectations. Expectations can be communicated through "teacher-student negotiations." In some classes, students learn that if they work quietly for 25 to 30 minutes, they can socialize with their classmates for the remainder of the class period. Such negotiation robs students of valued academic learning time, and over the course of a semester, many teaching hours are lost.

For Reflection 3.10, interview two students in a school in which you are completing a field experience — select students of different races and genders if possible — regarding

---

Reflection 3.10
Teacher expectations

Suggested Question for Students:
1. What does Mr./Ms. (teacher's name) think you will be when you grow up?

2. Does Mr./Ms. (teacher's name) think you are (a) smart, (b) average, (c) having difficulty? Why do you say so?

Suggested Questions for Teacher:
1. What do you think (student's name) will be doing when he or she grows up?

2. What kind of academic potential does (student's name) have: (a) smart, (b) average, (c) having difficulty? Why do you say so?

---

their teachers' expectations of them. Next interview the teacher about his or her expectations of the students you interviewed.

Compare the responses. Are the expectations of the students and the teacher close? If not, why do you think so, and what implications do you think this has for the student?

Teacher–Student Interaction   Expectations affect how teachers interact academically with students. On average, which of the following do you believe are true:

- Many teachers interact with, call on, praise, and intellectually challenge students who are White, male, and middle class more than other students in the same classroom.
- Many teachers reprimand Black male students the most.
- Teachers tend to give girls less attention than boys; boys get both more positive *and* more negative teacher attention than girls.
- If you believe all of the above are true, then you are correct, according to several research studies (e.g., Okpala, 1996).

Teachers often point out that students' behavior determines how teachers treat them. If students misbehave, teachers reprimand them. If students raise their hands, teachers call on them. If students fade into the background, teachers don't mean to ignore them, but that just happens. What is missing from this, however, is some analysis of how the teacher is interpreting the student. If a student wiggles constantly, what does that mean? Does it mean that the student is bored, lost, active, misbehaving, or needs to go to the toilet? When prevalent patterns are not interrupted, students who are White, male, and middle class tend to get a disproportionate share of the teacher's instructional attention.

A cycle of behavior then begins to develop in the classroom. Reflection 3.11 asks you to think about how you would react if you received the same patterns of attention or inattention, over the long run.

Now look at responses you wrote in relationship to their impact on teacher behavior. For example, if you were repeatedly ignored, would you demand attention? Fade into the background? Bother your friends? What kinds of teacher behaviors would your response likely trigger, and how would you respond to that teacher behavior? This cycle of behavior is important to examine because we have seen many classrooms in which a negative cycle of interactions between the teacher and some students develops. In such cases, both the teacher and the students assume their relationship is a product of the

---

Reflection 3.11
Does attention from the teacher matter?

If I were repeatedly ignored, I would _____

If I often received praised for mediocre work, I would _____

If I were constantly reprimanded, although I did nothing wrong, I would _____

kind of person the other is, rather than how they are interacting with each other. Often the students most negatively affected are culturally different from the teacher, and consequently misinterpreted by teachers who take for granted what they believe "normal" classroom behavior looks like.

Ability Grouping and Tracking Ability grouping, found extensively in elementary schools, and tracking in high schools in the major academic areas, help to institutionalize the bell-shaped curve by dividing students for instruction based on estimates of their academic ability. (Tracking means placing some students in college preparatory or basic/essential classes. The "bell-shaped curve" refers to the tendency for most people to cluster in the middle on many measures, with declining numbers of people distributed at the high and low ends of the spectrum.) You looked briefly at tracking in Reflection 3.5. Review your findings. Which kinds of students had most access to upper-level science and math classes? Which were clustered in vocational classes?

The pros and cons of ability grouping and tracking are continually debated by teachers, as demonstrated on the "Speak Out" page of the American Federation of Teachers' publication *On Campus* (Lucas, 1992; B. L. Mitchell, 1992). Here, two teachers argue their positions, one maintaining that ability grouping can create a label that lasts a lifetime, and the other that talented students must not be ignored. Although many people assume that ability grouping and tracking are best for most students, the evidence points to the conclusion that "no group of students has been found to benefit consistently from being in a homogeneous group," and that those in the middle and lower groups are often affected negatively (Oakes, 2005, p. 7).

Oakes's investigation of 25 secondary schools across the country in the late 1970s found extensive use of tracking, and illustrated how this practice institutionalizes inequitable access to quality instruction. In multiracial schools, upper-track classes were disproportionately White, whereas lower-track classes were disproportionately minority and lower class (see also Lucas, 1999). Upper-track students tended to get more teaching time, much more homework, many more varied teaching activities, clearer instruction, more emphasis on higher-level thinking skills, and much more exposure to content that would give them access to college than did lower-track students. Most upper-track students reported enthusiasm for school and feelings of personal competence, whereas lower-track students were often turned off to school and felt academically incompetent. Classes for gifted students are still disproportionately White, whereas classes for children with mental retardation and emotional disturbances are disproportionately African American (U.S. Department of Education, 2000). In some schools, Latino/a students are overrepresented in special education; in others, they are placed in bilingual education whether this is appropriate or not. Studies by Oakes and Lucas clearly show that students are grouped partly on the basis of race and social class and different methods are then used to teach them.

Grouping and tracking of students actively continues, and is increasingly carried out through the use of the large-scale achievement tests. Such tests are used by states and school districts to determine which schools, programs, or classes students are assigned to based upon their achievement level; whether or not to promote a student to the next grade; and whether or not a student will receive a high school diploma (National Research Council, 1999).

Access to Technology   Access to computer technology is inequitable, a situation aptly referred to as the "digital divide." Some call the age we are living in the "information age." Computer literacy is the necessary knowledge that is needed in order to to live successfully in the information age, and the necessary tool is a computer. In order to acquire both computer literacy and a computer one needs either money or a site where computers are available. Computer access correlates very strongly with the relative wealth of the particular school a child attends. Low-income children are far less likely to attend computer-rich schools than are children of professionals; and they are also far less likely to have access to computers at home. A recent study found 87% of White college students, but only 76% of Black students and 81% of Latino/a students, had used a computer frequently in 2004 (Farrell, 2005). As Farrell pointed out, "Black students are not keeping pace with other minority students, lagging five percentage points behind Hispanic students and 15 percentage points behind Asian-American students" (p. A32). The cost of high-speed Internet connectivity contributes greatly to the digital divide. Farrell noted that low-income communities are not considered significant markets for high-speed Internet, reducing technological access of young people in those communities. The digital divide, according to Gorski and Clark (2002), has a tremendous impact on second-language speakers of English as well as non-English speakers. Gorski and Clark report that most Web pages on the Internet worldwide are in English, whereas 57% of all worldwide Internet users are native speakers of languages other than English. The authors go on to state that it is unfortunate that as computer and Internet technology become more integrated into the sociocultural and educational fabric of the United States and the larger global society, very little attention is being paid to the have-nots, thus expanding the digital divide. Significantly pertinent to teacher candidates is Gorski and Clark's observation that, whereas "computer technology is a familiar tool in the language and second language development classroom, their manner of use in these contexts is most often in the vein of Eurocentric education 'skills and drills,' using computer software that grills students on phonics, grammar, vocabulary and verb conjugations" (p. 32).

Devaluation of Diverse People   In schools as well as in society at large, segments of people are persistently devalued in ways that can have devastating consequences; for example, take gay, lesbian, bisexual, and transgendered (GLBT) youth. GLBT people have little or no legal standing in society and expressions of disdain for them is so routine that many heterosexual people see it as normal. As a result, according to various reports, between 48 and 76% of GLBT youth have thought of suicide and between 29 and 42% have attempted it (Russell & Joyner, 2001). Gay and lesbian youth report greater depression, hopelessness, and suicidal inclinations than heterosexual youth. More than twice as many GLBT youth (30%) than heterosexual youth (13%) reported a prior suicide attempt (Safren & Heimberg, 1999). GLBT teens are also more likely to use and abuse drugs, become victims of violence and harassment, and get thrown out of their homes and end up on the street (Buce & Obolensky, 1990; Krucks, 1991; Uribe & Harbeck, 1991). As you work through this book, we will share strategies teachers can use to interrupt devaluation of people.

Children of GLBT parents/childcare providers also face difficult challenges in school. Reflection 3.12 asks you to interview a gay, lesbian, or bisexual man or woman who has a student(s) in school to ascertain how (if at all) their sexual preference influences the social or academic life of her or his child. Of course, such a person would likely need to be "out of the closet" for you to identify him or her as gay, lesbian, or bisexual. If you don't know whom to interview, that in itself is an indicator of an unaccepting climate in which people cannot reveal significant parts of themselves.

Did the interview help you become aware of at least one thing you can do to build a more inclusive classroom environment?

Over the last several pages, we have taken you through a number of related dimensions of schools and the broader society. Our intent has been to help you think critically about the persistent disparities in access to social and educational resources and to discuss the constraints which prevent the gaps from closing. Before moving on, Reflection 3.13 asks you to take stock of what you have read and thought about.

We have helped to increase your awareness about illusions of progress and how institutional constraints influence teaching and learning. Awareness is the first step to taking action. Creating academically challenging, culturally responsive, fair, and inclusive classrooms for all of your students is the best place to start. The rest of this book develops these ideas. New teachers will probably receive resistance from the administration and some other teachers if they try to disrupt established schoolwide practice, such as trying to get rid of tracking in a school where it has been in existence for years and is seen as a useful instructional tool. To begin tackling schoolwide equity issues, the new teacher can collect opinions from other staff members regarding their attitude about such concerns, and collect data on how the practice in question affects different student populations in the school. But the teacher must first identify those institutional con-

---

Reflection 3.12
Learning about inclusion

Possible Questions:
Has your child received any different treatment at school because of your sexuality?

Do other parents permit their children to socialize with your child in events or activities (e.g., birthday parties) outside of school?

Do teachers treat you or your child differently?

Reflection 3.13
Illusions of progress: taking stock

List two or three areas in which there has been significant progress in closing gaps over time.

1.

2.

List two or three areas in which there has been little or no progress so far, which are most important to you. Explain why they are important and what role you might play in addressing them.

1.

2.

---

straints where he or she can have influence and develop a plan along with goals to assess progress, and examine her or his own background to identify any personal issues that will serve as personal constraints to the effort.

Building Block 5: Setting Professional Learning Goals for Yourself

The patterns we have just examined have existed for some time and have been recognized and contested by many educators. In fact, areas of progress that we have noted have come about largely through the efforts of educators, working in conjunction with community and social movements, to make schools, along with other social institutions, fairer and more responsive to the needs of the students.

Now let's come back to you. You haven't yet started to teach, so you really don't have established patterns. The actions you take as a teacher, and the patterns they form, are yet to be constructed. Learning to become a fantastic teacher is an ongoing process that requires continual learning and reflection. In Reflection 3.14, take a look at your own

---

Reflection 3.14
Teaching that worked for you

Think back to your own elementary or secondary schools. If possible, use a yearbook to refresh your memory. Now, make two lists or descriptions.

Everything that supported you and your academic and social development

Everything that did not support you and your academic and social development

---

experience as a student. What kinds of teaching, programming, and other school experiences helped you most, and what didn't help you?

Compare your lists with classmates. You will most likely discover some similarities across your lists, and also some differences. Teachers base many of their ideas about teaching on their own experience as students. This is helpful, so long as you analyze that experience carefully, since your experiences and reactions to them are, in many ways, particular to you and may not apply well to students you teach.

Student Dialogue 3.6

Lisa: I didn't think about it until I completed Reflection 3.14, but I see some problems. No one pushed me in math, for one. To this day I hate math, and I'm worried that I'll discourage my students from liking it.

Gilbert: Not if you see that as a problem now and can figure out how to address it. Now, school was easy for me. It was like a game, a great mental game, especially history and French. Based on my experience, I don't believe kids should be coddled; that just holds them back. I had this history teacher who was hard, and kids gave him grief because of that, but I learned a lot from him.

Lisa: So, was there anything that didn't work for you?

Gilbert: Yeah, teachers who looked at me and said to themselves — "Black, single-parent family, so I should expect problems" — mixed race, actually.

Celia: Ah, more problems!

Gilbert: For me, academics was a great place to get away from whatever problems might have been going on between me and my folks. So I guess what worked for me was teachers who could see my potential and didn't let biases get in the way.

Celia: I sure went to a different school than you! Mine was mostly pretty boring. We just did the same thing every day, especially in high school. In my English class, you knew what day it was by what kind of work we did. Every Monday we did the same thing, every Tuesday the same thing — that got boring!

Lisa: So what I hear us saying is that all three of us liked to be challenged, right? Even if we complained at the time, we appreciated teachers who challenged us.

Every teacher candidate we have worked with has brought strengths to the teaching profession; and every teacher candidate has many areas for growth. Before plunging into the next chapters, take inventory of your own strengths and areas for growth. First, look back over self-inventories you completed in chapter 1, paying particular attention to the following:

- Your vision of a fantastic teacher (Reflections 1.1 and 1.13);
- Your analysis of what will sustain you as a teacher (Reflection 1.3);
- Your cultural roots learned through your home and community (Reflection 1.6) and groups you affiliate with (Reflection 1.9);
- Your analysis of your prior schooling (Reflection 1.7);
- Your beginning philosophy of education (Reflection 1.12).

Then review insights you gained about students in chapter 2, paying particular attention to the diversity among students in classrooms today, and insights students gave you regarding what will engage and empower them in the classroom. In this chapter, you have had to consider relationships between students' identities and backgrounds, and equity issues in schools and society at large.

As you examine all of these areas in relationship to each other, what do you see as central strengths you currently possess, and in what key areas would you like to learn and grow over the semester?

You have now created the beginnings of a professional development plan for yourself. The best teachers are open to ongoing learning and pay attention to what others tell them to learn, but also take charge over their own learning. Based on years of studying star teachers of children in poverty, Haberman (1995) emphasized that the best teachers look very critically at themselves, their prejudices, and their beliefs about children from different backgrounds, and their prior experiences; and they are willing to learn from that critical analysis. In addition, the best teachers are willing to continue to learn what works for the students they actually have. They don't stop learning; they always recognize areas in which they can continue to learn and improve. At the same time, they do not allow what they don't know to stop them from doing their best for children; they refuse to give up. Star teachers love to learn, and they establish classrooms in which everyone — including the teacher — is learning.

Putting It Into Practice

After class, Lisa went home feeling exhausted. She was exhilarated by many of the conversations she had been part of, and her mind was whirling in a thousand directions. As she entered her apartment, she realized that she was mentally exhausted, but not physically exhausted. So, she changed into sweats and running shoes, and took off for a four-mile run. As she ran, her mind began to slow down, although she couldn't get some ideas out of her head.

She knew that women had fought for equal access to athletics, and were still fighting on several fronts. In her high school, for instance, it was always a battle to get access to the best facilities during good practice times. But she had assumed that schools were working better for students of color, since they had been desegregated. And she realized that she simply hadn't paid attention to many things around her, like the ethnic homogeneity of the neighborhood she grew up in, as well as the neighborhood where she lived right now.

When she got home, she took a shower, put on a robe, and turned on the TV. She decided to just veg for a while before pulling out the books to get ready for class the next day. But as she watched TV, she began to realize that the shows she usually turned to catered to her demographic: young middle-class White people! As this realization hit her, she remembered Celia and Gilbert telling her to use experiences for learning, rather than feeling bad about them. So, she began to critically analyze the TV show she was watching, looking for the following:

- What are the race, gender, social class, and sexual orientation of the main characters? Secondary characters? Do any characters have a disability?
- What images does the show convey about diversity in the United States? Globally?
- What images does the show convey about equity in the United States? Globally?
- What kind of lifestyle are the advertisers trying to sell viewers on? Whose lifestyle is that? Who benefits most from that lifestyle? Who doesn't benefit from it?
- What other TV shows are going on at the same time that might offer a different perspective or cater to a different demographic? What might I learn if I changed the channel?
- Are there communities whose world simply isn't reflected much (or at all) in the TV shows that are available? Who benefits most from the array of shows available, and who doesn't benefit?

Within an hour, Lisa's head was spinning even more, but now, rather than being exhausted, she was excited! She was taking charge over her learning. She wasn't a passive observer to life around her, and she wasn't powerless. She realized that she had personal agency, at least over her own learning and behavior. She was so excited that she picked up her cell phone and called Celia to tell her about these discoveries.

Turn on a TV show you frequently watch, or if you aren't a TV viewer, any show that happens to be on right now. Use Lisa's questions to analyze it. Then write a paragraph about what you can learn by critically analyzing the media around you.

Answers to Reflection 3.4, Social class quiz: 1. 2.8%   2. 27.4%   3. 12.1% 4. 25% 5. 32.7%
Source: Arthur B. Kennickell (2003, November). A rolling tide: Changes in the distribution of wealth in the U.S., 1989–2001, Table 10. :Levy Economics Institute, Bard College, N.Y.

four
Building a Caring Classroom That Supports Achievement

This chapter will help you to answer the following questions:

- How do fantastic teachers develop positive student–teacher rapport?
- What does it mean to be a caring teacher?
- How can I use conflict resolution, and for what purposes?
- How can I use cooperative learning effectively?
- How can I conduct class meetings effectively?
- How can I help students address prejudice and stereotyping?

The first three chapters of this book set the stage for teaching. There, you examined yourself, students, and student-centered teaching as the basis for achievement, and you looked at classrooms in their wider social and historical context. Now it's time to move into the classroom, roll up our sleeves, and begin to build practice. Where do we start?

We believe the best place to start is with relationships, since they form the foundation for everything else that happens in the classroom. For students, learning involves taking risks — trying out new ideas, skills, and even identities, trusting that the teacher truly has their best interests at heart, and that classroom peers will support rather than discourage risk taking. As Meier (2002) noted, "Learning happens fastest when the novices trust the setting so much that they aren't afraid to take risks, make mistakes, or do something dumb. Learning works best, in fact, when the very idea that it's risky hasn't even occurred to kids" (p. 18). Teachers are responsible for building relationships that sustain learning and growth and the risk taking involved. But for teachers, building relationships involves risks, too, since caring exposes us emotionally.

Building trust, authentic caring, and trusting relationships involve work. Most educators agree that care is essential to good teaching. Care not only supports learning and achievement, but is also the fundamental glue that holds societies together. So, to help you get started, the first section of the chapter will unpack what it means to "care," applying this concept to teacher–student and student–student relationships. Then, the chapter will develop three building blocks:

Building Block 6: Using Conflict Resolution
Building Block 7: Addressing Prejudice and Stereotyping
Building Block 8: Using Cooperative Learning

Most of the reflections in this chapter involve you in analyzing ideas or connecting them with your own experiences. But for a few of them, you will need access to the following:

- The Internet (for Reflections 4.7, 4.12);
- Three people of any age to interview (for Reflection 4.3);
- About five young people you can talk with (for Reflection 4.8).

Care and Relationships in School

A study in the 1990s asked everyone inside four schools in Southern California (students, teachers, custodians, cafeteria workers, and so forth): "What is the central problem of schooling?" Interpersonal relationships — caring — emerged as the primary concern. People said that their best experiences in schools involved other people who cared, listened, and respected them. But they also noted that there was too little time throughout the day to cultivate personal relationships, and that too much fear and misunderstanding got in the way. Race, culture, and class were the second main concerns because these determined who had access to the most satisfying academic experiences and who felt understood and supported in school. One student summed up the research by saying, "This place hurts my spirit" (Institute for Education in Transformation, 1992).

Student Dialogue 4.1

Celia: Oh, that reminds me so much of my junior high! It was a mixed school, but there was a real pecking order. Someone like me with brown skin and a Spanish accent was seen as lower than low. I hated school then.

Gilbert: I wouldn't say I hated school or that it hurt my spirit. I've got a pretty tough spirit. But I know quite a few kids who never made it to tenth grade because they couldn't be themselves in school. They had to choose between being themselves or being a student. The way the school defined "student," they couldn't be both.

Lisa: I want to ask you two about your experiences because mine might have been different. But first I want to say that I'm glad we are dealing with trust building before getting into more heavy-duty topics. That last chapter was rough, and I don't know you two very well. Until I know you won't laugh at me, or think I'm racist or stuck up or something, I watch what I say.

Celia: I feel the same way. I don't worry about being seen as racist, but I worry about sounding dumb. I need to know someone and trust that person before I open up very much.

Lisa and Celia echo the feelings of many students. They want to speak up during class discussions, but are concerned about what others will think about their comments and actions. Building trust and providing a safe space, therefore, are the first order of business to the establishment of a productive learning environment. In addition, "race" arguably is the most difficult topic for a mixed racial and ethnic group of Americans to discuss. Gilbert's point about "being oneself" is also a challenge because of peer pressure and pressure from the school and teachers to conform to the school's way of doing things. This tug of war, we know from our own experiences and the experiences of others, lasts a lifetime. Working with all of this, however, does become a bit easier as you do it.

Probably no one intends to construct schools and classrooms in a way that hurts the spirit of teachers or students. Yet this happens unless we explicitly attend to the quality of relationships that are fostered. Below we examine teacher–student relationships, student–student relationships, and discipline.

Student–Teacher Relationships

Establishing caring relationships with every student may be the most important thing a teacher can do to begin teaching to high achievement and closing the "achievement gap" (Bell, 2002–2003). But, as with many educational concepts, there are different interpretations of what it means to care. Many beginning teachers use the words *care*, *love*, and *help* to express their reasons for entering the teaching profession. Look back at how you discussed loving and helping students in chapter 1. What did your discussion suggest that you do to demonstrate care? What have you done since reading chapter 1 to act on your ideas?

Students experience teacher care through what the teacher does. Noddings (1995) explained that "caring is not just a warm, fuzzy feeling that makes people kind and likable.… When we care, we want to do our very best for the objects of our care." Gay (2000) elaborated on what caring and uncaring relationships look like: "Caring interpersonal relationships are characterized by patience, persistence, facilitation, validation, and empowerment for the participants. Uncaring ones are distinguished by impatience, intolerance, dictation, and control" (p. 47). Teachers usually find warm, constructive relationships easy to build with some students and much harder with other students.

Reflection 4.1 asks you to take a brief inventory of your reactions to different kinds of kids. The more honestly you face your present reactions, the better you can examine and work with them. As you do this exercise, keep in mind that the real problem in classrooms isn't just how you feel about students. More significantly, it is about, on the one hand, whether you allow negative feelings to persist and shape relationships with some students and, on the other hand, whether you allow positive feelings toward other kids to privilege them and give them access that the first group of students is not receiving.

Examine what you wrote in relationship to Gay's description of actions that characterize caring and uncaring relationships. Which kinds of kids are you most likely to treat in ways that show patience, persistence, facilitation, validation, and empowerment? Which kinds of kids might you treat in ways that show impatience, intolerance, dictation, and control? Be bluntly honest here, now is the time to stand tall. Carl Grant recalls when Christine Sleeter pushed him to "stand tall" in developing his knowledge and interaction with students who have severe disabilities.

How you treat students affects how they regard you. Based on what you wrote in Reflection 4.1, which students will probably react to you in ways that make you feel competent, warm, and respected? Think carefully here about how kids will react to *your treatment of them*. Although students bring into the classroom a wide range of personalities, feelings about school, problems, and prior experiences from their lives outside school, most of their reactions to you will stem from how you treat them. It is quite possible that students will "read" your feelings about them from your body language even before you have thought consciously about those feelings.

Student Dialogue 4.2

Gilbert: Now, this is a profound idea, and it makes me think about my fifth-grade teacher, old Mr. Franks. Poor Mr. Franks, I think he was just a little bit old and out of step, but we tormented him! We thought he was strange and slow to figure things out, so we did all kinds of things to upset him, like putting tacks on his chair, talking when he wanted us quiet, and hiding his things. He thought we were incorrigible, mostly because about half of us weren't White. We respected our other teachers, so we didn't act that way with them, but he brought out the worst in us.

Celia: And I bet the whole time he thought your behavior was a product of your home environment, right?

Gilbert: Bingo!

Gilbert's thinking may make some teachers cringe. His reference to Mr. Frank's age, "little bit old and out of step," is somewhat hard to accept in a country where most are living longer and some are working well past 65, once considered retirement age. Before Gilbert rushed to his conclusion, it would have been wise to have a one-on-one with Mr. Frank. Such an interaction may have resulted in both of them having a better understanding of each other.

Chapter 2 discussed becoming acquainted with students. By listening closely to them, we can tune in to "the humanness of every child" and their capacities "to be creators, builders, and actors in their education and their lives" (Schultz, 2003, p. 35). We have found it very helpful as teachers to identify early on those students we find it difficult to relate to, and intentionally try to get to know them personally. We do not suggest snooping into the student's private life or looking for problems the student may have, but rather discovering what interests the student, what kind of person the student is trying to become, what hopes and dreams the student may have, what the student is good at. Most students respond when a teacher shows a genuine interest in him or her as a person.

As Reflection 4.1 illustrates, "care" is expressed as action. Reflection 4.2 asks you to consider the kinds of actions that best express care. Circle those that help to describe what it means to act on care.

Discuss with your classmates which terms you selected and why. How many of your classmates selected most or all of them? Which were not selected? Did those terms that were not selected deal with social justice, or did they deal with the less provocative issues regarding care such as "encouraging students to be their best?" You may be puzzled why we included some terms above.

We did so because ironically students who may need the most caring schools tend to get the least, partly because of a widening cultural gap between teachers and students that plays out in various ways. One reflection of this gap is the fact that the great majority of teachers are White, while student populations are rapidly diversifying. It is quite common that young White teachers worry about being seen as racist. In order to appear accepting of everyone, they are often inadvertently simultaneously friendly but condescending toward students of color. This stance is manifest when the teacher allows students to get by without working very hard, allows them to get away with things, avoids talking with their parents, or believes their parents can't be helpful in their education.

Student Dialogue 4.3

Lisa: Oh, no, I'm so embarrassed! I think I did that in my field experience classroom last term, and didn't realize it. I've never worked in a classroom that has a lot of minority kids in it, and, well, I was worried about whether I would be able to get along with them. I remember one day this Black girl was snatching a book away from a White kid, and I saw her but didn't say anything because I was so busy trying to make sure she liked me. I know that wasn't right, but I'm worried about not being racist.

Celia: I know you meant well, Lisa. But how will the little girl learn what's right and wrong if we don't teach her? You don't want to be cold when you are scolding someone; you can be kind and firm at the same time.

Gilbert: I think all of us worry about whether kids like us or not, it isn't just you. I do, too.

Celia: Yeah, I guess I do, too.

Gilbert: I think the problem is about learning not to think that being soft and being caring are the same things. Being soft really doesn't help kids. Being firm does help them. The hard thing is being firm consistently with everyone.

Another reflection of a cultural gap is the growing number of teacher–student relationships that cross some form of difference, including race, ethnicity, language, social class, or ability. Relationships are often thwarted when teachers leap to judgments about their students. Below, Marx and Pennington (2003) offer an example:

> The case of Rachel, a teacher candidate who described one child she met for just one 30-minute session as having an "apathetic attitude" toward English and education altogether. Crucial to her judgment was the fact that this child, Miguel, did not speak during their time together. In her journal, she wrote that, "I saw a child who was not proficient in even his native language, let alone in English" (Interview No. 4 with Rachel). Since she spoke no Spanish and, in their time together, neither did Miguel, there was no way for Rachel to know this. (p. 101)

We have worked with beginning teachers who assume that students do not receive love from homes affected by poverty, and therefore see their job as giving love they believe the student is not receiving otherwise. Sometimes this assumption, which can be laced with pity, is based only on children's demands to be hugged in school. However, based on research into child neglect, Finzi, Ram, Har-Even, Shnit, and Weizman (2001) point out that children who are truly neglected are more likely to withdraw from adults, than to seek affection from them. We have also worked with teachers who feel sorry for students with disabilities, describing them as "unfortunate." It is probably impossible to build supportive, authentic caring relationships on negative assumptions or pity.

It is also difficult to build respectful relationships on color-blindness, because when one claims not to see color, one ignores much of a person's identity. Thompson (1998) reminds us that a predominantly White teaching force will need to be mindful of how they demonstrate care because, "In contrast to most White feminist theories of care, Black feminist theories of care have paid close attention to the issue of race; and whereas color-blind theories of care tend to emphasize the innocence, Black feminist ethical theories emphasize knowledge" (p. 532).

In a study of a high school that serves mainly Mexican-American students, Valenzuela (1999) distinguished between two kinds of care: *aesthetic* and *authentic*. Aesthetic care attends to how students act or express themselves with respect to schooling. Teachers who assume an aesthetic stance toward care judge students on the basis of whether they adhere to the demands of the school, and see care as something students earn. Teachers reward students who show interest in school, and regard those who do not as "uncaring" and therefore deserving of teachers' low esteem. Authentic care, on the other hand, is based on a reciprocal relationship between teacher and student; building the relationship comes first. As an adult in relationship with young people, the teacher has a responsibility to know students as whole people, and to nurture their development. Valenzuela points out that this relationship is especially important to Mexican-American students who grow up in communities in which *educación* forms the basis of their learning. The term *Educación,* "refers to the family's role of inculcating in children a sense of moral, social, and personal responsibility and serves as the foundation for all other learning" (p. 23). The majority of the teachers in the high school she studied brought an aesthetic but not an authentic view of caring, insisting that students "buy in" to the assimilation function of schooling in order to earn teachers' care. The students, feeling uncared for at school, rejected schooling. Valenzuela argues that care must not subtract from students' important social and cultural resources, such as language. Authentic care encourages students to develop their language and culture, while at the same time, providing students with the opportunities and resources to develop academic skills and encouragement to strive for the best opportunities academically.

Student Dialogue 4.4

Gilbert: *Educación*? Celia, you speak Spanish, right? What are they talking about here?

Celia: Well, in my community, it's important to teach kids not just how to read and count, but also how to live right: how to be respectable and have good values, how to take care of themselves and other people.

Gilbert: Like, someone can be a well-educated idiot in real life, and that person wouldn't have *educación*?

Celia: Sort of like that. The thing that's important is that it's your responsibility to guide kids. You don't wait to see if they're interested. You're there for them, teaching them, helping them become good people. I grew up expecting that from adults. It didn't mean I was always good, but I expected adults to care enough about me personally to guide me. I think, Lisa, that is what it means to be firm and warm at the same time.

Lisa: I like that idea!

Lisa, Celia, and Gilbert all see *educación* as a powerful idea. An idea, we would have probably heard them say, if we could have listened in longer, that is not receiving its fair amount attention in schools, especially poor and urban schools.

Noddings (2005) sees care as an interpersonal relationship that rests not just on what a teacher does or feels, but also on the extent to which students actually feel cared for. She points out that, "The relational view is hard for some American thinkers to accept because the Western tradition puts such great emphasis on individualism. In that tradition, it is almost instinctive to regard virtues as personal possessions, hard-won through a grueling process of character building." Thus, the teacher who insists that his or her job is just to teach, or that students should simply ignore how the teacher feels about them, is rejecting the centrality of relationships, which many students find essential.

Gay (2000) claims, "teachers who really care about students honor their humanity, hold them in high esteem, expect high performance from them, and use strategies to fulfill their expectations. They also model academic, social, personal, and moral behaviors and values for students to emulate. Students, in kind, feel obligated to be worthy of being so honored" (p. 46). Feeling warm and sentimental toward students without translating care into acting on high expectations constitutes a form of "academic neglect" (p.

48), as does delivering content to students without building rapport. This is especially so with students for whom teacher–student rapport is essential to their learning.

Reflection 4.3 invites you to interview three people to find out how they view or remember their favorite teacher. The three people you interview can be of any age; try to select people from different backgrounds, in order to get a range of views.

When you finish, examine the three descriptions for evidence of teacher care. Then reread the material above from the work of Valenzuela, Noddings, and Gay; circle any words or phrases that reflected what you heard in the interviews. What have you learned from this activity that you will act on the next time you are with students?

In research studies, students usually describe their favorite teachers as "caring," but not necessarily as nice all the time (Alder, 2002; Gay, 2000; Irvine, 2003). Generally students have more regard for "warm demanders" than for teachers who let them slide by (Kleinfeld, 1975). Warm demanders expect a good deal from students, but also support students so they can achieve, and demonstrate that they like and respect their students as people. Did your interviews reveal favorite teachers who were both warm and demanding?

Caring teachers recognize the barriers that students face, and help students to deal with them. Stereotypes are significant barriers faced by students of color, female students, GLBT (gay, lesbian, bisexual, or transsexual) students, and students who are disabled. When students grow up seeing people like themselves repeatedly portrayed as incapable, they come to doubt their own capability. African-American students come to feel this way about their ability to take standardized tests, for example; female students often feel this way about their ability to excel in science or technology. Steele and Aronson (1995) explain that, "The existence of a negative stereotype about a group to which one belongs … means that in situations where the stereotype is applicable, one is at risk of confirming it as a self-characteristic, both to one's self and to others who know the stereotype" (p. 808). Students perform worse than they would otherwise when placed in a situation in which they are afraid of "living down" to an expectation. Caring relationships are essential to helping students get past this barrier. In an authentic caring relationship, a teacher demonstrates his or her belief in the student's capability by holding the student to high standards while supporting and encouraging the student along the way, and showing respect for the student's home background.

Student Dialogue 4.5

Lisa: I've got an example. It's math. I grew up with this phobia thing about math, you know, like, girls aren't supposed to be good in math.

Celia: Me too.

Lisa: Yeah, and like, when we had to take big tests in math, I just froze. I got terrible scores. I had this geometry teacher who didn't help any; he pretty much ignored the girls in class. Then we would take a test and not do very well, and he'd say, see? What can you expect? Well, he didn't actually say that, but he'd look at us girls like we were just lame. And that seemed to make us lame.

Celia: It's even worse being a girl with a Spanish accent! I was so afraid that I'd let my family down, I think the stress alone froze my brain.

A visit to a bookstore will show a fairly large collection dealing with "phobias." A quick scan will point out that the message the books try to get across is that you resist phobias. You work (sometimes with professional help) to reduce or eliminate them. Lisa, Celia, and Gilbert's recognition that students may have phobias, and that the ones related to academic achievement should receive the teacher's attention, will help to foster their relationships with their students.

Student–Student Relationships

For several reasons, students' relationships with each other, in addition to their relationships with the teacher, are central to caring classrooms. Students learn better when they feel emotionally safe than when they do not. Students also can learn a great deal from the diverse perspectives of peers, if teachers create a foundation for peer learning. In addition, since democratic life is social, preparation for life in a democracy should encourage learning to respect and communicate with people who are different from oneself. A story from a classroom illustrates:

A middle-school teacher who teaches in a fairly diverse school believes passionately in democracy, and strives to make her classroom one in which students get to know each other, develop respect for each other, and learn to discuss controversial issues. She told a story about what happened in her classroom right after September 11, 2001:

> I was having a debate with my students about whether we should bomb Afghanistan. The majority of my students said, "No, we shouldn't, because we would be bombing innocent civilians, we would be doing what was done to us, it wouldn't solve anything, et cetera." But I had two boys who said, "Yeah, we just need to bomb them, look what they did to us, we just need to bomb them." And I let the kids talk, and all the different people tried to

convince these boys that they didn't feel that this was right. Every day I try to create an atmosphere in the classroom where we can have this kind of discussion, where students feel free to disagree respectfully with one another as they explore their ideas. I'm not going to tell the students my own personal opinions … I want them to think for themselves. Finally one of the girls said, "Well, what about Ahmed? (Ahmed was a Pakistani student who disappeared two days after September 11. I think he went back to Pakistan.) And so the students asked, "What about Ahmed? He's over there. What will happen to him?" And those same two boys changed their minds and said, "Then we've got to come home.… We shouldn't bomb them." No great arguments, no amount of rationale would change their minds, only the human connection they had with their friend Ahmed. (Sleeter, 2005, pp. 173–174)

In this example, the teacher had built community among her students. She had enabled them to find common ground, develop empathy, and base decisions in empathy.

Building partnership relationships in the classroom helps students find common ground and build community with each other. Community and empathy do not come automatically, but they can be cultivated (Eisler, 2000). Empathy means being able to discriminate emotion in other people, take the role and perspective of another, and modulate one's own emotional expression as a result (Feshbach, 1975). Students need not necessarily agree with each other's viewpoints, but they can learn to appreciate that another student's viewpoint makes sense to him or her. They should therefore try to tune into how others feel about things they care deeply about (Feshbach & Feshbach, 1987).

As young people move from childhood through adolescence, they become increasingly preoccupied with identity and social relationships. Even very young children are busily constructing a sense of who they are, taking in clues from their social context. Van Ausdale and Feagin (2001) studied how children as young as 3 years old learned about race and racism in a day care center. Contrary to what some adults commonly believed, the children recognized differences in skin color. Although they had only begun to learn stereotypes associated with color in the wider society, the children used color to distinguish among themselves, and as a marker of exclusion and inclusion. Children also had some awareness of race relations in the wider society in that the White children began to act out authority over children of color. Carl's grandson, while in day care, was excluded from attending a birthday party because of his skin color. The child having the party, who was a good classroom and playground buddy, told the author's grandson that he could not come to his party because he is "Black."

According to Gifford-Smith and Brownell (2003), by middle childhood, "children can truly be said to participate in a separate world of their peers" (p. 236); over 30% of children's social interactions are with peers. Cliques and other groupings become more defined and structure who interacts with whom, when, and about what. As this peer structure develops, some young people feel liked and supported while others feel rejected and left out. As you can probably recall from your own adolescence, groups compete against each other, sometimes through mild rivalry and other times violently. Bullying has recently become recognized as a serious problem in student–student relationships; in the United States, for example, almost one fifth of elementary students report having been bullied (Drake, Price, & Telljohann, 2003). Bullying today takes place in ways not known in your mother's day. Students, Carl discovered during his recent observation in a school, send one another "I am going to get you after school" text messages on their cell phones.

By late elementary and middle school, societal, school, and peer contexts take a toll on the self-esteem of some groups of students more than others. These include disproportionately African-Americans boys (Madhere, 1991), Latina and White girls (U.S. Department of Education, 1998), and GLBT students. Like all young people, gay and lesbian students first experience erotic feelings around the age of 9, on the average. Unlike their heterosexual peers, however, by adolescence GLBT youth are struggling with feelings they have learned are considered socially unacceptable. As illustrated in chapter 3, this can take a huge toll on their self-esteem (Sears, 1993). Identity and self-esteem derive not just from peer interactions, but also from images and treatment of oneself and people like oneself outside of school.

While peer groups can contribute to stereotyping and exclusion, the good news is they can also counter negative images. For example, in her book, *Why Are All the Black Kids Sitting Together in the Cafeteria?* Tatum (1997) emphasizes that forming social groups with peers "like oneself" facilitates the formation of a positive identity as well as a sense of belonging. At times, too, group formation serves to protect students whose identities are devalued by the school setting and curriculum. Recall your middle school and high school days. Your circle of friends was important, not only because they provided you with someone(s) to hang out with on the phone in the evening, or go to the mall with on the weekend, but they also supported your self-concept, identity, and cultural values. Tatum stresses the need for appreciating the development of self-concept and engaging in conversations across currently existing racial and ethnic divides. For classroom teachers, the issue isn't one of preventing peer group formations, but rather of recognizing that children and youth bring into the classroom concern about who they are in relationship to peers, and experiences working through these concerns. In the classroom, and in that context of peer formations, how can teachers promote development of respectful and caring relationships?

Student Dialogue 4.6

Gilbert: Man, I wish my teachers would have understood this. I was a good student. I was a great student, in fact. But the other kids thought I was weird. The Black kids thought I looked too Asian, and the Asian kids were prejudiced against Black kids, so I didn't fit anywhere. To their credit, my parents tried to encourage me to appreciate being biracial, but that didn't carry over into how kids saw me. High school was the worst because by then all of the guys were trying to see how many girls they could get. All of that just isn't me.

Lisa: I would have liked you back then, Gilbert!

Gilbert: No, you wouldn't have. Lisa, you're the kind who ends up being popular.

Lisa: I wasn't exactly popular. I mean, I liked sports all my life, and especially tennis. But I hated being called a tomboy. In sixth grade, these two boys who I thought were cute told me that no one would ever want to marry me because I was too much of a tomboy. Well, from then on, I made sure I was feminine. I got my hair styled, started paying attention to fashions, wearing a little makeup. OK, you're right, I did want to be popular, but I had to work at it, because I didn't want to give up sports in order to be accepted.

Celia: In elementary school, most of the other kids spoke English without an accent, and they weren't as dark as I am. I wanted to be White!

Lisa: You're kidding!

Celia: No, I'm not. I used to drink white milk all the time to try to be White. I loved chocolate milk, but I didn't drink it because I was afraid it would make me even browner than I already am. What was so hard, though, was that I loved spending summers in Guanajuato with my grandmother, and she is even darker than I am! I felt at home there. Then I'd come back to Los Angeles and go back to school. I really felt torn because the people I loved most looked like the kids who were most harassed in my school — the kids I tried not to look like. I got good at pretending it didn't hurt. But it did.

Operating in a test-crazed environment and dealing with the pressures encountered during a typical work day, teachers sometimes don't give our full attention to the reality that students are confronting challenges of self-identity, group identity, and the many other social factors which influence becoming the person they hope to become.

Discipline

Many teachers argue that discipline is the top prerequisite for good teaching and student learning. However, there are differences among discipline, classroom management, punishment, and authoritarianism. Understanding these differences is pertinent to good multicultural teaching and improving academic achievement. As you read the definitions below, ask yourself which approach suits your style of teaching.

Discipline deals with how children behave in the classroom and the teacher's ability to influence that behavior. Discipline is directed toward oneself; responsibility comes from within the person. It is ongoing and central to the learning process, especially during this time of stress over students' achievement. Discipline helps students assume responsibility for their behavior through introducing the ideas of dignity and respect for both self and others (Fuller, 2001).

Classroom management is broader in scope than discipline. It includes everything teachers do to increase student involvement and cooperation and to establish a healthy, caring, productive working environment for students. In addition, classroom management includes the orchestration of a classroom — planning curriculum, organizing procedures and resources, arranging the environment to maximize learning, monitoring student progress, and anticipating students' needs and problems (Lemlech, 1991). From a multicultural perspective, classroom management refers to the teacher's ability to arrange classroom learning so that it welcomes and affirms all students, and it promotes cooperation and high expectations across ethnic, gender, and socioeconomic lines.

Punishment means paying or receiving a penalty for a deed or offense committed against a set of rules or authority. Students often perceive punishment in the classroom as an "us against them" situation — teacher against student. It usually indicates that someone in authority has the power to distribute the penalty. In schools, punishment may include the loss of privileges such as recess or consequences such as suspension or expulsion from school.

Authoritarianism is about control; teachers show students that the teacher is "boss." Sometimes teachers are unaware of the extent to which they are being authoritarian, attributing their behavior to tough love or giving students what they need. And sometimes in culturally diverse classrooms, teachers misinterpret ordinary student behavior as bad or challenging the teacher's authority. Of course, teachers are the legal and professional authorities in the classroom, and that is as it should be. However, when teachers show students care and respect by providing an engaging curriculum placed in a context that acknowledges the students' background, authoritarianism can give way to self-discipline.

A few of our education students tell us that they had thought being a teacher meant they should "control" the class — be the figure of authority or boss. Many, perhaps the majority, say that they want to help their students develop self-discipline by providing good classroom management and teaching them how to effectively relate to their peers. However, practically all of our students ask us what kind of discipline/classroom management we recommend. This query comes in the form of direct questions and what-if questions.

We try to provide you with some direction but we caution teacher candidates that there are no sure-fire, one-answer methods. Helping students to build self-discipline generally requires knowing the students and the context of the situation. We ask teacher candidates to think of their three favorite teachers and to recall whether they all ran their classes the same way. Most come to the conclusion that there is no little bag of tricks to help them with classroom discipline. We believe, however, that developing a caring classroom goes a long way in helping everyone to be friendly and respectful of one another: teacher and students.

Teachers can do quite a lot to build caring classrooms and schools. Positive relationships that nurture identity and self-esteem do not just automatically happen. In the remainder of this chapter, we will develop three building blocks for teaching that provide a foundation for building caring classrooms and schools:

Building Block 6: Using Conflict Resolution
Building Block 7: Addressing Prejudice and Stereotyping
Building Block 8: Using Cooperative Learning

Building Block 6: Using Conflict Resolution

Problems involving relationships are evident when there is conflict. The conflict might be a fight or an argument, a student talking back angrily, or a student snatching something away from someone else. As teachers we are often unprepared for conflict. We find it distressing because it upsets our emotional well-being, so we try to make it go away as quickly as possible. Discipline problems, for example, are often manifestations of relationship conflicts.

D'Ambra (2004) describes a spectrum of responses to conflict, in terms of the extent to which responses involve mutual participation in seeking a resolution. The responses include:

- Conflict suppression using force.
- Conflict management using force, adjudication, or arbitration. In a classroom, this would involve spelling out classroom rules, then applying them regularly and consistently.
- Conflict resolution, which involves negotiation to determine solutions to conflicts after they have arisen.
- Conflict prevention, which involves proactive negotiation and mediation to identify potential problems before they happen, and working out preventive solutions.
- Culture of dialogue, which involves assuming that differences always exist and need to be talked out in order to develop a respectful dialogue; which is not driven by problems but rather by compassion and the value of dialogue across differences.

Beginning teachers often resort to conflict suppression or conflict management, not anticipating conflict until it erupts. Reflection 4.4 asks you to recall an example of each of these responses to conflict in an education environment.

Which responses to conflict were easiest to recall? Which were the most difficult? Because conflict is usually uncomfortable, unless we are prepared to react differently to

---

Reflection 4.4
Examples of responses to conflict

Think of an example of each response to conflict in an education environment:

Conflict suppression:

Conflict management:

Conflict resolution:

Conflict prevention:

Culture of dialogue:

---

it, we usually react either by force or by trying to manage it. This is true of teachers as well as students. Stopping or attempting to manage conflict by punishment is a common response to classroom discipline problems. While conflict can usually be stopped through force or forceful management, these responses do not build an environment that works constructively with conflict. As Gathercoal (1993) observed, "Punishment leaves students hating and fearing educators. They respond by lying, cheating, withdrawing, and often becoming non-participants in school activities" (p. 17).

From a more proactive stance, conflict can be regarded as neither positive nor negative, but rather as a meaningful part of human existence. Most of us are involved in conflicts every day. People have conflicts with themselves over what to eat, or whether to go home for spring break or to go to Florida with friends. At home, school, or on the playground, conflicts often provide wonderful opportunities to learn that people's opinions can differ on almost any issue, and sometimes we need to rethink our own perspective based on encountering someone else's. Conflicts also provide opportunities to learn self-discipline, respect for others, respect for self, respect for the laws of society, and respect for diversity. The outcome from conflict may be negative or positive depending on the actions taken by the parties involved.

Because conflict resolution is so important to building caring classrooms with respectful relationships, conflict resolution programs have gradually become increasingly important. The first conflict resolution programs in schools emerged in the early 1970s, "sparked by the increasing concern of educators and parents about violence in the schools" (Girard & Koch, 1996, p. 111). Growing out of these earlier efforts, the National Association for Mediation in Education was established in 1984. The organization changed its name to the National Institute for Dispute Resolution (NIDR), and it works toward the development and implementation of conflict resolution and peer mediation programs in the schools.

Many schools today dedicate a great deal of time and attention to conflict resolution and the elimination of violence. Some states, such as Wisconsin, require that prospective teachers receive training in conflict resolution. Some states have programs where students can obtain an advanced degree in conflict resolution. Some school districts advocate teaching conflict resolution as early as kindergarten and the primary grades so children will be able to resolve conflicts such as playground disputes over balls and use of swings, and classroom conflict over pencils, computers, and friendships.

Conflict resolution programs can be quite extensive; reviewing them or showing you how to implement them is beyond the scope of this chapter. As Cirillo et al. (1998) point out, while no single program is a cure-all, when students are taught alternatives to violence, they have been found less likely to engage in violent behavior. In the next few pages, we will help you get started by showing alternatives.

One of the first steps in resolving conflict is to explain to students three common ways that conflict is handled, guiding them to think through which way is most productive and why. Table 4.1 presents three different ways to deal with conflict. You can

TABLE 4.1   Three ways to deal with conflict: Which do you think teachers recommend?

Denial: When someone is angry from a conflict, instead of saying he or she is angry, the person denies that anything is wrong. This does not allow for a resolution of the conflict because the second person does not know what is wrong or why the first person may be angry. If the situation isn't addressed, it can happen again.

Confrontation: When one or more students verbally or physically attack another student or students. The attack usually happens when the parties are not willing to listen to each other's side of the problem, or to discuss it. Instead they attack the other person or her or his ideas.

Problem solving: When the students work to resolve their difficulty. Each person listens to the other and looks for ways that their problem may be amicably resolved.

present these alternatives to students and ask which they see as preferable, and which method they believe that their parents would like them to use in conflict resolution.

The problem-solving approach is the one that teachers recommend and teach children. While this choice seems obvious, children do not automatically know how to make it work. In order to make it work, young students can learn skills such as communication skills, negotiation, mediation, apologizing, postponing gratification, and compromising. Below, we discuss two essential communication skills: "I messages" and active listening.

"I Messages" and Active Listening

The use of "I messages" can be important for maintaining good student–teacher rapport and avoiding more severe conflict. There is no ducking the issue: "I messages" get rid of "he said, she said" accusations and locate the speaking and feelings of the parties at a personal level.

Reflection 4.5 allows you to practice the three parts of "I messages": (1) state how you feel; (2) state the other person's behavior that prompts that feeling; and (3) state what you would like the other person to do. Notice that "I messages" do not lay blame on the other person or make value judgments about her or his behavior. Rather, they ask the other person to change behavior that is creating uncomfortable feelings for the speaker.

Reflection 4.5
Practice using "I messages"

I feel (name the feeling):

When you (describe the behavior):

I want (tell what would make the situation better for you):

To practice an "I message," pretend that you are in a classroom, and find out that a student told his former teacher that you are mean to him and pick on him every day. Write an "I message" that would let the student know how you feel about this.

How difficult was it to phrase your concern as an "I message" rather than as an accusation? "I messages" feel awkward at first, and they do not come automatically when we are feeling upset. You can have students role-play creating "I messages," so they get used to how they are stated, how they sound, and how they make each person feel.

Active listening is a useful skill that complements "I messages." Active listening means attending closely to what the other person is saying — actually hearing not just the words, but also the message behind the words. Often in a conflict situation, we are so busy trying to get our own point of view across that we do not hear the other person's viewpoint very well. Think back to a recent conflict you had with someone. Once you get the example in your mind, rewind your mind's tape recorder. Then play it back and assess your own behavior.

Evaluate your behavior with respect to the active listening skills below, which are recommended in Sunburst Communication's (1994) *Student Workshop: Conflict Resolution Skills*:

- Show that you are interested
- Ask questions if there is something you don't understand
- Listen for the feeling of the speaker
- Don't interrupt, change the subject or make up your mind before the person finishes speaking

Which active listening behaviors did you use? Which did you fail to use?

With practice, students can develop skill in active listening. Role-playing is a useful way to offer this practice. Some teachers also make creative use of puppets or theater in the classroom, inviting students to act out conflicts, disputes, and disagreements they see around them, using "I messages" and active listening.

Conflict Resolution Approaches

Conflict resolution skills help students get along with one another, and deal with the different people and perspectives they encounter. In addition, conflict resolution can limit the extent to which students become emotionally upset. Most models for resolving conflict recommend similar procedures. Tables 4.2 and 4.3 illustrate two models. Table 4.2 shows recommendations from Sunburst (1994). Table 4.3 shows steps in the Framework for Collaborative Negotiation proposed by Raider and Coleman (1992).

Reflection 4.6 asks you to compare the models in Tables 4.2 and 4.3 and identify their similarities. After listing their similarities, note where "I messages" fit in as a way of expressing feelings, and where active listening fits in as a way of hearing feelings.

TABLE 4.2   Conflict resolution procedures

1. Find a good time and place to talk.

2. Discuss the problem.

   Get the facts.

   Use Active Listening — show interest, ask questions, pay attention, repeat back to make sure you have it right.

   Use "I messages" to say how you feel.

   Focus on the problem, not the person.

   Avoid Communication Blockers.

3. Brainstorm for solutions.

   Be willing to compromise. Give a little to get a little.

4. Choose a solution that works for everybody.

5. Try the solution.

    If the solution doesn't work: go back to Step Three.

Sunburst (1994)

TABLE 4.3   Framework for collaborative negotiation

Stages	Tasks (examples)
Planning	Decide if the conflict is negotiable. Separate needs from positions. Try to see the other side's point of view.
Creating climate for negotiating	Establish trust and rapport.
Informing and questioning	Use "I" statements and inform the other side as to your needs. Ask about the other side's needs.
Finding common ground	Identify problems that affect both sides.Try to consider the issues in terms of shared needs
Brainstorming	Freely suggest ideas for solving the problem. Withhold judgment.
Choosing solution	Narrow down suggestions for solutions to the most promising ones for a lasting resolution.

Reflection 4.6
Similarities in conflict resolution frameworks

Now that you have a sense of how to build communication skills and strategies for conflict resolution in the classroom, let's look at a common format for working out problems: class meetings.

Class Meetings

Class meetings can be a powerful tool for resolving interpersonal conflicts and settling down the students, as well as addressing management and curriculum issues. The focus of any given meeting can vary widely, from a student seeking input on a personal issue to decisions regarding classroom policies. But class meetings are only truly effective when they involve genuine dialogue and include students' concerns, ideas, and voices. If the students are to take the process seriously, their voices should be at the heart of problem identification, discussion, and evaluation.

Class meetings are most effective when they occur frequently enough to serve as a negotiation tool, yet not so frequently that they become trivialized. They function best as one component of a democratic classroom in which opportunities for student input and idea sharing are continually sought and valued. The time taken to facilitate such ongoing discussion is repaid in student engagement and empowerment, and students feeling emotionally secure and safe.

Students should help to form the class meeting structure; the following components are essential:

- A way for students to identify and submit meaningful problems for group discussion.
- A regular time set aside for the meeting process, and arrangement of classroom space to accommodate face-to-face discussion (a group circle is ideal).
- Guidelines students help to establish for effective communication, such as refraining from using other student's names in problem description, and using a means for equitable turn taking.
- An effective means of evaluation that includes finding out from the individual or group who brought a problem as to whether they feel the solutions or advice are helpful. A brief follow-up discussion at the beginning of the next meeting might allow students to assess the quality of help given over time.

Student Dialogue 4.7

Gilbert: So part of our responsibility as teachers is to teach our students how to relate with each other? When I first thought about going into teaching, I thought mainly about teaching subjects, like history and reading. I enjoy working with kids, but to be honest, hadn't seen teaching things like "I messages" and active listening to be part of my curriculum.

Celia: Don't you think it would be worth it, though, in the long run? Think of all the aggravation you might head off before it happens!

Lisa: I like the idea, but need more information.

Gilbert's conception of teaching is held by many teacher candidates. There is so much more to teaching than covering the curriculum and transmitting information from one age group to the next age group. One of the roles of the teacher is teaching students how to get along with other students in ways that promote and respect one's voice and locus of control. Gilbert will have to modify his view ASAP, or he will place both himself and his students at an academic and social disadvantage.

A variety of materials that deal with conflict resolution are available. Increasingly, you can locate materials, organizations, and descriptions of program on the Internet. For Reflection 4.7, identify four websites that appear useful to you, and write a brief description of them.

Reflection 4.7
Websites about conflict resolution

Using an Internet search engine, locate four websites that appear useful to you. For each, write the URL, the name of the website, and a brief description.

1.

2.

3.

4.

This activity is one that some students will blow off, saying, "I can do this one later." But if you do so, you will miss both the intended and unintended learning that comes with completing such an activity. Most of the time when we go to the Web, we are surprised by the additional resources and ideas we discover. *So go to the Web, good ideas await you.*

Most teachers strive to be a neutral or fair party in the classroom, especially when it comes to political, religious issues, and many social issues. However, as you discovered in chapter 1, all teachers bring their baggage with them into the classroom. Teachers are influenced by their race or ethnicity, gender, sexuality, socioeconomic status, and religion. Any of these characteristics and their influence on one's everyday behavior, when not accepted by students or colleagues, can lead to conflict. G. Valentine (1997) suggests that in order to avoid such conflicts people need to have a clear understanding of their cultural perspectives, and how they influence attitudes and behavior. Understanding your own baggage, and helping students to realize that they too bring baggage with them, is critical in learning to work constructively with classroom conflict.

Building Block 7: Addressing Prejudice and Stereotyping

Students bring into the classroom perceptions about people through which they filter their understandings of everyone else. Classrooms themselves provide intense spaces for observing, interpreting, and reacting to different people. Describing an elementary classroom, Gallas (1998) observed, "What had once seemed routine and mundane was, in fact, peculiar. It was peculiar that, for the purposes of education, twenty or more children, all of the same age, would be confined for several hours a day in a room with a woman as their sole caretaker" (p. 25). She saw students' behavior in that environment as shaped by their gendered perceptions of their teacher, as well as by other categories through which they interpreted each other. After an extensive analysis of gendered behavior of primary-grade students, she concluded that, "I cannot orchestrate what ought to be when I do not understand what is" (p. 140). By this, she meant that we cannot change how young people perceive themselves and each other without first understanding what they perceive and why. This requires careful observation and attentive listening.

Reflection 4.8 offers a way to begin to tune in to perceptions young people bring into the classroom about categories of people. When our teacher education students have tried this reflection, they have found surprises; see if you do, too. First, select a sociocultural group you feel is often stereotyped. Some of our students have selected categories like "American Indians," "Black women," "Muslims," "White U. S. males during the days of the wagon trains," "gay and lesbian people," "Spanish-speaking people," or "people in wheelchairs." Then, find out as much as you can about how young people conceptualize the group, and how the group is portrayed in society. Interview about five young people to find out what they believe they know about the group. Simply ask them to describe the group, and where they remember learning about it.

Reflection 4.8
Depictions of a group

Group you are investigating:

How young people described the group:

Where they learned their perceptions:

How the group is depicted by:

Media:

Textbooks:

Other:

- Then, gather additional data about how the group is represented in various dimensions of society. For example, you might look at the following:
- Media that children or youth of that age consume: What images of that group are shown, if any at all? (You might select a TV cartoon show, a TV situation comedy, or a movie.)
- School materials, such as textbooks: What images, if any, are shown?
- Religious institutions young people attend: How is this group represented in this context?

From this investigation, to what extent did you find young people rely on stereotypes? Where does it appear they get their information? To what extent did their perspectives reflect images in popular media, such as TV or movies? To what extent did textbooks or other school materials replicate those images? Were you surprised by anything you found out?

Young people's awareness of human differences starts around the age of 3. Subsequently, they learn the social significance of differences from adults, media, schools, role models, religious institutions, and the like. Young people then act on what they have learned. To illustrate this idea we interviewed Yer Thao, a Hmong man who had immigrated to the United States as a child. He described how other children treated him when he arrived in America:

> We settled in a very poor area where we were mixed with Caucasians and African Americans, and we were the only Hmong family living in that area....We had neighbors [harassing us] like, they'd throw eggs at our door, they'd come and break our stuff, they threatened us. And it's like, they don't know who we are. My parents had to tell me, you go to school and you help us deal with this issue. But when you're out there, they call you names — You moved from the war and you are trying to find safety, but then you live in this country and you're living in fear. The people out there, they don't know who you are and you don't know who they are, and the way they react to you is very violent, and you feel like they could come and do anything to you at any time. And that is the most difficult part that I have been through.... During lunch hours, or before school or after school you run into some students who were giving very hurtful behavior toward you because you are a bit different and you have to deal with those issues. If you are in trouble, and you don't speak the language, most of the time the teachers or the principal don't know how to solve your problems. Most of the time incidents are happening in the hallway and no teachers see it, the majority will say, well this guy, we don't know what he's saying. So it wasn't your fault but you tend to be the one accused as the person who starts all the problems. (Sleeter, 2001, Immigrant Kids, p. 2)

Very likely many of the perpetrators were not intentionally trying to hurt him, and his teachers believed they cared about him. But at the same time, he looked "different," and initially spoke little English. Other students did not know how to interpret him, except through stereotypes of Asians, immigrants, and non-English speakers, which abound. Children in his school knew they could taunt him and blame problems on him, and get away with it, so they did.

Student Dialogue 4.8

Lisa: What do you guys think about kids calling each other "fag?" I hear that a lot in my field placement school, and no one does anything about it.

Gilbert: That word is like a punch in the stomach to me. Kids need to know it's wrong.

Lisa: But little kids, they don't know about homosexuality, they're just repeating what they hear. I always figured they'd outgrow it.

Gilbert: Outgrow it? Outgrow gay bashing? Look around you! If we don't teach kids, they'll model after what they hear and see.

Lisa: OK, but don't you think parents would get after you for teaching about gay issues?

Celia: I think you have two things going on here. One is whether to teach about gay issues as part of the curriculum. I think we'll get to that in a couple more chapters. But right now, if we are talking about creating caring classrooms where kids feel safe, we need to stop derogatory name calling. Period. Like Gilbert said, even if a kid doesn't understand what "fag" means, if throwing the name at someone is like throwing a rock at that person, it needs to stop.

Kids at a very early age learn to do things in ways that will minimize their getting caught. This skill, you probably remember from your own growing up, becomes more sophisticated with age. Teachers have to be mindful about the quality of attention the new student, as well as the student who is gay or lesbian, receives. It is naïve to carry on as if mean-spiritedness among students will not take place, and ignoring it can jeopardize the academic and social environment of the classroom.

Race, gender, physical size, and disability are markers of difference that play out in schools, as early as preschool. Based on an analysis of children's perceptions of race, for example, A. E. Lewis (2003) describes what she calls ascriptive processes through which markers of different identities are assigned to people through everyday interpersonal interactions.

These ascriptive processes work primarily through interpersonal interactions in which we attempt to assess what we know about another person, first through the instantaneous reading or interpreting of available clues (e.g., visible cues such as skin color or facial features, auditory cues such as accent, spatial cues such as neighborhood), and second through rereading or reinterpreting initial assumptions as additional information becomes available. These processes operate in a largely relational manner: some people are determined to be the "same" (or "like me") and others are determined to be "different." (p. 151)

Young children ask questions freely before they learn that some kinds of questions are considered impolite. Adults often treat questions about human differences as rude, so children stop asking them. For example, we have seen parents become embarrassed and quickly hush a child who innocently asks a question about race or disability. From such actions, children become bewildered about how they should handle their curiosities. Many respond by learning that such questions are taboo. They then base their ideas on what they hear from family and friends or encounter in the media. Often young people learn to verbalize feelings about differences in the form of jokes, snide remarks, and name calling.

Left unaddressed, students' interpretations of and attitudes toward peers who differ from themselves can degenerate into harassment and sometimes violence. According to Juvonen (2001), about one quarter of U.S. students "repeatedly either engage in or are the targets of bullying tactics that contribute to the climate of fear." Further, "children who view themselves as targets of bullying show high levels of anxiety and depression that impede their school performance." Harassment and bullying can escalate from name calling into physical violence. Educators who do nothing about it not only fail to teach young people how to live civilly together, but may also risk a lawsuit (Zirkel, 2003).

Caring teachers can begin to address stereotyping, prejudice, and harassment using a four-pronged approach: (1) Raising awareness of stereotyping; (2) teaching about what prejudice and discrimination are; (3) taking a stand against hurting people; and (4) helping young people learn to prevent or challenge discrimination.

Raising Awareness of Stereotyping

To begin raising awareness of prejudice and stereotyping, an elementary teacher we know taught her students to become "stereotype detectives," starting with stereotypes of American Indians. First, she asked students to draw a picture of American Indians. Then she read a children's book about American Indians, taking care to select one that is recommended by American Indians themselves (Slapin & Seale, 1998). The book had vivid illustrations of people who differed from each other, and as her students listened to the story and viewed the illustrations, they realized that their drawings were limited. After reading the book, she had students compare representations in the book with their drawings, and used this discussion to teach them what a "stereotype" is. She then took her students to the library, where they examined books to uncover stereotypes of American Indians. She continued to contrast the stereotypes with factual information, over the course of an extensive unit in social studies and literature (Sleeter, 2001, Rethinking Indigenous People). By the end of the unit the students knew what stereotypes are and how they limit perceptions, and they knew a good deal more than they had about indigenous Americans.

The process she used helped students to contrast what they thought were accurate conceptions of American Indians, with Indian representations of themselves. A problem with stereotypes is that we assume them to be true unless we have alternative information with which to contrast the stereotype. Aiello (1979) described teaching about disabilities by bringing to class guest speakers who had disabilities. In one example, children asked a blind visitor whether she could cook. She explained that she put Braille labels on foods in her kitchen, and that one of her favorite things to cook was spaghetti. A 7-year-old, after meeting her, exclaimed, "What a relief. I thought handicapped people cried all day!" (p. 30).

As children got to know people personally, they discovered that in addition to being different from each other, we are also alike in many ways. Derman-Sparks (1989) recommends that teachers introduce a variety of differences — cultural, physical, and gendered — that students actually see and experience, here and now. Rather than treating differences as exotic, treat them as normal, intentionally helping students to recognize when they are basing their ideas about people on stereotypes.

In addition to dispelling stereotypes by meeting people, students can also find out how a group might define itself by locating websites created by members of specific groups. For example, through a search, we identified websites produced by organizations of people who are often stereotyped. Table 4.4 illustrates what we found.

Students might browse websites that are appropriate to their age level, comparing representations with images they thought were accurate. As students develop an idea of differences between stereotyped images and more authentic representations, they can notice, seek out, and critique stereotyped images. At the same time, they begin to develop a more accurate basis for forming personal relationships with people whom they see as different from themselves.

Teach Directly About Prejudice and Discrimination

Teaching young people directly about prejudice and discrimination will give them language and conceptual tools to examine their school, community, and societal context, and to talk about forms of prejudice and discrimination that they experience. Recently we showed a videotaped session of a teacher teaching elementary children about discrimination. The audience consisted of other teachers and teacher candidates. The teacher in the videotape began explaining what discrimination is with reference to examples of sex discrimination that the children could relate to. She then went on to forms of discrimination that the children didn't see as obvious, such as discrimination against immigrants based on accent or language. In the course of this discussion, she asked children what they thought may or may not occur that day. Teachers in the audience were struck that she was able to teach such a lesson, and that the children were able to discuss it in meaningful terms.

TABLE 4.4   Sample websites created by specific sociocultural groups

Group	URL	Name of website
Indigenous people	http://www.nativeweb.org	Native Web
Black women	http://www.bcw.org	Black Career Women
Muslims	http://www.amcnational.org	American Muslim Council
Gay and lesbian people	http://www.glsen.org	Gay, Lesbian, and Straight Education Network
People in wheelchairs	http://www.wheelchairnet.org	Wheelchair Net

Like the teacher in the videotape, you can define prejudice and discrimination using examples your students are able to understand. Let's examine some definitions written for adults that can guide your construction of definitions to use with young people.

Table 4.5 includes four definitions and descriptions of discrimination. Study them and then, in Reflection 4.9, write a child-appropriate definition of discrimination that synthesizes key components in these definitions.

Several books and classroom resources are available to help teachers in teaching children and youth about prejudice and discrimination. We encourage you to visit the Teaching for Change website, where you will find many such resources (http://www. teachingforchange.org).

TABLE 4.5 Definitions of discrimination

National Institute of Environmental Health Sciences and National Institutes of Health

Discrimination is defined in civil rights law as unfavorable or unfair treatment of a person or class of persons in comparison to others who are not members of the protected class because of race, sex, color, religion, national origin, age, physical/mental handicap, sexual harassment, sexual orientation, or reprisal for opposition to discriminatory practices or participation in the [Equal Employment Opportunity]EEO process.

Federal EEO laws prohibit an employer from discriminating against persons in all aspects of employment, including recruitment, selection, evaluation, promotion, training, compensation, discipline, retention, and working conditions, because of their protected status.

http://www.niehs.nih.gov/oeeo/disc-def.htm

Law Office.com, West Legal Dictionary

Sex discrimination: Women and girls have long been excluded from many sports. In the 1970s Congress passed title IX of the 1972 Education Amendments … to ban sex discrimination in publicly funded educational programs….Title IX now gives women and girls equal access to sports programs in schools that receive any measure of federal funding.

Under Title IX schools must provide athletic opportunities to females that are proportionate to those provided to males. Courts do not require that complete equality occur overnight. Most courts engage in a three-pronged analysis to determine whether a school is fulfilling its obligations. First, the court examines whether athletic participation opportunities are provided to each sex in numbers substantially proportionate to their enrollment. If a school does not provide substantially proportionate participation opportunities, the court then determines whether the school can demonstrate a history of expanding the athletic programs for the underrepresented sex. If the school cannot so demonstrate, the court then asks whether the interests and abilities of the underrepresented sex have been accommodated by the school. If the court finds that the school has not accommodated student-athletes of the underrepresented sex, it may rule that the school is in violation of Title IX and order the school to take affirmative steps toward more equal treatment between the sexes.

Traditionally, courts have differentiated between contact and non-contact sports in determining a female's right to participation. A school may refrain from offering a contact sport for females if the reasoning is not based on an archaic, paternalistic, overbroad view of women. Courts are hesitant to mandate the creation of new teams, but most have no problem ordering that qualified females be allowed to play on exclusively male teams.

http://www.wld.com/conbus/weal/wsports1.htm

-continued

TABLE 4.5 Definitions of discrimination (continued)

Board of Public Education of the School District of Pittsburgh

The Board of Public Education of the School District of Pittsburgh requires that the School District maintain, at all times, an environment in which all stakeholders display and receive respect, tolerance and civility. Stakeholders include … all employees, students, families of students, residents and all entities interacting, or doing business with the School District in any capacity.… The Board considers human relations in the work and educational environment necessary to afford all stakeholders an opportunity to achieve optimal performance in a nondiscriminatory atmosphere. Therefore, the Board reaffirms its policy precluding invidious discrimination on the basis of race, gender, religion, age, national origin, disability, sexual orientation or socioeconomic background. Human relations is defined prescriptively and proscriptively as follows:

Human relations is mutual respect, tolerance and civility among all stakeholders.

Conduct reflecting human relations will result in equity for all stakeholders regardless of race, gender, religion, age, national origin, disability, sexual orientation or socioeconomic background.

Human relations precludes invidious discrimination on the basis of race, gender, religion, age, national origin, disability, sexual orientation or socioeconomic background.

Human relations precludes conduct, including language, overt and covert actions, which may create, or contribute to a hostile environment based upon race, gender, religion, age, national origin, disability, sexual orientation or socioeconomic background.

Human relations precludes overt and covert exclusionary behavior which limits access to school activities and curricula based upon race, gender, religion, age, national origin, disability, sexual orientation or socioeconomic background.

http://info.pps.pgh.pa.us/policies/human_relations.html

The National Association of School Psychologists' Position Statement on Racism, Prejudice, and Discrimination

The National Association of School Psychologists is committed to promoting the rights, welfare, educational, and mental health needs of all students. This can only be accomplished in a society which ensures that all people, including children and youth, are treated equitably without reference to race or ethnicity. NASP believes that racism, prejudice, and discrimination are harmful to children and youth because they can have a profoundly negative impact on school achievement, self-esteem, personal growth, and ultimately the welfare of all American society. A discussion of multicultural issues requires a definition of terms.

Prejudice: Prejudice is an attitude, opinion, or feeling formed without prior knowledge, thought, or reason.

Discrimination: Discrimination is differential treatment that favors one individual, group, or object over another. The source of discrimination is prejudice, and the actions are not systematized. Two forms of discrimination exist: *de jure*, which is discrimination based upon state policy; and *de facto*, which is discrimination, for example in school based upon housing patterns or the attitudes of people instead of state policy.

Racism: Racism is racial prejudice and discrimination supported by institutional power and authority used to the advantage of one race and the disadvantage of other race(s). The critical element of racism, which differentiates racism from prejudice and discrimination, is the use of institutional power and authority to support prejudice and enforce discriminatory behaviors in systematic ways with far reaching outcomes and effects.

http://www.nasponline.org/about_nasp/pospaper_rpd.aspx

Keep on thinking! Below are ideas for learning and reflection in the classroom.

- Even young children have common-sense understandings of what is fair and unfair. Children's sense of fairness provides a launch pad for expanding their awareness. For example, kindergarten children might agree that everyone has a right to a snack at snack time, and that it would be discriminatory to deny some students a snack.

- Historically, groups have fought and worked hard to make various forms of discrimination illegal. Learning about this history of struggle can help young people gain a deeper sense of the issues themselves, as well as how to bring about social change. You can find examples of how to teach about such struggles in books such as Turning on Learning (Grant & Sleeter, 2007) or the newspaper Rethinking Schools (http://www.rethinkingschools.org).

- As reflected in the definition of the National Association of School Psychologists, prejudice, discrimination, and racism are related but not the same. Students can examine how these concepts differ. Students can also apply this examination to construct definitions of sexism, heterosexism, and so forth.

- Some definitions suggest indicators of discrimination. Help students figure out indicators of discrimination in their own environment, such as on the playground or in how discipline is handled. Indicators can then be used to determine whether discrimination exists.

- At the same time, disputes arise because different people use and judge indicators differently, and bring different experiences and values to bear on them. Further, people disagree about what is fair for both the society as a whole, and for individuals and groups within that society. Creating a fair society is a process that is never finished; grappling with issues of fairness and discrimination is a way to learn to engage productively in that process. Take, for example, the matter of snacks at snack time. Is it discriminatory to serve snacks that some children do not like? What about snacks that some cannot eat (such as milk for children who are lactose intolerant, which is quite common, especially among children who are not of European descent)? Talking through how to balance individual and group rights in the real world helps young people learn to think through what "fairness" means.

Take a Stand Against Hurting People

Henning-Stout, James, and MacIntosh, (2000) argue that efforts to reduce harassment must have two immediate goals: "to increase safety for all children and youth, and to counter the heterosexism too often seen in school and community cultures" (p. 188). These goals were evident in programs that were effective in reducing harassment based on sexual orientation. Although Henning-Stout et al. examined schoolwide programs, their research offers insights that are useful at the classroom level for all kinds of harassment.

Think back to when you were in school. Do you remember teasing or name calling among children? (If you can't remember back that far, ask a young person who is in school right now to help you out on this task.) Reflection 4.10 asks you to identify specific instances of teasing, name calling, or other forms of harassment, and everything a teacher did to intervene.

What kind of harassment did you recall? Where did it occur? What effect did it have on students? What would you have liked teachers to do?

Often our teacher education students tell us that some teachers do not intervene when kids tease each other or put each other down. The teachers chalk it up to kids being kids, or if the teasing seems mild and not moving toward physical confrontation, they give students space to work it out on their own. We know that usually teachers are not aware of teasing or name calling because kids do it largely when teachers are not around. To what extent is your experience similar?

When we have asked children and youth what they think teachers should do, overwhelmingly they say that teachers should tell children to stop. However, saying "stop" is not enough. Teachers should publicly take a stand on matters that involve hurting other people. Teachers are role models, and when they do not take a stand, children assume that they condone hurtful behavior. It makes a difference when we teach children that hurtful behaviors and name calling are mean and destructive. Often children do not understand the extent of the impact of their actions on another person.

What names have you been called that were hurtful? Are they names that you would share with a peer, or names that you are embarrassed to repeat? The saying "Sticks and stones will break my bones, but names will never hurt me" is useful because it can serve as the first line of defense in a situation which has the potential to escalate. However, names do hurt, and as teachers it is our responsibility to get that across to all students. Students need to learn that names are not the only things that can hurt. Ignoring someone, taking someone's possessions without asking, and yelling at someone are other examples of hurtful behavior. Children need to know that a given name or behavior may not hurt them personally, but can still hurt someone else.

In a classroom, it is possible to generate a list of names and behaviors that students find mean-spirited and hurtful. Some teachers do this through open discussion, others ask children to anonymously write down names and behaviors that hurt; the teacher then compiles a list for public discussion. Explaining what those names really mean and why name calling is hurtful sends a message that certain behaviors are not condoned, and calling students certain names will not be tolerated. In addition, it makes the topic "concern and care for each other" a part of the normal classroom discourse.

Student Dialogue 4.9

Celia: I understand that we need to teach kids not to say derogatory things about each other, but won't verbalizing bad names give them ideas? What if they never thought about this until I bring it up in the classroom? Don't you think some kids will wait until the teacher is out of earshot and then start throwing some of these new words around?

Gilbert: I would have thought that until I watched a teacher work with this idea last term. She had the kids write down hurtful names, and then they talked about why the names hurt. She tried to get them to tune into what it feels like when you hurt. Then she did this little ceremony. She put the trashcan in the middle of the room, then one by one, the kids ripped up the paper where they had written the names they'd been called, and threw the pieces into the trash. Then the whole class took the trashcan out of the room and slammed the door. The teacher announced that these names would never again appear in the classroom. And as long as I was there, they didn't appear again.

Lisa: Wow, so she actually got them involved in stopping name calling. She brought peer pressure to bear on it. After a ceremony like that, the rest of the class will come down on someone who verbally hurts someone else!

A complicated issue is that of members of a racial or ethnic group calling one another derogatory names as a greeting and when in conversation with each other, where use of the term by anyone outside of the group could lead to conflict. Although a teacher cannot control the names students use to communicate to one another outside of school, he or she can let all students know that such terminology is off limits inside school, regardless of whether it is used as a term of endearment or in a mean-spirited way. In addition, a teacher should let students know that (re)appropriating a term that has a long history of debasement is difficult and perhaps not the best investment of their time.

As issues involving fairness and justice become more controversial, teachers often wonder if they should take a stand or attempt to remain neutral. For example, will knowing that a teacher supports gay rights keep students from honestly discussing their own feelings and questions about sexual orientation? Teachers are in a position of power in the classroom, so many students are unsure whether they can actually disagree with teachers. In our own teaching, both of us let students know our stand on issues, but at the same time encourage students to take their own stands. Debating and acknowledging different points of view are as old as the U.S. Constitution, and in caring classrooms people can participate. Discussing how he has wrestled with these issues when teaching about global sweatshops, Bigelow (2002) points out that he has "no desire to feign neutrality" because that only supports apathy and inaction (p. 132). So, he tries to present both sides of issues as fairly as possible, while letting students know his own position. This tension between taking a stand and encouraging honest discussion does not always work itself out cleanly, but pushing students to look at more than one side of an issue prompts real thinking and honesty.

Helping Young People Learn to Prevent or Challenge Discrimination

Teachers cannot create caring classrooms by themselves; teaching children or youth to participate in caring means helping them to establish expectations to live by. Centralizing decision making turns the teacher into the classroom "cop." This can undermine care in the classroom in at least two ways. First, centralizing decision making does not help students learn to take ownership of rules for social living and of their own actions. It leaves them in a passive role. Second, children sometimes deliberately break rules set by the teacher as a way of challenging authority. If the teacher is the classroom cop, some children deliberately hurt other children to rebel against the cop figure.

An alternative to running a classroom like a dictatorship is to help students learn to exercise democratic decision making within the classroom, involving them in making decisions about the work of the classroom. Sharing authority with students does not mean abdicating authority to them. Rather, it means guiding students in the process of learning to make decisions in a democratic fashion. A starting point is to help students brainstorm, discuss, and vote on rules and expectations for classroom behavior. Students can also help to establish consequences of behavior. Involving all students in this way helps them to develop ownership of caring behavior.

For example, students might decide that there will be no stealing. Many teachers encourage students to reword such an expectation so that it tells students what they should do, rather than what they should not do, such as: "We will respect each other's property." What are the consequences of following this expectation or of failing to follow it? As students consider these kinds of questions, they can learn to act on caring, and to take responsibility for their own behavior as well as the behavior of their peers.

These kinds of activities can help reduce prejudice and stereotyping. Based on a review of research on curricular interventions addressing racial and gender stereotyping (e.g., using a story where an Asian-American kid is having difficulty with mathematics and science to dispel the stereotype that all Asian kids are experts in these areas), Banks (1995) found that some studies report that interventions make no difference, while other studies report a positive change. Banks concludes that teachers should use curricular interventions and materials to help them, but they should pay attention to the impact of the interventions on students so that they can make adjustments as needed. Young children seem particularly influenced by curricular interventions — elementary teachers have an especially important opportunity to develop open and democratic attitudes in children. In chapter 8, we will again take up the issue of teaching for democratic participation.

Building Block 8: Using Cooperative Learning

Cooperative learning has a strong and consistent track record in improving student–student relationships across race, gender, and ability/disability lines as well as boosting student achievement (Bowen, 2000; Cohen & Lotan, 1997; Gillies & Ashman, 2000; Johnson, Johnson, & Maruyama, 1983; Slavin, 1995). For example, Sall and Mar (1999) documented a deaf-blind student's experience with inclusion in his neighborhood school. Specialists teamed with regular classroom teachers to help accommodate his instructional needs. In addition, teachers used cooperative learning and peer tutoring to help involve him with peers. The researchers noted that interactions with some peers that began as assistance, gradually expanded into social interactions as he and some of his peers discovered mutual interests. As we will discuss below, cooperative learning is a carefully planned form of small-group work; how well it works depends on how well it is planned.

Many teachers resist cooperative learning, confusing it with garden-variety group work. Reflection 4.11 asks you to reflect on your own experiences with group work. Write down (1) instances in which you remember group work being used when you have been a student; (2) what worked for you; and (3) what did not work for you.

Now let's compare group work you have experienced with four characteristics of cooperative learning: (1) heterogeneous grouping; (2) careful planning to make sure each

---

Reflection 4.11
Group work

When do you recall having participated in group work in school?

What worked for you?

What did not work for you?

Reflection 4.12
Characteristics of cooperative learning

Characteristics of cooperative learning	Group work you experienced
Groups are heterogeneous in terms of ability, race/ethnicity, gender, social class, etc.	
Work is carefully planned so that every student has a role; roles are switched as activities change; all students are accountable for their work.	
Students must work together to complete the task; the task requires interdependence.	
Students are taught cooperation, group process, and conflict resolution skills.	

student has a role; (3) work that requires interdependence of group members; and (4) students are taught cooperation and group process skills. In Reflection 4.12, these four characteristics appear in the left column. The right column asks you to compare instances of group work you described in Reflection 4.11 with these four characteristics.

How did the group work you have experienced fit those four characteristics? To what extent have you experienced cooperative learning?

Let's look more closely at each of the four characteristics in relationship to building a caring classroom that supports achievement. Grouping students heterogeneously means mixing them by gender, racial or ethnic background, primary language, skill level, and so forth. Doing this disrupts patterns of segregation that may be developing among students, and provides opportunities for them to get to know peers who differ from themselves. Heterogeneous grouping, when used along with the other three characteristics, makes diversity an asset to draw on rather than a problem to solve. For example, what kind of project might students be able to accomplish if one is a good writer, another is good at drawing, another is a good organizer, and yet another has strong computer skills? Of course, you would not want to pigeonhole students into using the same ability all the time rather than broadening their skills and abilities. But this example illustrates thinking of diversity as an asset to work with.

Cooperative learning requires planning so that each student has a role. The biggest complaint usually lodged against group work is that a few students do most of the work while the others coast. Planning so each student has a role can take a variety of forms. For example, everyone in a group might have a different task to contribute to the group effort. Or, the group might be responsible for making sure all members learn material such as spelling words, because only one member will be called on to represent the group.

Students' roles must require interdependence — working and talking together. If students can complete a task through an assembly line process that does not require communication until the end when they assemble individually produced pieces, they will not reap the benefits of cooperative learning. The task must be structured so they have to discuss, exchange ideas, or help each other.

Finally, the teacher needs to teach students how to cooperate. Most students do not automatically bring cooperation skills to class. Turn taking, encouraging others to speak, checking for understanding, or asking each other for help are behaviors that need to be learned. Teachers who can make cooperative learning work usually teach one or two cooperation skills at a time, and start with fairly simple cooperative learning tasks. As students become better at engaging in cooperative learning, tasks can become more complex.

Student Dialogue 4.10

Celia: I enjoy working with other people, especially if there's enough guidance and structure so we know what we are doing. Without that, sometimes we just sit there and talk.

Gilbert: I don't enjoy it, or at least I haven't in the past because I end up doing most of the work. But if everyone had an assigned task, and we all knew what each person was responsible for, then maybe it wouldn't be so bad. I still might not like working in groups as well as I like working by myself, but at least it wouldn't be a real pain.

Lisa: I like the idea of having to interact about academics, as we are doing here. I'm learning quite a bit from the two of you. And I'm starting to learn to trust you.

Gilbert: Well, me too.

Various models of cooperative learning exist. The *group investigation model* requires students to contribute different talents, skills, interests, and roles to the creation of a group project or solving of a group problem. The project may be as elaborate as a multimedia production in which students synthesize information they have gathered about a topic; or it can be as small as a list of ideas generated during a short discussion (Johnson & Johnson, 1999). The *complex instruction model* organizes fairly open-ended problem-solving activities around a central concept or big idea. The activities are designed to require higher order thinking. Students are taught different roles that contribute to the task, such as "facilitator" and "materials manager." Teachers publicly identify something in particular that students are doing well and let the group know what is good about it, making sure that everyone gets recognized for doing something well, and that everyone is participating (Cohen & Lotan, 1997).

The *jigsaw model* involves two connected groupings. First, the class is divided into groups and each group studies a different but related subtopic of a larger topic. Group members work together to make sure they all understand the material and become "experts" on it. Students are then regrouped, so that each new group has one or two "experts" on

EXAMPLES OF COOPERATIVE LEARNING

Model	Example	Reflection
Group investigation		
Complex instruction		
Jigsaw		
Student team learning		

each subtopic. A task is then given requiring students to pool their expertise. Many teachers like this model because it ensures that everyone has expertise to contribute. In the *team games model*, students practice academic skills while working together as a team. Then teams compete against other teams in a tournament. Team members have a vested interest in making sure everyone on the team has learned the material (Slavin, 1986).

It is fairly easy to find examples of cooperative learning, either by talking with teachers or on the Internet. Using whichever resource you have most access to, locate an example of each of the four models of cooperative learning, for Reflection 4.13. Describe it briefly and then write a reflection on the strengths or weaknesses of that example.

After you have completed Reflection 4.13, identify the example that seems least complicated, the one that you might be able to start with. As you work with reflective activities in subsequent chapters that ask you to plan some curriculum and instruction, come back to Reflection 4.13 for examples of cooperative learning.

Putting It Into Practice

By Elizabeth Day and Kim Wieczorek (1998), University Wisconsin–Madison

You are student teaching in Mrs. Stroman's third-grade classroom at Nolan Elementary School. The school is predominantly White and middle class, with a growing number of immigrant students. Some of them are from Mexico, and others are from Bosnia and Pakistan. In your student teaching classroom are two immigrant students — Carlos, who is new to the school and whose family is from Mexico, and Habiba, who came from Pakistan the previous year. So far as you can tell, things seemed relatively peaceful in the classroom — until last Friday.

Last Friday, Tracy, one of the White students, went home crying, telling her parents that Mrs. Stroman had grabbed her, spun her around, and in the process, hurt her. On hearing what happened, Tracy's father Bill Sloane called the principal who then set up a meeting for Monday morning.

At the meeting, Tracy hid her head in her mother's coat. Almost all the adults asked her to tell them what happened in the classroom. In a whisper, Tracy said that Mrs. Stroman had grabbed her and hurt her, because she took some paper away from some other classmates. But no one had asked her why she took the paper away. Mrs. Stroman explained that she had seen Tracy interrupting a small group of students who were working at a table near Tracy's seat. Tracy was talking loudly and had even started to grab a paper that one of the students was working on. Mrs. Stroman had gone over to Tracy and thought that Tracy had heard her say she should return to her own desk. When Tracy seemed to ignore her, Mrs. Stroman reached out her hand to physically guide Tracy back to her own seat. She certainly had not meant to hurt Tracy.

Mr. Tanner, the principal, lowered himself physically so he was eye-level with Tracy, and asked her why she had grabbed the paper. Tearfully, Tracy said that it had some nasty words on it, and a drawing of Habiba. Kids were making fun of Habiba, and Tracy didn't know how to get them to stop, so she took their paper away. Then Mrs. Stroman had grabbed her and hurt her. Tracy was afraid and didn't know what to do, because sometimes in the past she had made up stories in class, so people didn't always believe her.

Mrs. Stroman looked bewildered for a moment, and then asked Tracy if she still had the paper. Tracy said, no, it got torn up in the process, and she didn't know where the pieces were. Mr. Tanner asked her how she knew that kids were making fun of Habiba. Tracy replied, "They do it all the time on the playground. They know they'll get in trouble if a teacher hears, so they wait until a teacher isn't around."

As a student teacher, what would you do? What would you suggest that Mrs. Stroman do? Create a plan that addresses the immediate problems of this crisis, and a more long-term way of improving and building classroom relationships.

five
Using Students' Assets to Facilitate High Achievement

This chapter will help you answer the following questions:

- What factors affect student achievement, and which do teachers have control over?
- What do cultural assets have to do with teaching?
- How can teachers use students' interests and backgrounds when teaching?
- Why is language important to learning?
- What are learning styles, and how can teachers find out their students' learning styles?
- How can teachers work productively with parents?

As a teacher, your main responsibility is to facilitate students' academic learning. Students come to school with cognitive, physical, linguistic, cultural, and other assets that facilitate learning. It is the teacher's role and responsibility to help students to develop these assets. The development of students' assets is the greatest testimony to loving and helping students. However, teacher candidates entering the profession will face both a *social* and an *instructional challenge* to make this happen. The *social challenge* comes from the many people (e.g., colleagues, friends) and messages (e.g., in the media, education material) that argue that some of your students lack or have limited learning assets. The *instructional challenge* is about you and your commitment to take advantage of the opportunities and available knowledge for learning how to teach all students in a way that does not rob them of the culture they bring to school.

Because of the complex interrelationship among culture, achievement, and teaching, the chapter begins with a discussion of these in relationship to teacher expectations. Then, we develop four building blocks that will help you identify assets students bring to school to use as springboards for academic instruction:

Building Block 9: Making Students' Interests and Background a Focal Point in Teaching

Building Block 10: Using Students' Learning Styles When Planning Classroom Instruction

Building Block 11: Making Students' Language a Valuable Learning Resource

Building Block 12: Connecting With Parents and Community

In most of the reflections in this chapter, you will connect ideas with your own experiences, ideas you have learned in previous chapters, and observations and interactions with others. For some of the reflections you will need access to the following:

- About six students to interview or observe (for Reflections 5.2, 5.7, and 5.11)
- Adults who work with students (for Reflection 5.4)
- Adults from a community that is culturally different from your own (for Reflections 5.5 and 5.6)
- Two friends who approach learning in different ways (for Reflection 5.10)
- A group of people talking in a public place (for Reflection 5.13)
- A TV show presented in a language you don't understand (for Reflections 5.12 and 5.13)

Culture and Cultural Capital

All students have culture and come to school with cultural knowledge. Understanding the role of culture, cultural knowledge, and cultural capital is significant to teaching. We looked briefly at the concept of culture in chapter 1, where you surveyed your home and family culture. According to Barrett (1984), culture, is "the body of learned beliefs, traditions, and guides for behavior that are shared among members of any human society" (p. 54). Edward Hall (1977) states:

> Culture is a man's medium; there is not one aspect of human life that is not touched and altered by culture. This means personality, how people express themselves (including shows of emotion), the way they think, how they move, how problems are solved, how their cities are planned and laid out, how transportation systems function and are organized, as well as how economic and government systems are put together and function. (p. 16)

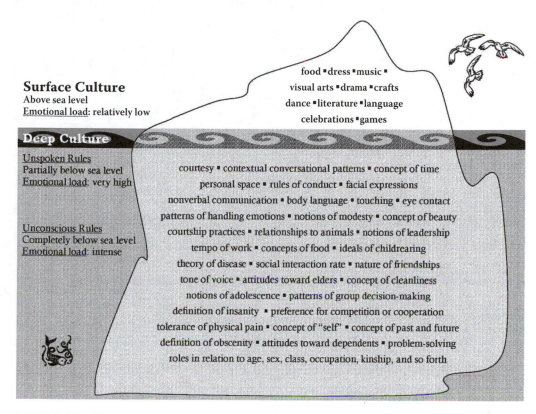

Surface Culture
Above sea level
Emotional load: relatively low

food ▪dress ▪music ▪
visual arts ▪drama ▪crafts
dance ▪literature ▪language
celebrations ▪games

Deep Culture

Unspoken Rules
Partially below sea level
Emotional load: very high

Unconscious Rules
Completely below sea level
Emotional load: intense

courtesy ▪ contextual conversational patterns ▪ concept of time
personal space ▪ rules of conduct ▪ facial expressions
nonverbal communication ▪ body language ▪ touching ▪ eye contact
patterns of handling emotions ▪ notions of modesty ▪ concept of beauty
courtship practices ▪ relationships to animals ▪ notions of leadership
tempo of work ▪ concepts of food ▪ ideals of childrearing
theory of disease ▪ social interaction rate ▪ nature of friendships
tone of voice ▪ attitudes toward elders ▪ concept of cleanliness
notions of adolescence ▪ patterns of group decision-making
definition of insanity ▪ preference for competition or cooperation
tolerance of physical pain ▪ concept of "self" ▪ concept of past and future
definition of obscenity ▪ attitudes toward dependents ▪ problem-solving
roles in relation to age, sex, class, occupation, kinship, and so forth

FIGURE. 5.1 The iceberg concept of culture

The Iceberg Concept of Culture can help you to go below the surface when considering the relationship between culture and learning. When thinking about the culture students bring to the classroom, often teachers see only the most obvious manifestations of culture and miss its more fundamental expressions. As the illustration in Figure 5.1 demonstrates, like an iceberg, nine-tenths of culture is below the surface. Cultural forms such as food, dress, music, visual arts, drama, craft, dance, literature, celebrations, and games are at the surface level. For instance, at the University of Wisconsin football games, students and alumni know to stick around for the "Fifth Quarter." They're waiting for the marching band to take the field and step away from the pomp and ritual of the first four quarters. Band members place their hats on backwards, play, sing, and dance along with the crowd.

However, most forms of culture are located below the surface or in the realm of "deep culture." For Reflection 5.1, examine Figure 5.1 and list the forms of culture that you are surprised to see.

Let's explore the significance of a "below the surface" cultural form. Consider body language. Strike a pose that you believe communicates each of the following:

- A desire to be included in a social situation;
- An interest in what someone is saying to you;
- A desire to be seen as important;
- What a "good student" looks like.

Each pose represents use of your body to communicate something to others. You depend on others reading your body language in the way that you intend. But all of the poses are learned, and none means the same thing in all cultural contexts. In some contexts, for example, a "good student" sits quietly, facing forward, while in others, a "good student" talks, moves about, asks questions, and responds to other people. In some contexts, interest in what others are saying is communicated by eye movement; in others, it is communicated by an occasional "mm-hmm"; and in still others, by touching the other person's arm lightly. Body language works when people share assumptions about what movements mean. When assumptions aren't shared, miscommunication happens. Unfortunately, however, the people involved do not necessarily realize they are misreading each other culturally. Instead, they often interpret the other person through their own cultural lenses. So, for example, while one culturally defined expression of interest may be misread as aggression, a different expression of the same thing could be misread as passivity.

This example probed just one element of "below the surface" culture. When you consider classrooms as cross-cultural meeting sites, you can see how complicated it can become to understand culture. "Cultural knowledge is the 'collective memory' of a people," contends Gordon (1997). Spindler (1982) adds that culture consists of "the knowledge participants … use to guide their behavior in the various social settings they participate in" (p. 5). Obviously, a teacher won't be able to acquire depth of knowledge of the culture in which every student participates. However, if you learn to view student behavior (not to mention teacher behavior) through an understanding of culture, you'll ask useful questions before jumping to conclusions. Activities and reflections later in this chapter will offer you some guidance in questions to ask.

Culture is related to, but not the same as, cultural capital. Capital refers to a resource that can be used to generate wealth. It can be "cashed in," invested, or used as a stepping-stone to move up. Cultural capital can be likened to what M. F. D. Young (1977) describes as "high-status knowledge," or the cultural knowledge of upper status groups in society. Although all students come to school with culture, they do not all come with the cultural capital valued by the White middle class and on which most school knowledge is built. According to Giroux (1981), the term *cultural capital* "refers to the socially determined tastes, certain kinds of prior knowledge, language forms, abilities, and modes of knowing that are unevenly distributed throughout society" (p. 77). Acquiring cultural capital, or high-status knowledge, usually requires money or access to places where it is available. For example, some students come to school with knowledge gained from frequent travel to European and Asian countries, vacationing at the better hotels in cities throughout the United States, attending Broadway plays and classical concerts, visiting art museums, subscribing to magazines and newspapers, and dining at fine restaurants.

Lei (1997) clarifies the relationship between culture and cultural capital, explaining that the value attached to cultural capital is socially defined, not inherent to any specific manifestation of culture. She elaborates on three economically informed sociological and anthropological premises on which cultural capital is based. First, "seeing culture as capital implies that the value of any piece of capital is culturally arbitrary." In other words, its value is determined, consciously or unconsciously, by sociocultural convention. For example, many regard knowledge of William Shakespeare's and the Brontë sisters' literary works as of more *academic* value than knowledge of Gwendolyn Brooks's and Countee Cullen's literary works. But the academic value of bodies of literature derives largely from what knowledge is expected at the next level of education. Second, "in any one society the exchanges of cultural capital with other, more generally recognized, forms of capital (economic and social) are set within an overall hierarchal distribution of capitals." For example, if students become stockbrokers, lawyers, or teachers, you may correctly guess that their earning and access to middle-class living will be greater than if they become maids at motels, clerks at McDonalds, or stockers at the local Wal-Mart. The cultural knowledge students use to become a stockbroker versus a maid is valued differently because these classifications of work valued very differently in social terms. Third, like economic and social capital, cultural capital is time dependent; over time both accumulation and loss of cultural capital are possible. For example, a librarian's knowledge of the card catalog system for locating books for students became outdated with the advent of computer technology.

The point is that while everyone comes into the classroom with a great deal of cultural knowledge, some cultural knowledge has much greater "currency" in a stratified society than other knowledge. For example, algebra may not seem practical in everyday life, but knowledge of algebra is one of the keys to college admission. Moses and Cobb (2001) argue that ensuring that everyone has access to high-status knowledge such as algebra is a very important civil rights issue.

Students who have had little access to learning the "culture of power" of the dominant society depend on schools to teach them that culture much more than students who are immersed in it every day. At the same time, high-status culture may be alienating to students from lower-status backgrounds, requiring teachers to think creatively about how to both affirm the cultural backgrounds students bring with them, and build bridges between students and the cultural capital that will give them access to opportunities.

Reflection 5.2 has you interview three students of different racial/ethnic or social class backgrounds, asking them to describe examples of cultural knowledge and cultural capital they bring to school. Of course, students won't be familiar with these terms, so you'll need to provide them with examples. Questions regarding cultural knowledge might include:

- Are there ways of thinking and acting among the students you hang out with about how to prepare for tests?
- What have you learned at home about dating, and about asking a person to go on a date?
- Which area of the school campus is *yours* and why?
- What kinds of things do your family or friends typically do on weekends?

Questions regarding cultural capital may include:

- Do you have knowledge of Shakespeare's plays?
- How much have you studied scientific principles, such as Newton's laws?
- What are the names of the musical instruments used in a classical orchestra?
- Do you have the ability to speak French or German?

Reflection 5.2
Who has cultural knowledge and cultural capital?

	Cultural Knowledge	Cultural Capital
Student 1		
Student 2		
Student 3		

Discuss with your classmates how an understanding of culture, cultural knowledge, and cultural capital will assist you in preparing curriculum and students' assignments.

Student Dialogue 5.1

Celia: I'm confused about this. What if a girl I interviewed said that she and her friends blow off tests, haven't heard of Shakespeare or Newton's laws, and spend their time trying to make themselves attractive to boys? I could easily conclude that this girl isn't school oriented, and to forget about trying to make her interested in school. But I don't think that's where the chapter wants us to go.

Lisa: I'm having the same question. I interviewed a kid who knows some Italian and has actually been to the opera! Can you imagine that? He and his friends think tests are stupid, but they compete to see who can do the best on them. What am I supposed to do, work Italian into assignments? I'm confused.

Gilbert: Lisa, your kid is getting some priming for getting ahead somewhere. Celia, yours isn't. I think the point is to figure out how to start with your student's interests, to get her into schoolwork. She doesn't bring a whole lot of high-status knowledge to school, so teachers need to help her develop some. Somehow.

Lisa: Like, starting with makeup to teach Newton's laws in science? Is that what this is saying?

Gilbert: Which of your two students is smarter? (Silence) See, you don't actually know. It would be easy to say that the Italian-speaking kid who has been to the opera is smarter, but all you're reacting to is the status of opera.

Lisa: True. OK, I see that, I can see where we started to assume that opera signals smarts and makeup doesn't. It looks like that's the next topic.

Student Achievement and Teacher Expectations

As a teacher, your responsibility is to help students achieve. Although pressure you may face to raise students' achievement levels can lead at times to mind-numbing, drill-and-kill approaches to teaching, it should lead to an exploration of how your own students learn best, and what assets they bring that you can build on in instructional terms. Many different reasons are given for why students from some backgrounds achieve in schools better than others; let's look critically at them, because sometimes such reasoning can get in the way of seeing students' learning assets.

The National Assessment of Educational Progress (NAEP) is a standardized test that has been given to a nationwide sample of students ages 9, 13, and 17 in reading, mathematics, and science since the mid-1970s. It serves as a useful yardstick for tracking student academic learning in the United States and for raising questions about student learning. Table 5.1 shows average achievement scores of 13-year-olds in reading, between 1975 and 1999, by race. Examine the table, and then, for Reflection 5.3, write about the trends or patterns that you see.

TABLE 5.1 NAEP reading scores, age 13, by race

	1975	1980	1984	1988	1990	1992	1996	1999
White	262	264	263	262	262	266	266	266
Black	222	226	233	236	241	238	234	238
Latino	233	237	240	240	238	239	238	244

Campbell, J. R., Hombo, C. M., & Mazzeo, J. (2000). NAEP 1999 trends in academic progress: Three decades of student performance. Washington, D.C.: U.S. Department of Education.

Reflection 5.3
Achievement trends, by race

Trends and patterns in NAEP reading scores are:

Read the discussion by Celia, Lisa, and Gilbert, who offer different ideas about what they think these data mean. What do you think about their reasoning?

Student Dialogue 5.2

Celia: The Black kids made quite a bit of progress, especially until the mid-1980s. The Latino kids made some progress, but it was more up and down.

Lisa: The White kids stayed about the same from year to year until the 1990s, and then they went up a little.

Celia: I'm trying to figure out why the Latino kids' scores went up and down. I wonder if it has to do with immigration, and the fact that every time this test is given, there would be a whole bunch of new immigrants taking it.

Gilbert: That could be. I'm reflecting on how, in the 70s and 80s, I think, a lot of teachers began to be aware of culture, and made their teaching more relevant. Whatever was going on then was starting to close the racial achievement gap. You can see that when you compare 1975 and 1990.

Lisa: Yeah, but there are still really big gaps. Don't you think it has something to do with the culture at home, you know, like parents reading to their kids and getting involved with school? I mean, Celia, I know you came from a home that pushed you, but a lot of kids don't, especially in the inner cities.

TABLE 5.2   NAEP reading scores, age 13, by parents' level of education

	1975	1980	1984	1988	1990	1992	1996	1999
Less than high school graduate	239	239	240	246	241	239	239	238
High school graduate	256	255	253	253	251	252	251	251
High school graduate plus	270	271	268	265	267	270	269	270

Campbell, J. R., Hombo, C. M., & Mazzeo, J. (2000). NAEP 1999 trends in academic progress: Three decades of student performance. Washington, D.C.: U.S. Department of Education.

Now look at Table 5.2, which shows how 13-year-olds were reading in relationship to their parents' level of education between 1975 and 1999. What patterns do you see?

Student Dialogue 5.3

Lisa: See, I told you it had to do with what goes on at home. Parents that didn't graduate from high school just don't value education, and don't push their kids to learn. They don't read to their kids, or come into the school. Education just isn't a priority with them.

Gilbert: I don't exactly see it that way. Lisa, you're talking as if student achievement all comes from what happens at home. Like it keeps saying in this book, teachers are part of the equation! My take is that it has a great deal to do with the education of the parents/caregivers. As their graduation rate goes up, not only can they teach their kids the cultural capital schools expect, but teachers also expect more. Black high school graduation rates have gone up, right? At the same time, Black kids' reading levels went up. Why is that? Well, in my experience, not only could better educated parents help their kids, but teachers also figured that kids of educated parents could learn more, because of the cultural capital they display in school.

Lisa: This isn't about race Gilbert, it's about the conditions of the home. The table doesn't say anything about race, you're adding in race.

Gilbert: I am not!

Lisa: Listen, there were some poor white families where I grew up, and they just didn't know very much. Some of them were unemployed, this one family had problems with alcohol, this other lady had three kids by different fathers and was on welfare. No wonder their kids had problems in school!

Celia: I know some Latino teachers who think the same thing about Latinos from poor families. But I came from a poor family, and I know a lot of poor families where the parents didn't have much schooling. We need teachers to school us. To me, all of this comes back to how much power the teacher has to make a difference with kids.

Gilbert: I agree. But check this out: Between 1975 and 1999, there was no average improvement. And the gap you saw in 1975 was still there in 1999. So it seems like whether achievement gaps were closing depends on which data you are looking at.

Lisa: We've got a lot of work to do, folks!

Lisa, Gilbert, and Celia are trying to make sense out of a complicated set of variables that include race, social class, and parents' level of education. We believe that the most fundamental thing for teachers to address isn't so much what variables explain achievement differences, but rather what teachers can do to support academic learning among their own students. Supporting academic learning doesn't mean being blind to students' race, ethnicity, social class, or parental background, but rather figuring out how and when to use knowledge of students' backgrounds for instructional purposes. This means being a very critical consumer of the reasons people give you for achievement gaps. An excellent question to ask is: To what extent does reasoning we hear about achievement gaps suggest how to teach students better? To what extent does it suggest that students won't learn very well no matter what you do?

Reflection 5.4 asks you to investigate the reasons people give for why some students achieve more than others. Select two or three adults who work with kids for a short interview, following the directions below.

Reflection 5.4
Explanations for achievement differences

Ask two or three adults who work with kids the following question, and write their responses below: What do you think are the main reasons why some kids do well in school academically while others do not?

Adult 1 said:

Adult 2 said:

Adult 3 said:

Underline responses that put the burden for learning on students' homes and communities; put a square around the responses that put the burden on parents' education; and circle those that put the burden on schools and teachers. To what extent did the responses focus on factors within the student's world (e.g., economics) that teachers can do very little about? To what extent did responses highlight what teachers can do, and what schools have control over?

Research studies report a variety of reasons why there are gaps in student academic achievement. Some broad clusters of reasons include:

- Teacher knowledge of subject matter: You cannot teach well what you do not know well; evidence links teacher subject matter knowledge with student achievement (Stigler, Gonzales, Kawanaka, Knoll, & Serrano, 1999). But the best prepared teachers tend not to teach in low-income schools, which results in students having unequal access to knowledgeable teachers (Boyd, Hamilton, Loeb, & Wyckoff, 2004).

- School organization and climate: Research on "effective schools" links student academic learning with the extent to which the school as an organization cohesively and actively supports clearly defined student achievement (e.g., Lezotte, 2003).

- Prior academic learning: Students who have been academically prepared at earlier grade levels have the tools to achieve better at later grade levels than those who are underprepared.

- Students' perception that school achievement will pay off: Students in high-poverty neighborhoods, in which there is a scarcity of jobs, often question the extent to which school will actually help them (A. A. Young, 2004). Further, students who believe that people like themselves are routinely discriminated against, and that the main purpose of schools is to make them like their oppressors without actually equipping them with real opportunities, often reject schooling. Strategies in this book help bridge students' and teachers' communication gaps in order to reach an understanding that enables those issues to be addressed.

- What teachers actually do with students in their own classrooms: Fantastic teachers, as we observe them teach, are convinced that their students can learn, expect a lot of their students, and find ways to make whatever students bring to school a learning *asset*. Some learning assets, they admit, more directly relate to school policy and practices; nevertheless with effort, they are able to use what students bring as teaching resources (Haberman, 1995).

This latter point is increasingly supported by research. For example, Thomas (2000) studied factors that account for differential math achievement across ethnic groups in the United States. He found quality of instruction to be one of the main factors affecting student achievement. Students' academic self-perception was also important; students who believed they could learn math achieved better than did students who questioned their ability to learn. Thomas pointed out that perception of ability to learn also hinges on what happens in the classroom. So, throughout this chapter, we will focus on factors that teachers can control because these factors matter. By control we mean teachers have a major say in what takes place in the classroom, as well as how it takes place.

Generally, teachers who help students to learn at high levels take a good deal of responsibility for student learning, rather than attributing the ability to learn to factors teachers can't do anything about. Such teachers are able to capitalize on the cultural knowledge students bring. In addition, they are aware of factors and conditions that serve as barriers to student learning, and figure out ways to deal with them. For example, a teacher may learn that a student's caregivers/parents did not finish high school and therefore lack cultural knowledge helpful to getting their kids ready for college. Nevertheless, the teacher knows that the parents/caregivers are working extra jobs to have the money to send their child to college. Thus the teacher provides the "nuts and bolts" knowledge to help the student prepare for a college education.

Teacher expectations are the linchpin of student achievement. When teachers expect students to learn — not simply hope that they do, but expect that they will — they take responsibility for making sure learning happens. Rosenthal and Jacobson (1968) and Jones (1990) argue that teachers' expectations can have a self-fulfilling prophecy effect on student achievement. In other words, students respond to the expectations set for them. When students mentally tune out, don't do their work, misbehave, or fall sleep, many teachers see this as evidence of the students' inability to learn. Some teachers with low expectations engage students in activities that are fun, but academically lead nowhere (Grant & Sleeter, 1996). Fantastic teachers expect a lot, actively take responsibility for student learning, and search for strategies that will enable students in their classroom to succeed.

Building Block 9: Making Students' Interests and Background a Focal Point in Teaching

All children bring to school what the psychologist L. S. Vygotsky called "living knowledge" (Moll, 1990, p. 10) that they learn outside school, in their homes and communities. The more different the child is from the teacher, and the more different the child's areas of competence are from traditional school knowledge, the less likely the teacher is to recognize this living cultural knowledge. Teachers who become familiar with children's interests — what they already know and the knowledge networks they engage in every day outside school — can tap into valuable teaching and learning resources. This knowledge allows teachers to provide temporary scaffolding within what Vygotsky (1978) calls a zone of proximal development (ZPD), to assist students in learning academic knowledge.

Scaffolding works like the training wheels on a bicycle that are removed as the child gains competence. When teaching children to write a book report, for example, scaffolding might include assessing what students already know through discussion, using trade books that the children can relate to, and providing an outline of a book report with spaces to guide children's writing. As children gain practice in writing reports, the outline is removed; children write complete and increasingly complex reports on their own. Recently, one of the authors saw an excellent example of scaffolding in a fourth-grade class. The teacher first modeled strategies and knowledge for doing long division. Next, the students attempted to do as the teacher had done. They drew upon the previous chalk-and-talk discussion with the teacher as they directed her when, where, and how to carry out long division procedures as much as they could. After repeating the procedure several times, with the teacher giving help and support when and where needed, the majority of the students were able to do long division problems alone.

Here we can see why Vygotsky (1978) regards learning as a social activity. He argued that intellectual development takes place in natural interactions involving a child and an adult. Within a zone of proximal development, which is the space between what a student can do independently and what the student is not yet ready to do, a student can be assisted to learn new things and make mental connections. Activities need to be meaningful (this is why knowledge of students' interests and background is significant) and difficult enough to stretch the student but not so difficult as to be overwhelming. Assistance within the ZPD may take many forms, including modeling, giving feedback, structuring new ideas or skills, questioning, and instructing (Gallimore & Tharp, 1990). The emphasis is on the *student*'s active mental engagement and on the sense the student is making of the content, rather than the assistance itself.

Culturally relevant pedagogy complements use of students' zone of proximal development. Culturally relevant pedagogy makes use of students' interests and background, and directly connects students' academic learning to their ethnic culture, home, and community. According to Gay (2000), this kind of teaching:

> filters curriculum content and teaching strategies through their [the students'] cultural frames of reference to make the content more personally meaningful and easier to master. It is radical because it makes explicit the previously implicit role of culture in teaching and learning, and it insists that educational institutions accept the legitimacy and viability of ethnic group cultures in improving learning outcomes. (pp. 24–25)

Teachers who take the extra step of finding out about students' cultural background can build cultural continuity between home cultural knowledge and school. Cultural discontinuity happens when students have to cross two quite different cultural contexts, with minimal assistance. Discontinuity may be particularly aggravating for the child who is expected to function within the school's culture without being taught that culture, and who must leap between cultures twice a day — once when arriving at school, then again when going home. Imagine the confusion and frustration of children who are expected to replace their home culture with school culture by teachers who define school knowledge as "proper" and home knowledge as incorrect.

The larger the cultural gap between the child and the school, the harder schools need to work to construct bridges to minimize cultural discontinuity that students experience. For example, Phelan, Davidson, and Cao (1991) distinguished among four kinds of relationship between the worlds of the student and the school:

- Congruent worlds among home, school, and peer group, with smooth transitions from one setting to the next;
- Different worlds with boundary crossings from one to the next that are manageable;

- Different worlds with unbridged boundary crossings that are hazardous for the student; and
- Different worlds with insurmountable barriers.

They found that students did reasonably well academically with teachers who tried to adapt their teaching to the students. When forced to choose between the peer group and the school, or between home and school, many students did not choose school and consequently failed academically.

You can find out a good deal about students' interests and backgrounds by asking them to share themselves in the classroom, and by exploring their world outside of the classroom. In the preface of their book *Funds of Knowledge*, Gonzalez, Moll, and Amanti (2005) recommend that teachers and teacher candidates learn from their students and their communities. They state that "learning does not take place just 'between the ears,' but is eminently a social process. Students' learning is bound within larger contextual, historical, political, and ideological frameworks that affect students' lives" (p. ix). They go on to contend that people are competent, they have knowledge, and their life experiences have given them that knowledge. This they refer to as *funds of knowledge*, which "refers to these historically accumulated and culturally developed bodies of knowledge and skills essential for household or individual functioning and well being" (p. 72).

Following are several reflection activities to guide you in identifying community funds of knowledge. Howard, Rhodes, Fitch, and Stimson (1998) define three types of communities that are useful to the reflection activities:

1. An area of neighborhood — a "group of people living together with a location."
2. Social relationships — "a set of social relationships mostly taking place within a geographic location."
3. Identity or common interest — "a shared sense of identity such as group" (p. 33).

The three community-based investigation activities below can help you explore the learning assets, experiences, and interests students bring to the classroom. However, before you head out into the community, study Box 5.1, which discusses ethics and guidelines for entering the community and asking questions.

Reflection 5.5 involves interviewing adults from a community or neighborhood that is different from your own, to gain "insider" perspectives about the community and its assets. (School secretaries and custodians are often excellent sources of information.) Although most communities have problems of one sort or another, often problems are all outsiders know of some communities, especially if their residents are low income or people of color. In fact, the community may well have a number of strengths and assets that you can become familiar with by talking to people who live there.

When you are finished with Reflection 5.5, write a description of the community assets that you have discovered. Share these with your classmates. To what extent did these interviews change or broaden your perspective about the community?

Reflection 5.5
Community assets

Select five adults from a community that is culturally different from your own, or from the neighborhood of a school in which you are doing a field placement. Tell them that you are learning to teach, and have been encouraged to get to know the community being served by the school. With their permission, ask questions such as the following:

1. What do you see as the main assets of this community?

2. What are people in this community especially good at doing?

3. Describe how you would like to see the community 10 years from now.

4. What assets can help the community reach this vision?

5. What barriers will the community face in working toward this vision? What is being done about those barriers?

6. How can the school serve the community most effectively?

Box 5.1 Tips for Entering the Community

"To act ethically is to act the way one acts toward people whom one respects" (Graue, Walsh, & Ceglowski, 1998, p. 56). Ethical behavior is about the attitude that teachers bring into the community and bring to their interpretations. Acting on your ethical behavior, you would do the following:

Preparation for Entry

1. Be clear about what you want from your visit. Who is your population of interest? Who do you want/need to talk with?

2. Identify and contact gatekeepers or key respondents (people who have special knowledge or individuals who can facilitate contact). If the school has a community worker, ask that person to make the first few visits with you. If no community worker is available, an upper-grade student is an excellent companion.

3. Acquire background knowledge about the community, including how to act in culturally appropriate ways.

4. Prepare questions or observation plans, and decide how you are going to take notes.

5. Plan exactly when, where, and at what time you will meet with key respondents.

6. Explain the reasons you wish to visit the community. You may briefly explain the curriculum for the year, including any field trips, assemblies, guest speakers, and so forth. Teachers are not known for visiting their school community, so if parents are suspicious at first, that is OK. Tell them why you are there. Carl would visit the homes of all of his students within the first two weeks of the semester. During this time he would get parents to sign off on any permission slips for field trips, etc. When he first

started teaching at the school, he would take one or two students with him who knew the area and the community residents.

Entry

7. Develop rapport with gatekeepers, key respondents, and community population, and be polite. Politeness may differ from community to community. Ask the traveling companions for help in this area. For example, you may ask: "Is there anything I need to know to show my politeness and sincerity during the visit to this home or community site?"

8. Be aware of where you place your personal items (e.g. hat, coat, etc.). Trust your feelings; it you don't feel comfortable, leave.

9. Reciprocity, or both parties getting something out of the relationship, is highly important, particularly in communities that universities have used but have not collaborated with. Offer your assistance or invite suggestions about what you can do to assist the community. Write a thank you letter after the visit.

While you are there

10. Explain why you are taking notes and collecting materials. Take notes openly. By this we mean, don't hide what you are writing. Instead, share it and tell folks why you are writing things down. Carl told his host that he had to write because he was lousy at remembering names, and did not want to mix up the information collected between the first and fifth home visits. The host would show understanding and some hosts would contribute stories about their own memory. Such swapping of little tales also serves as an ice-breaker.

11. Be nonjudgmental. Remember that your observation is only a thin slice of the ongoing activities. Any judgment you make needs to take that into consideration.

12. If possible, ask questions that will help to clarify any concerns or questions you may have about what you are seeing or hearing.

13. Be patient. Don't hop about from one location to the next.

When you are finished

14. Conclude your visit with invitations to come and visit at school. Explain the procedure for entering the building and stopping by the office to get a guest pass. Also, tell them that you will let the office secretary know that you will be expecting guests throughout the semester. This will take the sting out of the formal but necessary procedure for entering the school and visiting your class.

Ideas for these tips come from: Batchelor, Beel, and Freeman (2006) and Grant and Sleeter (1996).

Reflection 5.6 continues your exploration of the community, by looking into household funds of knowledge. Every household contains a good deal of knowledge necessary for survival in everyday life. People develop expertise in various jobs and roles that are useful to and needed by the household and the community. Even in the most impoverished home, people develop skills and areas of expertise. These funds of knowledge can serve as connections between what parents and other community members know (knowledge that children have access to at home) and school knowledge (Gonzalez et al., 2005).

Elaborate on the community description that you started with Reflection 5.5, using what you learned in Reflection 5.6. Now imagine that you are teaching students from this community. How might you work with the community assets that were identified, to connect academic material that students do not know with what they or their parents do know?

Reflection 5.6
Adult areas of expertise

Find out about what kinds of jobs adults in the community have, and through talking with a few of them, develop an "inventory of knowledge" people have related to their work. Ask questions such as, *"I don't know much about what a person actually does in that job, can you tell me how a day goes?"* In addition, explore informal areas of expertise such as fixing cars, cooking, planting and growing things, and so forth. Ask questions such as, *"What kinds of things are some of the women/men in your neighborhood good at doing?"*

(Note: Do not probe into illegal activities. Children sometimes volunteer information they shouldn't; older children and adults sometimes simply look uncomfortable if they suspect you are investigating illegal activities. You can direct conversations with examples, such as asking, *"What about repairing things? If your bike is in need of repair, would you take it to someone in the neighborhood to repair?"*)

Reflection 5.7 offers an additional way of getting to know about students' everyday life experiences, by asking what they do when not in school.

You should now have a set of tools (ideas) to help you find out more about students' worlds. You may be wondering how to use these tools to connect concepts and skills in the curriculum with what the students know, care about, or find interesting. Reflection 5.8 invites you to practice making those connections, using data you have gathered in Reflections 5.5 to 5.7.

For Reflection 5.8, identify an academic concept that is commonly taught in school. By "concept," we are referring to an idea or skill that might be taught in a lesson, such as how to add two-digit numbers, what a continent is, or what the term *oligarchy* means. Select something that would be appropriate to an age or grade level you plan to teach. Then list as many connections as possible between this concept and the community assets and student experiences you learned about.

Reflection 5.7
Students' lives outside of school

Find out what kids spend time doing when they are not in school. If possible, spend some time hanging out with a group when they are not in school. In addition, ask them to talk about what they do that you don't see. Probe areas of activity such as: houses of worship, chores at home, community center activities and clubs, jobs, and activities with friends. Walk around the neighborhood where they live. Look and listen for things you can use as examples in lessons or as ideas to develop lessons to help teach concepts in your curriculum. Pay attention to such things as geometric shapes in building designs, the kinds of plant life and rocks that are present, the types of stores that are present, the styles of music played, or the kinds of games children play. Identify 8 to 10 specific interests, activities, or items from the environment that you can connect with specific concepts in the curriculum.

Reflection 5.8
Connecting academic concepts with students' lives

Academic concept:

Connections you discovered with students' lives:

We have been scaffolding your learning in this section. We first explained the importance of the zone of proximal development (ZPD) and culturally relevant pedagogy, then differentiated it from cultural discontinuity. Next we sent you into the community to learn first-hand about the students' cultural knowledge, including the assets found in the community. Simply put, we are modeling: providing knowledge and strategies through interactive activities about how to become a fantastic teacher.

Student Dialogue 5.4

Lisa: I didn't think about actually going out into the community to ask these kinds of questions. When I did these reflections, people were more open than I would have thought.

Celia: Yeah, I like how you even got the mayor in a low-income community to talk with you!

Lisa: I'll admit I was scared. Gilbert, you gave me the idea of sending him an e-mail, and I was flabbergasted when he invited me into his office. I was pretty nervous, but people were a lot more open to talking with me about school and the good things that go on around here than I would have thought.

Gilbert: I think my biggest revelation was that the school secretaries know a lot about the community because they live there. It never had occurred to me to ask them about what's going on, and who is good at doing what.

Celia: I discovered that the mom of one of the kids in my classroom knows how to make candy. Wouldn't it be interesting to connect what she knows about things like boiling points of different substances to the science curriculum? She never went to college, but she has this knowledge that relates pretty directly to what they are calling "high-status academic knowledge."

Building Block 10: Using Students' Learning Styles When Planning Classroom Instruction

Being familiar with a student's learning style can help you interpret his or her behavior and think through strategies that might engage her or him. According to Gay (2000), "A learning style is the process one habitually uses for cognitive problem solving and for showing what one knows and is capable of doing" (p. 150). Learning style involves how people perceive, process, store, and retrieve information. In a learning situation, what cues does a student attend to? How does the student connect cues? What strategies does the student use to make sense of new information or ideas?

Everyone develops a learning style. For example, some students learn a concept better when they read about it, others when they actually see it, and still others need to use a combination of sensory modalities, such as seeing, hearing, touching, or writing. Some students need a great deal of structure (such as a time schedule, a task schedule, or writing guidelines), while others prefer little structure, employing their creativity when doing an assignment.

Christine used to be a special education teacher. Her learning-disabled students struggled to read, so she had to figure out how they could retain reading skills as well as how they learned other concepts. She found that if she identified how each student learned best, she was able to constructively adapt her teaching processes to her students.

How would you describe your own style of learning? For Reflection 5.9, think about your experiences tackling new or difficult material, and the kinds of processes you use or prefer that work well for you.

Reflection 5.9
Your learning style

In the space below, write a description of how you believe you learn best, especially when material is new or difficult.

To some extent, learning style arises out of a person's unique psychological makeup, and to some extent it arises out of family child-rearing patterns. For example, in families in which children are expected to share and work together, children experience learning as social and collaborative. Families that encourage independence and individualism produce children who tend to approach learning in an independent style. Since child rearing relates to culture, learning style very roughly overlaps with cultural background. For example, Jordan (1985) and her colleagues identified a few key practices that interfered with the effective learning of native Hawaiian children who spend considerable time working with peers outside of school; if they are punished for interacting with peers in the classroom, and especially if punishment involves isolating them, they put their energy into establishing illicit contact with peers. If a moderate level of peer interaction is allowed, they tend to stay on task. Wan (2001) found Chinese college students to have difficulty in U.S. classrooms because they are too unstructured, chaotic, and not teacher-centered enough. During a visit to Taiwan, we observed that the elementary and middle school classes maintain a very structured environment, which explains Wan's observation of why Chinese college students find U.S. classrooms chaotic.

Shade (1989) distinguished between *analytical* and *synergetic* cognitive styles. Analytical learners are competitive and independent, and they focus well on impersonal tasks. They learn well through print, focus best on one task at a time, and work in a step-by-step sequence. Synergetic learners, on the other hand, prefer to work cooperatively rather than independently; they attempt to integrate personal relationships into learning tasks. Synergetic learners are stimulated by multiple activities and become bored when only one thing is happening. They often prefer kinesthetic (bodily movement) and tactile (touching) involvement as well as discussion. Shade argued that teachers who are analytical learners often misread the behavior of synergetic learners, viewing them as talking too much, being off task, or cheating (discipline problems) rather than building on their preference for cooperative work. But synergetic learners need not be low achievers or discipline problems; a synergetic teaching style is much more engaging to them.

In Reflection 5.10 identify and observe a friend who is an analytical learner and a friend who is a synergetic learner. Observe or interview both of them to find out how they prefer to learn new or difficult academic material.

Reflection 5.10
Analytic vs. synergetic learners

What the analytic learner prefers:

What the synergetic learner prefers:

How similar or different were their preferences? Compare what you learned about their learning styles with your own style as you described it in Reflection 5.9. Are there any key differences you see among the three of you? Would you add anything to what you wrote about yourself?

Student Dialogue 5.5

Gilbert: This gives me some insight about why I found school pretty easy. I guess I must be an analytic learner, since the way I prefer to work fits the description here, and it fits how my teachers thought students were supposed to work.

Celia: I'm kind of in between, but lots of the kids from my neighborhood must have been synergetic learners. Like, they have music on all the time while doing homework, talk while they work, and like to work in groups. I like to work in groups, and I do get bored if there isn't enough stimulation, but I'm not one of those kids who talks all the time in class.

Lisa: When I'm doing homework, I don't just start at the beginning, I hop all around. I thought there was something wrong with what I do, but maybe I'm just using my learning style!

Celia: What's a little scary to me is that we'd need to be able to figure out how to reach the kids who approach things differently from us. Gilbert, you'd need to be able to accommodate to Lisa, and Lisa, you could have some Gilberts in your class!

Most students can learn to approach tasks in more than one way. At the same time, all students have ways of approaching problems that work best for them. Learning style strengths and preferences probably matter most when material is new and difficult. When trying to figure how to teach so that the students will become engaged, it helps to think in terms of how the majority of students learn best, even if that is not what would work best for the teacher. Then, individualize as needed for students who aren't getting the ideas or skills and need a different approach. At the same time, it is important not to stereotype groups based on what you think their learning style is. Get to know the students and work from there.

Reflection 5.11 can serve as a tool for getting to know students' learning style. Gather the information below by either interviewing or observing six to eight students. (The thought of interviewing a whole class of students may seem forbidding because of the anticipated amount of time involved, but what you will learn will make the time spent well worth it.)

Analyze the data by tallying the responses you get for each question. How would you describe the learning styles of the students? Do some students have different preferences according to subject matter? Are you surprised by anything that you discovered? When teaching, Carl was always surprised by what he discovered each year. The number of students who preferred detail versus the overall picture, or structured

Reflection 5.11
Learning styles

<u>Working alone versus working with others</u>: Many students work best cooperatively with a partner or small group, whereas others work best individually.

Possible questions: *Tell me if you prefer to work with others or alone. Also, tell me if there are times when you prefer one way of working more than the other way.*

<u>Preferred learning modalities</u>: This term refers to the sensory channels that students prefer to use for acquiring new information or ideas.

Reading

Listening

Discussing

Touching

Moving

Writing

Possible question: *What is your favorite way to learn something new and hard?*

<u>Content about people versus content about things</u>: Some students are more interested in content related directly to people and social issues, while others are more interested in content related to impersonal abstractions or mechanics.

Possible questions: *What engages you the most, learning about people and social issues, for example poverty and AIDS/HIV, or learning about technical or impersonal issues, such as the development of space flight? Which people or issues are you interested in, or which technical and impersonal issues strike you the most?*

<u>Structured versus nonstructured tasks</u>: Some students prefer tasks that are structured, while others prefer to create their own structure. Students who seem lost or do poorly on open-ended assignments probably need structure; those who seem bored with structured assignments probably need open-ended work.

Possible question: *Do you like a lot of step-by-step directions when given an assignment, or do you prefer to figure things out on your own?*

<u>Details versus the overall picture</u>: Some students do meticulous work, are attentive to details, and can work through small steps to arrive at the larger idea. Others need to view the larger picture first and may become bored or lost with details or small steps. Although all students eventually need to work on both details and the big picture, some will have trouble if the teacher emphasizes one or the other too soon.

Possible questions: *When starting on a new project, do you prefer that the teacher explains each step as you go, or would you prefer starting with an overall explanation of the finished product, then get help figuring out the steps only as needed? Which holds your attention on a project the longest?*

versus nonstructured learning changed from year to year, making him realize that it is important to check out each class each year.

Gardner's (2000) concept of multiple intelligences, while not the same as learning styles, is related. Gardner posits eight different kinds of intelligence: linguistic intelligence and logical–mathematical intelligence (which schools focus on most heavily); musical intelligence; interpersonal intelligence; intrapersonal intelligence; spatial intelligence; bodily–kinesthetic intelligence; and naturalist intelligence. Everyone has a profile of strengths and weaknesses. Students who are not as strong in verbal skills as in other intelligence areas often do not do as well in the classroom as they might if their stronger intelligence areas were supported. Gardner's work on multiple intelligences helps get beyond seeing intelligence as one-dimensional — some people have more of "it" than others — and to look for areas in which every student demonstrates intelligence. Gardner (1995) recommends that teachers delve deeply into fewer rich topics rather than covering many topics superficially, and in delving, approach topics through a variety of ways of knowing that will engage the variety of students they are teaching.

Expressive and communication styles relate to learning style. Expressive style includes language and dialect, use of body and gestures (movement), and style of dress. In almost every school, you will find some students who have a distinct expressive style. For example, some students may announce their presence dramatically, while others appreciate being less obtrusive. Also some students display their sexuality openly, while others tend to hide it. Teachers should consider how they can use the students' expressive style to enhance their learning.

Communication style refers to the variety of strategies and behaviors used in interpersonal interactions. For example, some students will rarely interrupt when another student is speaking; other students will not only interrupt, but may engage in multiple conversations simultaneously. Some students talk continuously, while other students are hesitant to talk at all. Some students will say "hi" robustly and simultaneously give a high-five; others will give a more traditional modulated greeting, "What's-up?" or "How are you doing?" Everyone has an expressive style and a communication style. And, when they are asked why they do what they do, a number of students will tell you that this is the way they feel comfortable. They will contend that the way they express themselves helps them in the school setting. It is just who they are. They are not trying to show off or to monopolize a discussion. Students sometimes have not figured out that their communication style influences their learning. Culturally responsive teachers recognize and affirm the expressive and communication styles of their students, while at the same time helping them to develop a communication style that best represents them in the present and future.

Use Reflection 5.12 to find out more about the communication and expressive styles of several students when they are not in school. For this reflection, go to a public place (such as a playground, a fast-food restaurant, or a recreation area), where you can unobtrusively observe young people who are of the same cultural background as they interact with each other.

Reflection 5.12
Communication and interaction patterns

Watch members of the same cultural group talking naturally (on more than one occasion, if possible). If you can do so unobtrusively, write descriptions of their behavior as they talk. Look for things such as:

What distance do they maintain between each other?

What kinds of gestures are used?

In what contexts do people touch each other? How do they touch, and where? (Some cultural groups touch a lot, others very little.)

What do they do to indicate they are listening?

How does a person "get the floor" when she or he wants to speak? (e.g., does the person simply start talking, wait for an opening, or use a hand gesture?)

What level of loudness or softness of speech do people maintain?

If you are able to watch an adult giving directions to, or reprimanding a child who is a member of the adult's same sociocultural group: What does the adult say? What nonverbal behavior does the adult use? How does the child respond?

To what extent do people "code-switch" from one set of interaction patterns to another if they move to different settings?

Compare your findings with classmates who have observed in similar, and in different settings. What patterns do you see? Do you notice any ways in which expressive and communication style might conflict with behavioral expectations in the classroom? If so, how can you reasonably make classroom behavioral expectations fit a broader range of styles? How can you communicate and teach classroom expectations in a way that helps students to learn which style to use in what context (for example, the playground context versus the classroom context)?

It is important to realize that young people can learn to switch between two different cultural styles, if they see a reason for doing so, and do not feel that they have to "give up" the cultural style of their community. For example, you can (and should) teach young people how you would prefer they behave in your classroom. But if they bring into your classroom a different behavioral repertoire, you need to make clear that you are not trying to force them to accept your way as the "right" way (implying that their home way is the "wrong" way). Rather, you are teaching them your expectation, which they should add to their repertoire of communication and interaction styles.

Student Dialogue 5.6

Lisa: I'm in a classroom this semester where some of the kids really strut in, and, like, act like they are the center of the universe. It's been driving me nuts. I don't understand why they can't just walk in and sit down.

Gilbert: If those kids just walked into the classroom like you do, their friends would laugh at them. Just like your friends would laugh at you if you started to walk into a room like these kids do.

Celia: Like, some of my friends went to school wearing high heels and lots of makeup. They copy the *telenovela* stars. That's what kids do.

Lisa: So we are supposed to just let kids do whatever they want?

Gilbert: Of course not. But we've got to learn what rules are really important, and what aren't. If a kid struts into class and gives his friends high fives on his way to his seat, then sits down and gets to work, where's the problem? But if he sits there and blows off class work, then there's a problem.

Celia: From doing Reflection 5.12, I can see how helpful it is to get out into community settings where kids act like themselves, and adults who are from their community set them straight. It gives me a sense of perspective.

Building Block 11: Making Students' Language a Valuable Learning Resource

Garcia (1999) tells teachers, "Language is a critical social repertoire, a set of skills that enable children to function in a world of social interaction" (p. 187). The discourse component of any social interaction most often determines the general quality of that interaction. As such, language carries special significance for culturally and linguistically diverse students. Students who are good with their language, teachers argue, will be successful in school.

This thinking connects to Vygotsky's (1978) observation that language acquisition is the momentous occasion when internal mental representation and external reality converge. Key to Vygotsky (and to teachers' knowledge and understanding of students) is that the "external reality" is first and foremost cultural; in the development of language through interpersonal experiences, children begin to construct meaning. In this view, language functions significantly as a tool of thought, and thus as a valuable learning tool. Hamer and Blanc (1989) claim that the shared representations and scripts, which are basic to language proficiency, arise in the interaction between the child and the people in her or his life spaces. The representations the child will construct of objects, people, and ideas are highly dependent on shared social representations in his or her environment. Children internalize those language functions that are valorized and used with them; it is through the socialization process that they become cognizant of functions and representations. Teachers play a paramount role in constructing how a student's language will serve the student. This is why many teachers who are advocates of multicultural education and multilingualism argue that respect shown toward a student's home language will influence how students accept their home language and use it with pride, and more fundamentally how students will accept themselves.

Students may interpret acceptance of their native language as a significant act of social justice. If you have traveled outside the United States, you probably have noticed people moving easily and fluently between two or more languages. Research now shows cognitive benefits to being bilingual. Based on a summary of this research, Baker (2001) points out that people who are fully bilingual develop more cognitive flexibility, better analytical thinking abilities, better language and metalinguistic awareness (e.g., awareness of ways in which language is being used), and are more creative thinkers than monolinguals. People who are only partially bilingual perform more like monolinguals. It is not until fluency in a second language is achieved that cognitive gains appear. This comes about as a result of having learned two language systems, and the contexts in which each is used.

Some of you will become bilingual teachers; most of you will not. However, the great majority of you will have some students whose first language is not English, and some of these students may enter your classroom struggling. One of the first things to understand is that all students bring knowledge and linguistic skills to the classroom, even if they do not bring Standard English. If what they know is in a language other than English, one of the teachers' tasks is to provide an environment in which students can connect new language skills and new knowledge with what they already know.

The student who understands little English will not learn new academic content taught in English, or be able to demonstrate competence in tests given in English. If an English language learner is to learn academics, teachers must teach in ways that are comprehensible to that student. The student's first language is generally the student's strongest language foundation. Students with well-developed first-language skills acquire their second language with greater ease and success than those who are still learning their first language. Cummins (2000) explained this phenomenon with his "common underlying proficiency" model of language acquisition, which holds that many language skills and attitudes, once learned well, can be translated into any language and that they are best learned in one's strongest language. For example, Christine was talking with a Maori adolescent in New Zealand who had learned to read in Maori. The student's mother pointed out that the student had also taught herself to read in English while browsing teen magazines, which she loved to pore over.

Research suggests that it will take a student between five and seven years to develop adequate proficiency in a second language to support academic learning (Baker, 2001; Cummins, 2000). Academic language is much more complex than social language. Children may pick up English fairly quickly on the playground, and often teachers believe prematurely that they are fluent in English. But using social language is different from using academic language to understand a new abstract concept, to compose a paragraph, or to analyze an event. In everyday social situations, there are usually plenty of context cues (such as facial expressions, objects) to assist comprehension, and the language itself is often fairly simple. In academic learning, however, context cues become reduced as one moves up the grade levels, and the vocabulary and sentence structures become more and more complex; language becomes the primary means by which new concepts are taught (Cummins, 1996).

Reflection 5.13 asks you to watch a TV show or movie in a language you do not
understand, for about half an hour, to increase your awareness of context cues that help
supplement language. As a teacher, you may not be able to speak the languages of your
English learners, but you can make context cues available to them. (Given the proliferation of TV channels, most readers will be able to identify such a show. Many video
outlets have movies in foreign languages, which also work well, as long as you can turn
off English subtitles.)

Let's reflect on what this exercise reveals. First, you entered the viewing with stocks of
knowledge that help you interpret what you see. For example, you were already familiar
with TV genres such as drama, comedy, or talk show, and knowing a genre helps interpret what is going on. If a familiar story line is enacted, you can follow it to some extent,
even without understanding the language. Second, you used a number of cues such as
body language, facial expressions, voice tone, setting, and props. You may or may not
interpret them correctly, however, if the cultural context of the TV show is not familiar
to you; but you probably tried as best you could to identify and use cues. Third, when
concentrating on understanding meaning when you do not know the language, your
attention probably waned quickly. To what extent did you get mentally tired doing this
exercise? If you had been able to view the show with someone else who understood the
language, and could discuss it with you in your own language, to what extent might you
have understood more?

Reflection 5.13 suggests several strategies a teacher can use to make the curriculum
more comprehensible to second language learners. Some additional strategies are discussed below:

1. Provide key background information students will need to understand a lesson and opportunities for them to connect this background to what they already know. To the extent possible, encourage students to talk about, draw pictures about, or dramatize what they already know in relation to what will be taught. Help them to connect what they already know to the main new ideas in the lesson. Having them talk or draw pictures will give you a glimpse of the knowledge they bring, and it will help them make connections.

2. Teach key vocabulary words students will need. To the extent possible, connect those words to meaningful discussion rather than simply presenting words in isolation. Keep the number of words manageable, and make sure students hear and see the words.

3. Use pictures, demonstrations, manipulatives, artifacts, and dramatizations while you are talking. Give students as many nonlinguistic cues as possible to help them get the ideas you are teaching. Hands-on activities can be very helpful. Keep in mind how strongly you rely on these cues when watching a TV show or movie in another language! Also keep in mind that listening to a lot of talk in a new language, with few cues, is very tiring and stressful. Whole class discussions can be even more difficult for an English language learner to follow than listening to just one person (i.e., the teacher). As much as possible, supplement oral language with cues that will help second language learners follow the main ideas.

4. Use diagrams to map concepts, since they help illustrate concepts and relationships visually. For example, the Venn diagram in Figure 5.2 can be filled in to show similarities and differences between plants and animals.

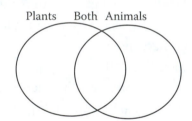

FIGURE 5.2 Characteristics of plants and animals

5. Use cooperative groups. Although not all students prefer cooperative learning, it helps second language learners to talk through an idea or even listen to peers talking through the idea. If several students who speak the same language are in the classroom, it is OK to group them together, since they can help each other make sense of what is going on. In most cases the students are hearing English a great deal anyway; working through an academic concept with someone they can talk to can help them learn the concept without sacrificing English language acquisition.

6. Pull the main ideas of the lesson together at the end. Fantastic teachers do this anyway, but second language learners can benefit even more by having the main ideas stressed again. If students are able to read, write the main ideas on the board during a short concluding discussion. Again, this visual reinforcement helps.

Students who are learning English also need instruction in the English language. Simply throwing them into an English environment without teaching English leaves many students floundering. It is beyond the scope of this book to describe English language development strategies, but if you have English language learners in your classroom, we encourage you to make sure they are receiving instruction in English (Carrasquillo & Rodriguez, 2002).

Dialect is an important dimension of communication. Several different dialects in addition to Standard English are spoken within the United States, including Appalachian, Hawaiian Creole, Spanglish, Chinglish (Chinese mixed with English), and Black English. Dialects are linguistically sound, governed by their own rules of phonemics, syntax, morphology, and word meaning (Labov, 1969).

Reflection 5.14 on the next page can help you gain some awareness of linguistic patterns of dialect you hear people use. For this reflection, sit somewhere such as in a student lounge where you can hear people interact in a dialect different from yours. Use the guide below as a tool for careful listening.

What patterns did you detect? Did you identify any linguistic patterns shared by members of the group that you had thought were errors? The more widely a community of speakers shares patterns of speech, the more likely it is that these patterns reflect a dialect that the speakers are using correctly.

Smitherman (1981) argued that the attitudes of educators toward the "Blackness" of Black English are a larger problem than communication mismatch per se. Speakers of Black English come to school having mastered one dialect, and cognitively equipped to master a second one — Standard English. For example, African-American students who exhibit competence in oral games, such as sounding, bring figurative or creative language abilities that can be capitalized on in language arts instruction. Unfortunately, they are often penalized by being required to take tests that assume competence in Standard English before they have been taught to use it. If they don't do well on those tests, teachers often assume that Black English is poorly learned language and that those who speak it are incapable of advanced learning. Reflection 5.15 on page 153 offers a suggestion for how to hear creative or figurative language used by students; if you are in a community in which students play with language while jumping rope, using creative or figurative language expressions to count and keep pace and rhythm.

All students in U.S. schools need to learn to speak Standard English. Some African Americans may be very resolute about using only Standard English in the classroom, because they know that it is the official language of the marketplace. Others may argue that since Black English is a legitimate language, teachers should accept both dialects. These African Americans understand the commercial value of Standard English and know that it is important for their children to learn, if only for marketplace purposes — but they don't want the students' home language trashed. Further, most speakers of Black English understand Standard English very well and have the ability to be bicultural and bidialectal. This means becoming thoroughly knowledgeable of dominant cultural patterns presented by mainstream institutions, including the mass media and

---

Reflection 5.14
Dialect difference

Listen closely to how people are talking. See how many patterns you can detect.

Phonemes (sounds)
- Are some consonant sounds pronounced differently from the way you are used to? Does it matter if the sound is at the beginning, middle, or end of the word?
- Are some vowel sounds pronounced differently from the way you are used to?
- Are consonant sounds that you pronounce dropped when they appear in certain places in words (such as at the end)?

Grammar
- Compared with the way you speak, are there differences in the way the past tense is indicated?
- Are there differences in the way the possessive is indicated?
- Pay attention to how "do" and "be" are used; look for patterns that differ from what you are used to.
- Are there differences in word order?
- Pay attention to patterns indicating the negative.
- Are there differences in use of pronouns?
- Are there differences in use of adverbs or adjectives?

Vocabulary
- Listen for words you are unfamiliar with; find out what they mean.
- Listen for words you are familiar with but seem to have a different meaning from the one you are used to.
- Listen for phrases you are unfamiliar with or you do not use.
- Pay attention to words and phrases you use regularly that are not used regularly by the students you are working with.
- Pay attention to figurative or creative use of language.

Nonspoken Language
- Are facial expressions used differently from what you are used to?
- Are gestures used differently from what you are used to?
- Are voice inflections used differently from what you are used to?
- Is rhythm or speed of talking different from what you are used to?
- Do people sit or stand at the same distance from each other that you are used to?
- Do people talk as loudly/softly as you are used to?

Social Context
- Do individuals switch dialects around different people or in different settings?

---

mass marketing, while retaining cultural and linguistic patterns from home, and knowing when it is most appropriate to use each (Tobin, 2000; Valentine, 1971). Teachers, we believe, should be sensitive to both the views of African Americans who support Black English and the reality and harshness of the marketplace.

Teaching a new dialect is much like teaching a second language — the differences between the two "languages" must be made clear, and continued practice is essential. Delpit (1995) described a teacher of Athabaskan Indians who referred to the student talk as "Heritage English." This teacher helped the students to appreciate their language by savoring the words and discussing its nuances. However, it must be made clear that

---

Reflection 5.15
Figurative language

Check to see if the girls in the school area jump rope. If so, observe the figurative language they use when counting. If possible, jump with them and try their counting routine. If necessary, ask the girls to write out what they are saying. If the girls are in your class, discuss with them how these sayings can be included in a creative essay.

"everyday talk" is to be used with friends or outside of school and "school talk" must be used in school. Most students accept this distinction as long as they are not asked to choose one dialect as the "correct" way to talk in all situations.

Delpit (1997) suggests several ways teachers can teach children to use a second dialect. Constant "correcting" is not recommended — it is frustrating to the child, and focuses attention on rules of speech rather than ideas. Children who are constantly corrected often begin to do worse rather than better because of the stress of monitoring every utterance. Some stop participating altogether. Young children can become "language detectives," listening for different types of speech they hear on TV and in their surroundings. Children are good imitators, and can learn to mimic how different people talk. Through role play, they can pretend they are members of different speech communities, and act out scenes, trying to use the speech of their character as accurately as possible.

Student Dialogue 5.7

Celia: Why is it that during a time of concern about raising student achievement, bilingual programs are being scaled back and eliminated rather than strengthened? If we want all children to attain high levels of learning and cognitive functioning, U.S. schools should help all children become proficient in two languages.

Gilbert: I agree with you because during my visit to South Korea, I would not have had as much fun if I could not speak the language.

Lisa: Yes, I agree with both of you. I can speak French and German. Each year I try to vacation some place where I can practice my languages. The English-only argument for students in school, I think, is pretty stupid. In Germany many of the kids that I meet can speak several languages.

Celia: Plus, don't forget, Lisa, that your schooling was all in your first language. That's what your teachers spoke, that's what your curriculum reflected, and that's how you were tested. Imagine if you had to do it all in German, even though English was your first language.

Lisa: Oh goodness, I would have struggled. I didn't think of that; I might not have made it into college if my whole school experience was in a language I hadn't learned at home. At least that point of view gives me something to think about. That relates to the idea of equity, huh?

Language is vital to students' learning and their successful functioning in the social world. Making use of students' language can greatly benefit their learning. Most scholars who study language and teachers who work with students whose native language is not English argue that students' native language is a valuable learning tool when teaching the 3Rs and, as such, is a tool that teachers should use to help students achieve.

Building Block 12: Connecting With Parents and Community

Multicultural advocates encourage strong, respectful home–community school relationships. They believe that when it comes to the education of children, parents and community members must be more than mere spectators, simply attending graduation ceremonies, open houses, or sporting events. Just as citizen participation is fundamental to democracy in the United States, so too is parent and community participation fundamental to student academic achievement. Gough (1991) argues:

> Effective parent involvement programs include —but go far beyond — encouraging parents to read with their children. Such programs also deal with parents' needs for information on effective parenting; on available social services; on school procedures and curricula and other ways to help their youngsters. At the same time, effective parent involvement programs acknowledge the fact that parents are a child's earliest and most influential teachers. Trying to educate the young without help and support from home is akin to trying to rake leaves in a high wind. (p. 339)

Most teachers regard parents as important partners. Developing sensitivity and skill in working with parents and other community members from diverse backgrounds takes work, however.

For Reflection 5.16, think about the ways in which schools usually try to connect with parents.

Reflection 5.16
Ways of connecting parents and teachers

In the space below, write all of the ways and means you have seen or experienced that attempt to connect parents and teachers.

What kinds of things are on your list? How many of them require parents to come into the school? How many require teachers to visit parents on their own "turf"? Which of the items you listed build communication and working relationships between parents and teachers *before* teachers need to talk with parents about problems? Now consider a parent who may be:

- A single parent with other small children at home;
- A school drop-out, with little self-confidence around school personnel and poor reading skills;
- A speaker of a language other than English;
- Working two shifts in order to make ends meet;
- An educated person of color who has already experienced being stereotyped as poorly educated or uncooperative.

Circle the strategies you wrote above that would work for these parents. How might the school regard the parents if they do not respond as educators expect?

Teachers, Fuller and Olsen (1998) argue, "must accept that parents are their children's first and most important teachers, and further, that the attitudes, language, values, and cultural understanding that help guide children and young people are learned most fully within families" (p. xi). Ultimately, we believe that school–parent relationships should be worked out through direct communication between parent, community members, and the school. Professional educators bring their own assumptions, experiences, and biases about procedures they think work, and these may not fit with parents' expectations. For example, while many teachers expect parents to help with homework, some immigrant parents see teaching as the teacher's job, while the parent's job is to make sure children arrive at school healthy, clean, and cared for.

At the same time, teachers sometimes make inaccurate assumptions about parents. We know several immigrant parents who are stereotyped as being uneducated because they have accents, or because the job they have in the United States requires considerably less education than the job they had in their own country. Teachers from other countries, for example, usually cannot obtain teaching jobs in the United States. A student from Russia in Carl's class, who had earned both an undergraduate and a master's degree in education in her native country, and who had obtained U.S. citizenship, was required to complete a teacher preparation program in the United States before teaching.

While parents may not always be comfortable or able to tell professional educators how to relate to them, community leaders and social service agencies can often assist. We have worked with community center directors and religious leaders, for example, who have communicated very productively with teachers and principals on behalf of adults in the community. They recommend strategies such as those that follow.

Start by advertising children's success to their parents, and letting parents know what an excellent teacher you are. You can do this in several ways:

- Send home examples of children's best work, with positive comments written on it.

- Call parents at home early in the year to tell them how much you are looking forward to working with their child, and to tell them at least one positive characteristic of their child you have noticed.
- Mail the child a postcard right before school starts to introduce yourself and tell the child something exciting that will be happening in your class.
- Call parents, or send home a short note periodically when the child does something well.
- Make sure communication to parents is in the language parents understand.

Parent conferences and open houses can be very stressful for parents as well as for the teacher. Most parents will come to a conference if they feel it will be useful (and conducted in language they can understand), if it is scheduled at a time and place they can attend, and their child insists that they go. Children urge parents to go if they believe parents will hear good things about them. We know of teachers in very low-income schools who have had 90% or better parent turnout by making sure children knew the parents would hear some good things about their academic work, and by trying to make the experience as welcoming for parents as possible. It is helpful to explain to parents what their children will be learning in school, how their children's growth as learners will be assured, what special effort will be made to support their children if they begin to struggle, and how they as parents can be most helpful to their children's academic learning beyond school (Fuller & Olsen, 1998). Conferences should be constructed as two-way conversations rather than one-way in, which the teacher talks and parents just listen.

Parents do not need to be entertained at an open house; most often, they simply want to meet the teacher and find out what he or she is teaching and what is expected of the children. For instance, if you have a homework policy, this may be the parents' only opportunity to hear it clearly explained.

Schools can also plan creative ways to engage parents and teachers together. Parents will come to performances in which their children have a role; concerts or plays can be followed by short informal teacher–parent conversations. Some schools work with neighborhood churches to organize pot-lucks. We know of one school that organized a laundry night: parents and teachers brought laundry to a local laundromat and the school supplied the quarters. Some schools organize an open gym night, in which children's "ticket" into the gym is to bring a parent or other significant adult along.

We also recommend that teachers go into the community themselves, where they can meet parents and other community people on their own terms. For example, if you attend a church, mosque, or synagogue that some of the families attend, or attend a community event, you may get to know parents and children in a very different and more constructive light than if you only expect to meet them in the school. It probably seems as if we are advocating that teachers take the first steps in constructing home–school relations. Your observation is correct. Many poor parents and parents of color have been turned off by school officials and teachers. This does not mean that they don't want their children to attend school and get a good education. They do. Nevertheless, the trust level may not be there, and you may need to be the one to build it. Building trust is often facilitated by your having some knowledge of the community to begin with. Revisit Reflection 5.5 and use the information you acquired, along with your knowledge of the students, to help you forge alliances with students' parents.

In this chapter, we have discussed culture, the role of cultural knowledge and cultural capital. We have pointed out that Black, Latino, and American Indian students, students living at the poverty level, and student with disabilities have demonstrated they can be higher achievers, but thus far, on the average, do not achieve on par with White students. We have shown that teachers who have high expectations, make students' interest and backgrounds a focal point of teaching, provide instruction which takes advantage of students' learning styles, and uses students' native language to facilitate instruction are teachers who help all students achieve. Now it's your turn to apply these insights.

Putting It Into Practice

During student teaching Celia was placed in a first-grade classroom in which about one-third of the students were middle-class White, one-third were low-income African American, and one-third were low-income Hmong. Even though most of the Hmong students conversed with their peers on the playground in English and in Hmong, they were still developing classroom language and content vocabulary in English. Often Hmong students supported each other's classroom learning by using Hmong to clarify concepts and directions. Celia noticed that many of the African-American students liked to work together and in places other than their desks. She also noticed many African-American students talking through the activities before beginning their work and checking in periodically with each other throughout the work period. Many of the White middle-class students seemed to enjoy working independently in a designated area. Celia sensed the middle-class White students were more focused than the other students in the class on structured activities, such as working on problems from textbooks.

Celia is supposed to design an integrated unit on the life cycle of plants. During one lesson, students are supposed to learn the following vocabulary words and how the words relate to the way plants grow: *sprout, shoot, roots, stem, leaves, water, soil,* and *sunlight.* They will also plant bean seeds for further investigation during the unit.

Imagine you are Celia. Write down the following:

1. How would you go about finding out what assets the students bring that you could build on for this unit? In other words are there things from their background, community, or understanding of language that will be helpful to your instructional planning and their academic learning?

2. Are there ideas generated in discussions with your classmates that will be useful in helping to teach the instructional concepts Celia is expected to teach? (Hint: Review Reflection 5.8.)

Here is what Celia did. As a part of a unit, students had an observation folder where they could keep any information they had collected about plants, both inside and outside of class. Celia wanted to include a series of diagrams that would help illustrate the vocabulary she wanted students to gain during this lesson. Celia knew that most students would bring a lot of prior knowledge and experiences about plants including some of the vocabulary she hoped students would learn. However, she also anticipated that many of the Hmong students would need language support in English in order to build the bridge between the concepts and vocabulary they already knew in Hmong. Celia thought that having a visual representation to refer back to would allow students to review information as they needed throughout the unit.

Celia first asked students to look around their house and neighborhood for plants and bring one or two of them to school. At school, students left their plants at their desks while they walked around the room, making observations about what kind of plants their classmates had collected and discussing where their plants had been found. Next, Celia had students use their plants to label the class-size diagrams. As they talked about each part of the plant, students located it on their own and their neighbor's plant. As they talked about the leaves, stem, and roots, they also connected it to what plants needed to grow and labeled the diagram accordingly.

Celia knew that most likely no one would have brought in plants that had sprouts or shoots. In order to illustrate these concepts, she used one of the students as a seed. The student curled up on the floor and began to grow the beginning of a root, which is called a sprout. She then explained to the class what a sprout was and labeled it on the class diagram. Each child then acted out the process of a seed growing a sprout. She continued to move through the vocabulary in a similar manner, always referring to the class diagram, until students could begin as a seed and "grow" into a plant with roots, a stem, and leaves. At the end of the lesson, students went to their desks and labeled a set of diagrams to put into their observation folder.

Celia's cooperating teacher also shared with her that one of the Hmong student's families sold vegetables at a local farmers market. With the help of the school's Bilingual Resource Specialist, they found a date when the mother and her two young children could come teach the class how to plant bean seeds. During this time, the mother would model the process of planting bean seeds as well as teach the class some of the vocabulary words in Hmong.

six

Planning Curriculum That Is Multicultural

This chapter will help you answer the following questions:

- What is my definition of curriculum?
- How do I plan a multicultural curriculum?
- What is the teacher's role in producing and maintaining an unintended curriculum?
- Where do I locate good multicultural teaching resources?
- How does a fantastic teacher use curriculum standards?

Debates about what schools should teach are not new. By the 20th century, according to Kliebard (1982), four main currents had developed in these debates in the United States.

1. *Humanists* believe the main purpose of curriculum is to help young people learn to reason. They argue that everyone can learn to reason; they dispute the practice of dividing students by ability such that those in upper groups are taught critical thinking while those in lower groups are taught mainly to

memorize information. Humanists believe that young people learn to reason by being taught to do so with practice, and by studying well-reasoned thinking. Humanists who believe that the clearest thinking is reflected in the Western classics argue that these should be central to curriculum.

2. *Developmentalists* believe that the main purpose of curriculum is to support child and adolescent development. They argue that children differ in interests, abilities, and developmental rates. To accommodate these differences and to support the natural process of growth and learning, curriculum should fit each child's level of development and personal interests. Good teachers are good psychologists; they are able to analyze developmental needs of their students and tailor their curriculum and teaching methods to fit them.

3. *Social efficiency* educators see the main purpose of curriculum as preparing young people for the needs of an industrial or postindustrial society, as defined by business leaders and employers. Curriculum should be planned according to measurable learning outcomes; students should be taught to those outcomes and tested for mastery of them. Students should also be divided based on ability so that the more able students would be prepared to lead, and the less able would be prepared to follow and take up less intellectually demanding work.

4. *Social progressives* see curriculum as preparing citizens to address social, community, and global issues such as justice, poverty, or environmentalism. Social progressives see children of today as tomorrow's citizens. As such, curriculum should prepare them for active participation in democratic institutions; skills such as communication and collaboration are particularly valuable. Basic concepts and skills can be embedded within society-oriented projects.

Different currents have surfaced in importance at different times. As we showed in chapter 1, multicultural education reflects social progressivism; and as chapters 4 and 5 illustrate, it also draws some teaching/learning implications from developmentalism, as well as the humanist emphasis on thinking. At present, however, social efficiency drives most school curricula. A central question for you, a prospective teacher, is this: How can you navigate these conflicting currents when deciding what to teach? This chapter considers what curriculum is and whose knowledge appears in textbooks. Then we consider curriculum in relationship to the standards movement to establish a context for planning curriculum that is multicultural in your own classroom. Following that, this chapter will develop two building blocks:

Building Block 13: Developing Concepts From Multicultural Perspectives
Building Block 14: Locating Multicultural Teaching Resources

To complete the reflections in this chapter, you will need access to the following:

- A K–12 textbook (for Reflections 6.3, 6.4, 6.9, and 6.11)
- The Internet (for Reflection 6.5, 6.7, 6.12, and 6.13)
- At least two teachers to interview (for Reflection 6.8)

Curriculum, Texts, and Standards

Before plunging into curriculum planning, we will examine some useful concepts. We will look broadly at curriculum, including unplanned curriculum, since students learn not only what you plan but also things you didn't plan or intend. Then will we look at whose knowledge is in textbooks, and other curriculum documents, including standards. Following that, we will consider the standards movement and its implications for multicultural curriculum planning.

Intended and Unintended Curriculum

Let us begin by considering what curriculum is. Reflection 6.1 asks you to write your definition of curriculum, then compare your definition with one offered by two curriculum theorists.

Reflection 6.1
Definition of curriculum

Write your definition of curriculum.

Compare the definition you wrote with the following by Beyer and Liston (1996). They describe curriculum as "the formal, overt knowledge that is central to the activities of teaching, as well as more tacit, subliminal messages — transmitted through the process of acting and interacting within a particular kind of institution — that foster the inculcation of particular values, attitudes, and dispositions" (p. xv). Their definition includes several features:

- The "what" of teaching and learning: What the teacher teaches and what the students learn.
- What is in texts and other materials that are used in the classroom; as well as the all important "curriculum in use" — what actually transpires between teacher and students, and among students in class, regardless of whether it is in the text or not.
- Both planned and unplanned learning: This includes not only what the teacher intends to teach, but what students learn as a result of being in the classroom and school, intended or not. As a result of how a particular classroom is run, for example, students might learn that knowledge consists of right answers or that only certain students are smart and the rest are slow.

Circle words or phrases that are common to their definition and yours: Underline words or phrases that appear in *either* your definition *or* in theirs. Did Beyer and Liston suggest dimensions to curriculum that you hadn't thought of?

Sometimes the unplanned curriculum ends up teaching in more powerful ways than does the planned curriculum. Kumashiro (2004) illustrates this point with an activity he did with teacher candidates. He made two columns on the board designating "planned curriculum" and "unplanned curriculum." Then he asked for examples of learning about gender in school; he recorded these as either planned or unplanned. Examples of planned curriculum included items such as women's history month, lessons on women writers, or lessons on gender discrimination. Examples of unplanned curriculum (which turned out to be a much longer list) included items such as lining up for separate restrooms; girls and boys going to different spaces to play different games; inclusion of more literature by male than female authors in the planned curriculum; and having boy–girl couples on prom courts. Students learned a lot about gender through processes that were not in anyone's lesson plans. Further, many of them may undermine the planned curriculum or cause teacher candidates to look critically at the planned curriculum.

As a teacher, you will be concentrating on the planned curriculum because you will be expected to do so. It is important, however, to think more broadly about what students actually learn from your classroom as a whole, particularly when those unplanned lessons contradict or undermine what you plan to teach. Kumashiro points out that there is no formula for learning to think broadly and anticipating what students might actually learn, so he urges teachers to accept uncertainty as fundamental to teaching, and to use uncertainty as a tool for reflecting on your curriculum.

To connect these ideas to your own experience, in Reflection 6.2, reflect on a class in which you were a student. Write down the teacher's main goal for that class. Then think about what you learned that was related to that goal, through the unintended curriculum of the classroom or through the way you experienced the classroom.

Reflection 6.2
Unintended curriculum

Write a teacher's main goal for class:

Write what you learned related to that goal through the way you experienced the classroom.

As you reflect on what you wrote, ask yourself the extent to which you believe the teacher was aware of what you were learning, and whether it might have made a difference to you had the teacher been more aware. Compare with some classmates what you and they wrote, and ask them whether they too thought that if the teachers knew about the unplanned things students were learning, it would have made a difference to their planning. Based on your comparison, do you see any significant issues that teachers should consider as they plan and teach curriculum?

Student Dialogue 6.1

Celia: I have an example of unintended curriculum. You know that I grew up speaking Spanish, and that my parents wanted me to be fluent in both English and Spanish. Well, throughout most of elementary school I was in an ESL program part of the day, where they worked on my English. By the end of elementary school I had "graduated" into all-English, and didn't need ESL anymore.

Lisa: Good for you! It must be great to be fluent in two languages!

Celia: Yeah, but the unintended curriculum was that English matters and Spanish doesn't. The middle school and high school I went to had ESL programs, and most of the students in them were Mexican. It worked kind of like a lower track for Spanish speakers, because the ESL students seemed to be scheduled into the easier classes. It was like two schools, one for the English-speaking students who got harder work, and another one for the Spanish-dominant students, who got easier work. Out of all of that, I learned that it's bad to speak Spanish, so I stopped letting anyone know I could speak it. I started equating Spanish with being either foreign or dumb.

Gilbert: That message probably didn't help your regard for your parents, I bet.

Celia: You're right, it took a long time for me to work through feeling that they didn't know much, because so much of what they know, they know best in Spanish. *Unintended curriculum:* Now I've got a word for how I was taught to hate Spanish and look down on my family. Ironically, this was all done with good intentions, I realize now.

Celia is correct that the unintended curriculum was that "English matters and Spanish doesn't matter." Celia's example allows us to return to our discussion of power from chapter 2. Her example illustrates how power acts both invisibly and visibly. It operates visibly as the school openly provides only a program for English as a Second Language (ESL), but not for other languages, thereby demanding that the students learn English, and expecting that they will become proficient enough in English to be able to attend classes where English is the only language in which the subject (e.g., math) is taught. Power operates invisibly in that the actions (demands and expectations) of the school and Celia's teachers have informed her that students have to know how to speak English, otherwise they will be relegated to the "lower track." The remainder of this chapter works primarily with the planned curriculum, although in the context of considering it, we periodically draw your attention to unplanned lessons students might take away.

Whose Knowledge Is In Curriculum Documents Today?

Textbooks have, for years, tended to standardize what schools teach (Wang, 2002; Zimmerman, 2002); if you go into a school today, can you find a text that is very much like one you used as a kid? As a beginning teacher, you will be handed curriculum guides, standards documents, and textbooks which are explicitly meant to serve as instructional materials or guides for your classroom. Keep in mind that with those materials, you've been given someone's curriculum (e.g., textbook publisher, board of education, or textbook selection committee) *and* an invitation. The invitation is not merely to accept the materials and teach from them, but also to review and examine them for their relevance to your student's needs and interests. You may not have a choice about *whether* to use the materials, but you will have some choices as to *how* you use them.

In chapter 3 we summarized an analysis of textbooks that we did several years ago. Now, we would like you to start conducting your own analysis. You might begin by asking whether textbooks have become more inclusive since our research. Select a textbook, curriculum guide, or standards document that is currently being used in the schools. The easiest way to estimate whose knowledge this curriculum document includes is to count the people represented in the text according to race/ethnicity and gender. (You can use additional descriptors such as disability, social class, or religion if you are able to identify these.)

Reflection 6.3 guides you in taking an inventory of who, most or least, appears in the document. Count pictures of people, and if possible, names of people; use the space below to tally your results.

Share your findings with your classmates. If you pool your findings from five or 10 texts, what patterns prevail? Whose knowledge seems to predominate? Who appears but to a lesser extent? Who is absent? Were you able to detect any recurring stereotypic roles?

As we noted earlier, in the 1970s, people of color, women, and people with disabilities were absent from most texts and other forms of curriculum. Publishing companies today scrupulously count pictures of and references to different groups so that they appear roughly in proportion to their representation in the population as a whole. This means that Whites predominate, receiving the most sustained attention and being shown in the widest variety of roles. Numerically, African Americans are the next most represented group. Asian Americans, Latinos, and Native Americans are included, but usually in very sketchy form, and Arab Americans are invisible. People with disabilities appear occasionally. So the results of your tally are probably very familiar to publishers, who planned what you see.

But there is a deeper question: Whose point of view guides the knowledge in curriculum? Since the late 1960s and early 1970s, scholars in ethnic studies, women's studies, disability studies, gay–lesbian studies, and cultural studies have generated an enormous amount of research that offers alternative points of view.

Reflection 6.3 Textbook or document tally			
	Male	**Female**	**Both sexes**
Arab American			
Asian American			
African American			
Latino American			
American Indian			
White American			
Race/ethnicity Ambiguous			
Mixed Group			
Disabled American			

For example, in 1972 Rodolfo Acuña published *Occupied America: The Chicano's Struggle toward Liberation*, a book that is now in its fifth edition (Acuña, 2003). Prior to this book, Mexican Americans were depicted as immigrants who came to the United States to escape poverty, but struggled because of poor education, lack of English language proficiency, and so forth. Contemporary K–12 textbooks usually still take that viewpoint. But Acuña and other Chicano scholars completely shifted the analysis, focusing on how the United States colonized northern Mexico, and then executed political and economic structures that locked Mexican people into low-wage labor for the benefit of Anglos and institutionalized repressive policies that have continued to keep Mexican Americans subordinate. Acuña's and other Chicano authors' writings directly challenge the perspective in most textbooks. If one is teaching history or social studies, an inclusive curriculum should not only include some Mexican Americans, but also their perspectives.

As another example, disability studies scholars such as Simi Linton (1998) challenge the view that people with disabilities are defective. In her book *Claiming Disability*, she points out that although people with disabilities have symptoms that are "sometimes painful, scary, unpleasant, or difficult to manage," the symptoms themselves are not central to disability. Rather, from the point of view of people with disabilities, "what we rail against are the strategies used to deprive us of rights, opportunity, and the pursuit of pleasure" (p. 4). In K–12 curricula, when people with disabilities are included (which isn't often), the theme usually focuses on how individuals lead more-or-less normal lives despite the disability. Although this is a constructive theme, it is limited. Disability studies looks at society from the vantage point of disability, examining the range of institutional structures that need to be changed in order to accommodate a much broader range of human needs than is currently the case. Despite the strong presence of special education in school, as Linton points out, much of special education is actually not designed *by* people with disabilities. As a result, it generally focuses too much on trying to fix what is wrong with children rather than on changing institutions that impede progress of people with disabilities.

But discussions of disability rights or the wage structure might not fit the topics in a textbook. We often hear teachers wonder whether planning multicultural curriculum means dragging in information that doesn't fit.

Student Dialogue 6.2

Gilbert: When I was a senior in high school, I took a computer class. I'll be darned if the teacher, who was a woman, didn't add into the class bits of information about women in computer science. Who cares?! How was that going to help me learn computer programs?

Lisa & Celia: *We* care.

Lisa: Women are way underrepresented in computer science! Do you know that most girls have no idea we could learn to program computers? In my high school, there were two girls in an advanced computer science class. And, the guys tried to laugh them out.

Celia: The proportion of women majoring in computer science in universities actually dropped from 40% in the mid-1980s, to only 10% in the mid-1990s. That's what it says in this article I just read ("Computer Software Industry," 1997). Take a look at the video and computer games on the market. Most of them are violent. They don't appeal to me, and if that's what computers are about, then I wouldn't be interested.

Lisa: I'm not really good with computers myself, but I had a teacher who used to talk with us about women and minorities in the computer field, and how the field might become different if we were there. It really helped me see, yeah, this is something I can do, and I wouldn't have to create the same kinds of programs that men create.

Gilbert: So you're saying that what fits depends on your point of view.

Celia: Exactly.

Inclusion, exclusion, or "othering" are major challenges teacher candidates have to master on their way to becoming fantastic teachers. How and where do I include those who have been left out? The curriculum is highly significant, but it is only one place in the classroom where certain groups are underrepresented or left out. There are many other areas in a class where underrepresentation takes place and needs attention. For example, when students construct projects, who is on the inside and who is on the outside of decision making and participation? Is the nature of conversations within the group, and are the artifacts used by that group, free of bias and stereotypes? Is "othering" serving as an unintended curriculum, invisibly operating as power, in that the students who are included are being taught that those who possess certain accoutrements or characteristics can expect to be included, and those who do not should not expected to be included?

What do you do if you are the teacher in the following situation? The mother of a girl (Joy) having a birthday party says to you, the teacher: "We have put the names on the invitations of the students that Joy wants to come to her party. Will you please see that the students and their parents receive the invites, when the parents come to pick up their kid from school? Thanks." Only one little girl (Mary) in your class is not invited. If you pass out the invitations and Mary does not receive one, have you become part of "othering?" What would you do? We hope you will take some constructive, alternative action. Saying to Joy's mother that you will not have time to pass out the invitations shows some action, but is it a cop-out? Objecting to "othering" (or excluding) is critical to becoming a fantastic teacher.

Now let's take a closer look at knowledge produced by sociocultural groups that were underrepresented in the textbook or document you examined. There are several ways to do this. If you have taken a course in ethnic studies, disabilities studies, or women's studies, you can compare the content of that course with a school textbook in the same general discipline. You can also do some research in the library and on the Internet.

Reflection 6.4 asks you to compare how a topic is treated in a text, curriculum guide, or standards document with how it is treated in a broader set of documents. First, select a topic that appears in the text or other curriculum document (such as "families," "electricity," or "supply and demand"), and describe how it is treated or what kind of information appears about it.

Reflection 6.4
Textbook perspectives

Write down a topic, and summarize how it is treated or what information appears.

Now, using an Internet search tool, enter the topic plus the name of a subordinate sociocultural group such as the following: Indigenous, African American, Arab American, Asian American, Hawaiian, Filipino, Latino, Chicano, Puerto Rican, women's studies, disability studies, Deaf, gay, lesbian, working class. (We capitalized "D" in Deaf to indicate affiliation with Deaf Studies and the Deaf community.) Many combinations will give you a great number of websites, indicating a tremendous amount of work that is available. But not all combinations will yield helpful websites; you may need to play with search terms. For example, you are not likely to find something called "Deaf algebra," although you may find websites regarding strategies for teaching algebra to deaf students, and you will certainly find websites about Deaf history or theater.

Some combinations will likely yield information you did not expect. For example, several websites are devoted to indigenous science. You might discover the Indigenous Peoples, Indigenous Science, and Sustainable Development Project (http://www.sppf.org/indscien), or lively discussion boards where North American indigenous people are discussing science in indigenous communities, or websites by African, Pacific Islander, or Australian indigenous scientists. You may also find topics in the websites that do not appear at all in the text. For example, a women's studies issue is violence against women, but this topic may not appear anywhere in the planned curriculum.

Student Dialogue 6.3

Gilbert: I have a personal issue that this group business brings out. I just don't fit. You know that I'm biracial, Korean and African American. This is hard because I never, ever, ever talk about this stuff. I'm also gay, but not out, exactly. I mean, I think I am, although I'm not in a relationship right now. Can you deal with that?

Lisa: Oh — yes. Keep talking, we won't tell anyone anything you don't want us to.

Gilbert: OK. Here we are in this teaching program, where they're telling you, "In order to become a fantastic teacher you must first know yourself." Well, here I am, working on that. Now, I'm not Asian, and I'm not African American, I'm both. So I can't just check a box. But I'm also not about to tell people my personal business. I haven't even seen my Ma in the past two years, although I talk with her on the phone sometimes. She's the Korean side. I haven't been home since my Korean uncles, Ma's brothers, were teasing me during a family dinner. It started when Uncle Keun Kyu asked, "When are we going to meet your girl friend?" And then, "You do have a girl friend, don't you?" This quizzing went on throughout dinner. I was so embarrassed, and I was annoyed at Ma for not coming to my defense. See, they were dissing my very personhood. In my family, we never talked about sexuality, and I was confused and didn't know what to say. My folks split up when I was 13, and my Ma had never encouraged a frank discussion with me about my sexuality. I think she thought I didn't want to talk about myself 'cause I was working through being Black and Korean. Although, when she and Dad were together, they both tried hard to make my biracialism a positive thing. I gotta hand it to them in that department. Anyway, now here we are, clarifying ourselves and identifying people as this or that, Black or Asian, straight or gay. I don't fit the categories. And I sure as heck don't want to announce my issues to the world.

Lisa: Thank you for trusting us enough to share that. I just had an epiphany! Maybe none of us fits the categories, exactly. OK, you see me, white bread whatever, right? Well, my dad's side was mostly British and my Mom's side was mostly Irish. Now, I don't know if that matters to my everyday life or not, but on some level, it matters.

Celia: I think what I'm seeing is that the group categories are tools to get us to see whose ideas are at the table and whose aren't. The categories were invented, they aren't biology. No one fits them to a "T": We can use them as tools to ask who gets left out of curriculum and whose voice dominates, while being aware of their limitations.

Lisa: And Gilbert, you're helping me appreciate that students have a right to keep private business private.

The students' discussion illustrates how easily social issues can prompt uncomfortable personal discussions. Later in this chapter we consider students' lives as part of curriculum. For now, let's return to background research. If possible, make sure you are locating websites not only *about* groups, but also *by* members of those groups. The point of view represented in any body of knowledge depends in part on who is creating and writing about the knowledge; outsiders often take different points of view from insiders. You cannot always determine who created the website, but you should at least attempt to do so. In Reflection 6.5, compare how the general topic was treated in the text with how it was treated in the websites you located.

You may find some information that can be added rather easily onto the content of the textbook or curriculum document you analyzed. You may also find bodies of information that don't seem to fit. A teacher in one of our courses experienced a crisis

---

Reflection 6.5
Comparing perspectives

Treatment in:

Curriculum document (Reflection 6.4)   Website(s):

---

when looking into American Indian perspectives about the 13 colonies. She began her research assuming that she would find information she could add to a unit on the 13 colonies, but instead found that American Indians view the entire colonization experience as one of conquest and genocide. She struggled with what to teach her fifth graders, as she became aware that the textbook and indigenous people's writings present conflicting points of view. She decided to organize a short unit around a trial, in which the Haudenosaunee people of Massachusetts bring the colonists to trial for misusing the natural resources of the area. Students role-played the trial and in the process debated opposing points of view (Sleeter, 2005).

How should a teacher decide whose perspectives to include in curriculum, given the large number of groups that exist? As a tool for thinking about this question, Style (1996) conceptualized curriculum as offering students both windows and mirrors. She wrote, "If the student is understood as occupying a dwelling of self, education needs to enable the student to look through window frames in order to see the realities of others and into mirrors in order to see her/his own reality reflected." For example, if one's students are largely Filipino, a generic curriculum that barely mentions Filipinos teaches the unplanned lesson that Filipinos do not matter and have no significant history or culture. Why should Filipino-American students value education in which they are never reflected? Evidence suggests that students learn more when they can see themselves and their communities mirrored in their curriculum (Gay, 2000). At the same time, all students need to learn to respect and empathize with other people's experiences and viewpoints. Banks's (1995) analysis of research on the impact of curriculum in developing students' attitudes about people different from themselves suggests that a well-designed curriculum can make a difference. So, when selecting readings for the curriculum, it is useful to ensure that all students regularly find both mirrors and windows.

Oh yes, one more thing. Are you thinking about Gilbert's dilemma? Good, here are our thoughts. We believe that Gilbert has a pretty good handle on his problem. He still has a way to go to work things out, including concerns about dealing with what his

---

Reflection 6.6
Who should decide?

Who should decide what and whose knowledge young people should learn?

Place a percent in the space:

Teacher__ Community__ School Board__ Federal Government __ State Government __

Principal__ Students__ Parents __ Religious Body ___

Or:

All of the above should share equally___ Yes ___No

---

mother and uncles may think. However, he does have two good and caring friends to lean on as he works things out. Such may not be the case for some other students who are facing challenges within themselves and from others about their identity. In many ways Gilbert is "othering" himself. People, including students, do this when they don't feel comfortable or that they belong. Teachers must stay aware for students who are challenged beyond what they can individually handle.

Curriculum and Standards

Years ago, the philosopher Herbert Spencer (Turner, 1996) asked the recurring question: What knowledge is of most worth? We've added to Spencer's question: *Whose* knowledge is of most worth? Who do you believe should answer these questions? Reflection 6.6 asks you to consider how much weight various segments of society should have in deciding what young people should learn.

How does your response compare with what you believe actually happens today? Teachers' latitude in deciding what to teach has been restricted in the last few years. Since the mid-1990s, every state except Iowa has passed legislation authorizing curriculum standards. What does this change mean for you in developing curriculum beyond what is already in textbooks and curriculum guides?

Student Dialogue 6.4

Lisa: I was wondering when we were going to get to this. I'm doing a field experience right now in a low-performing school, and the curriculum is already there. Teachers even have a script to follow for part of the day. They can't just go and redo the curriculum, they have to follow what's in the standards and the textbook.

Celia: It isn't that way in the school I'm in. Teachers are supposed to follow the standards, but they can make up their own units, as long as they can show how they are addressing the standards.

Lisa: Really? I thought maybe this chapter was one of those "good idea" theory kinds of things that teachers can't really do anything with.

Celia: I think it depends on where you are and how much support you have.

Gilbert: I understood the whole idea of standards as helping to improve the quality of teaching. There seem to be different notions about what "standards" means. Can't we have high standards without standardizing, like you are describing, Lisa?

Many education reforms, such as standards, are handled in different ways at different schools. Often, however, the school principal's thoughts about the students in the school — their academic achievement level, socioeconomic status, ethnicity, and English language proficiency — will play a role in determining the amount of flexibility teachers receive. Teachers in schools in which the achievement level is below norm, students are living at or below the poverty level, proficiency in English is below average, and the student population is mostly from minority groups are instructed to stick close to the standards. While on the surface, the school administrator seems to be looking out for the students by adhering to a structured basic curriculum, this may not be the case because the structured curriculum may not have been developed with the students at the school in mind. By this we mean that the curriculum may not connect with their background or challenge them. In addition, instructing teachers to stick to standards suggests that teachers are not capable or don't have the professional ability and skills to plan their own curriculum.

Curriculum standards serve as a double-edged sword. On the one hand, they can provide helpful guidance; on the other hand, they can act as a straitjacket. The word *standard* refers simply to level of quality or excellence. For decades, people have advanced standards as a tool to improve services or outcomes, such as standards for air quality, fairness in journalism, or basic funding for schools and other public services. Standard setting is not a new idea; many people use it for a variety of things (Sherman & Theobald, 2001). *Performance standards* specify how well students are expected to master a given body of knowledge or skills; distinguishing among performances that are inadequate, proficient, or excellent provides a yardstick for communicating how well students have learned.

Content standards specify what students should know (A. Lewis, 2000), and have become the basis for determining what students should be tested on, and how performance should be measured. Today's content standards originated with the first President Bush and the state governors, who in 1989 called a summit to set goals for improving schools. The resulting National Education Goals Panel attempted to establish national goals for student learning. The Improve America's Schools Act, passed in 1994, and The Goals 2000: Educate America Act established national discipline-based groups to construct national curriculum standards in math, science, history, English, and other disciplines. For example, the National Council of Teachers of Mathematics (NCTM) established a set of mathematics standards that have subsequently been used by most states. National standards documents were drafted in other disciplines, but due to philosophical disagreements over what all students should know, attempts to finish and adopt them waned, and states were left to determine content standards.

Although all states have developed content standards, states vary widely in the degree to which they specify content in detail. Some states set fairly broad standards, while others have voluminous documents listing hundreds of content standards for each grade level. Content standards can provide coherence by guiding teachers in what to teach at each grade level, reducing unnecessary redundancy, and making sure that there is a meaningful sequence of learning. Standards can also be used to ensure that all students have access to grade-level curriculum. For example, many students, particularly those in high-poverty schools, do not get access to algebra concepts until high school. But, if students are to be prepared for college, they should learn algebra much earlier, so states such as California specify content standards that start teaching basic algebra concepts in kindergarten. Doing this is supposed to help raise teacher expectations by focusing on grade-level skills and content, which is critically important in high-poverty communities where students are too often routinely undertaught.

At the same time, highly prescriptive content standards assume consensus about what everyone should know and what teachers should teach, undermining the efforts to make curriculum more inclusive of the historically marginalized perspectives discussed earlier. The use of content standards can also solidify top-down decision making, reducing the authority of teachers to make professional decisions. *Standardization* is a consequence of standard setting when attempts to improve student learning become bureaucratized, curriculum is defined in detail, and all teachers are expected to teach the same thing, regardless of the interests and backgrounds of their students.

Content standards are not neutral; they tend to push curriculum toward one philosophical current and away from others. To explore this idea, let us look into how one prominent group that has shaped the standards movement views the purpose of curriculum. The Business Roundtable has been a leading organization behind standards-based reform. According to this organization:

> The first step to solving our nation's education problems is to substantially raise academic standards and verify achievement through rigorous testing.... To those of us in business, it is obvious that large segments of our education system are failing today. We are the ones, after all, who get the first real-world view of the young people emerging from the American education "pipeline." Unfortunately, many of them arrive at our doors unable to write a proper paragraph, fill out simple forms, read instruction manuals, do essential mathematical calculations, understand basic scientific concepts or work as a team.

The Business Roundtable makes a very clear connection between educational standards, accountability testing, and the ability of the United States to maintain its position in "today's global, information-based economy" (Business Roundtable, 1997).

Reflection 6.7 asks you to identify which of the four educational currents that were discussed earlier (Humanism, Developmentalism, Social Efficiency, and Social Progressivism), best fits the Business Roundtable's position, and why you think so. You may wish to explore their website for more information (http://www.businessroundtable.org/).

Reflection 6.7
Business Roundtable and the purposes of curriculum

Circle your choice and then explain your thinking.

Humanism   Developmentalism   Social Efficiency   Social Progressivism

Why you think so:

┌───┐
│   **Reflection 6.8**   │
│   **Teachers' experiences with standards**   │
│   │
│ Tell me a little bit about the curriculum standards you are expected to use. │
│   │
│ In what ways do you see the standards helping you teach better? │
│   │
│ In what ways do standards get in the way of your ability to teach? │
│   │
│ To what extent are standards helping raise expectations for student learning? │
│   │
│ How much latitude do you have to plan curriculum, given the standards you are expected to │
│   follow?   │
└───┘

Which purpose did you select? What implications do you think this purpose has for curriculum you might teach?

A good way to start to think about how content standards impact the work of teachers is to talk with teachers. Reflection 6.8 asks you to interview two or three teachers to find out their experiences with content standards. Interview both a beginning teacher and an experienced teacher, since their perspectives may differ considerably. Also, if possible, interview a teacher in an affluent school and one in a school that serves mainly students of color or students who are poor.

Share the results of your interviews with classmates. How did the various teachers respond? Were there differences between perspectives of beginning and experienced teachers? If so, why do you think that is? Did you discover any differences between teachers teaching in different schools? If so, were the differences related to the race or social class of their students?

Teachers cannot simply ignore standards, but in most cases teachers can work with them strategically. We distinguish between *standards-driven* and *standards-conscious* curriculum planning. Standards-driven curriculum planning means starting with the standards, and directly planning curriculum around them. The standards become the backbone and definers of the curriculum. Other inputs, such as knowledge from ethnic studies, teacher interests, or students' interests may be added on, but the curriculum originates from the standards.

In standards-conscious curriculum planning, the standards are not necessarily the starting point, and do not define the central organizing ideas of curriculum. The teacher plans curriculum based on other primary inputs, including those examined in this book. After the curriculum has been drafted, the teacher then maps it against the required standards to identify what it addresses and what needs to be added in order to bring the curriculum into compliance. We have seen teachers do both. An excellent example of standards-conscious planning is an interdisciplinary unit a first-grade teacher developed on Monterey County agriculture (see Sleeter, 2005). She focused the unit on experiences of Mexican farmworkers in California, farming in Mexico, crops grown in the county, and the development of the United Farmworkers Union. She then connected the unit with state content standards in reading/language arts, social studies, math, and science. She used textbooks along with many other resources, including parent guest speakers (for social studies) and graphs made to depict local crops and jobs of students' parents (for math).

As a new teacher, you may find it very difficult to question the extent to which curriculum should be determined by the state, and backed up by state-mandated achievement tests. However, we encourage you to examine the curriculum carefully, and to learn to work with standards-conscious planning, even if the most you are able to do initially is to relate the curriculum you are given to your students. Ultimately, the way you work with curriculum in your classroom will rest on your beliefs about the purpose of schooling and your knowledge base. Paulo Freire (1998) insists that for teachers "critical reflection on our conditioning by our cultural context, on our way of acting, and on our values is indispensable" (p. 79). The more clearly you understand assumptions that ground your beliefs about purposes of school and what is most worth teaching, the more honestly you will be able to teach. Although textbooks, curriculum guides and standards, and your school's policies will push you in particular directions, you will be the one to shape the "curriculum in use" in your own classroom.

Building Block 13: Developing Concepts From Multicultural Perspectives

Often teachers who first begin to design lessons or units that are multicultural assume that such curriculum needs to teach *about* a cultural group. But with the pressure to raise achievement as measured by tests today, many teachers assume they don't have time to do this. These assumptions, however, misunderstand what it means to develop concepts in the curriculum from multicultural perspectives.

Rather than taking time away from academics to teach various cultural groups, we advocate teaching much of what is already in the curriculum from multicultural perspectives. As your textbook analysis probably showed, most curricula develop concepts in relationship to experiences and perspectives of Whites (particularly middle-class or affluent White males) more than any other group. How might a teacher change this pattern?

Identifying Major Concepts or Skills in Your Curriculum

Let's begin with what it means to develop a "concept." In curriculum planning, a concept is a central idea that students should understand, or an important skill they should be able to use by the end of the unit or lesson. For example, first graders need to learn to use the mathematical concept "more than/less than"; middle school students learn to write a focused, coherent essay that conveys an idea to an audience.

Curriculum should be organized around important concepts — not lists of items to know, subject areas, activities to do, book titles, or book chapters. Your best, most experienced teachers probably had a very clear idea of the central concepts they wanted you to learn, and consequently they were able to focus their energies on teaching those concepts and making sure you learned them. In contrast, teachers from whom you learned less may have covered a lot of material, but weren't clear about what the main concepts were, so they did not routinely connect new material or skills to central concepts, and as a result you probably forgot much of what they tried to teach you (see Brophy & Van Sledright, 1997; Wharton-McDonald, Pressley, & Hampston, 1998).

In her book *Teaching for Understanding*, Wiske (1998) uses the term *generative topics* to refer to major concepts. By "generative," she means that a concept is:

■ "Central to a domain or discipline. Curriculum built around generative topics engages students in developing understandings that provide a foundation for more sophisticated work in the domain or discipline."

■ "Accessible and interesting to students. Generative topics are related to students' experiences and concerns."

■ "Interesting to the teacher.… A teacher's passion, curiosity, and wonder serve as a model of intellectual engagement for students who are just learning how to explore unfamiliar and complex terrain with open-ended questions."

■ "Connectable. Generative topics are readily linked to students' previous experiences (both in and out of school) and to important ideas within and across disciplines. They often have a bottomless quality, in that inquiry into the topic leads to deeper questions" (pp. 64–65).

Curriculum guides and state content standards can be helpful sources of concepts around which to build lessons or units. In fact, you will likely be expected to build your curriculum around the content standards of the state in which you are teaching.

Student Dialogue 6.5

Lisa: I'm trying to get this. Is something like science a concept?

Gilbert: No, science is a discipline. Something like "gravity" is a concept.

Celia: Gravity, hmmm. I'm looking at this list of characteristics of "generative topics." By itself, I'm not sure gravity fits this list. It might be central to understanding physics, but how interesting is gravity to students?

Box 6.1

If you are still having trouble sorting through the relative importance of ideas and skills in the text or curriculum guide you are examining, try sorting material into the three categories suggested by Wiggins and McTighe (2005):

Worth being familiar with. This consists of ideas and skills that you believe students should learn, if there is time, but if need be, can be skipped over.

Important to know and do. These ideas and skills should not be skipped over; they are more important than those above.

Enduring understandings. This is what students will be able to use and remember long after they have left your classroom. What is important to know and do can be hooked onto enduring understandings. Enduring understandings are central concepts.

Gilbert: OK, the word *gravity* by itself probably isn't that interesting. How about the question of why things always fall to the earth?

Celia: But things don't always fall. Like, birds fly. How does that relate?

Gilbert: Birds and airplanes, and anything else that flies still have to reckon with gravity.

Lisa: I think what I'm seeing is that you can't just plunk a concept like gravity down in front of students, because often, who cares. But like, with this one, you get in an airplane and you care a lot. So, a teacher needs to play around with a concept from a discipline to figure out how it links with real questions that students have.

To practice identifying a concept, locate a textbook or curriculum guide. In it, identify a main idea or skill that has all four characteristics that Wiske described. In Reflection 6.9 below, write how this concept fits her four characteristics. If you have difficulty seeing how it does, you may have started with something either too broad or vague (such as "life science") or too narrow (such as "correct use of commas") to serve as a central concept for curriculum planning. In that case, keep looking until you identify a concept that fits all four characteristics.

Typically, beginning teachers have difficulty identifying major concepts because everything seems equally important. Teacher candidates may wish to discuss what central concepts guide curriculum at specific grade levels with their supervising teachers or university supervisor. We stress the importance of planning curriculum around central concepts (enduring understandings or generative topics) because concepts can be developed in a variety of different ways. Planning how to develop them from multicultural perspectives gets us away from covering facts and adding bits of multicultural information into those facts. It also gets us away from seeing multicultural curriculum as lessons about "others," to add if there is time.

Reflection 6.9
Identifying a concept or "generative topic"

What the concept is: _____

How is it central to a domain or discipline?

What topics, skills, or experiences can be connected to it?

How relevant or interesting can it be made to students?

In what ways does it interest you or relate to your experience?

Elaborating on Concepts From Diverse Perspectives

Now let's elaborate on concepts from diverse, multicultural perspectives: Multicultural theorists have developed typologies to examine and evaluate different models of multicultural curriculum design (Banks, 1989; Sleeter & Grant, 2007; Tetreault, 1989). Below is a synthesis of them; they are illustrated by using the concept of "wellness" from the health curriculum.

1. *Contributions, add-and-stir, or human relations.* This is the "heroes and holidays" approach, in which the teacher adds on famous people to study (heroes), holidays and celebrations, and lessons about differences and similarities. The overall curriculum ideas, however, don't change; marginalized groups still appear as "bits and pieces." For example, a unit on "wellness" might add healthy foods from non-Anglo cultural groups to examples of healthy menus that are in the textbook. This alone is not the approach we recommend, but it is common because it doesn't require much rethinking of curriculum.

2. *Ethnic studies, women's studies, or single-group studies.* In this approach, concepts are taught in depth from the perspective of one marginalized group, be it an ethnic or racial group, women, people with disabilities, gays, or others. Earlier we gave examples of how Chicano studies and disability studies scholars have reworked major ideas. Ethnic studies curricula give students of color a sense of their own history and identity in U.S. society, increase their awareness and self-confidence, examine why their group has disproportionately less than its share of resources, and discuss what strategies the group has used to challenge inequity (Suzuki, 1980). Women's studies envisions "a world in which all persons can develop to their fullest potential and be free from all the ideologies and structures that consciously and unconsciously oppress and exploit some for the advantage of others" (National Women's Studies Association, 2005). In Reflection 6.5, you examined a textbook topic in relationship to the knowledge and experiences of a marginalized group. This approach to curriculum emphasizes a nondominant group's knowledge and viewpoint.

   A health unit on "wellness" from a women's studies perspective might critique beauty images that emphasize thinness, examine eating disorders such as anorexia, and develop positive self-images that embrace good nutrition, exercise, and appreciation of one's natural beauty. Or, from an Indian studies perspective, it might examine major health issues facing Indian people currently (such as diabetes), why many Indian communities lack access to good health care, and how traditional tribal health care can be connected with contemporary health care systems.

3. *Transformative multicultural.* Banks (1993) defines transformative academic knowledge as "concepts, paradigms, themes, and explanations that challenge mainstream academic knowledge and that expand the historical and literary canon. Transformative academic knowledge challenges some of the key

assumptions that mainstream scholars make about the nature of knowledge" (p. 9). In your research into subordinate communities' knowledge about a concept, you probably tapped into transformative academic knowledge. Transformative multicultural curriculum regularly teaches concepts through two or more groups' viewpoints and experiences. Rather than adding on contributions to the traditional perspective, the teacher makes an effort to identify perspectives members of a group tend to share about an event or issue. As much as possible, the teacher identifies diverse groups whose experiences offer diverse angles from which to consider the concept. A unit on "wellness" might compare and contrast what it means to be well or healthy from three different cultural perspectives, such as Chippewa Indians, Western medicine, and Chinese acupuncture.

Figure 6.1 further illustrates the transformative multicultural approach with respect to two literature units. The first unit develops the concept of "hero" through works by an African-American author, a European-American author, a Deaf author, and a Chicano

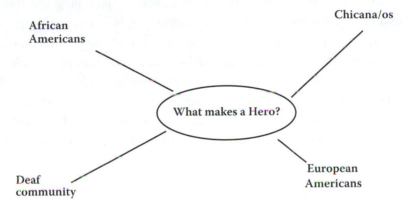

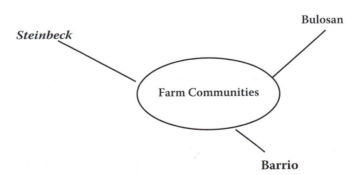

FIGURE 6.1 Design for literature units. See "Literature on Migrant Workers and Exploitation," developed by Anne Fairbrother, in Grant & Sleeter, 2007.

author. The second unit develops the concept of "farm communities" through works by three authors writing about farming in California: John Steinbeck, Raymond Barrio, and Carlos Bulosan (see Fairbrother in Grant & Sleeter, 2007, p. 238–242).

In another example, a language arts teacher might organize a poetry unit around a theme such as "identity" or "family," selecting poetry written by members of a variety of groups. Note that in both examples, the central concept is developed through multiple sociocultural groups' knowledge. Because it is impossible to teach the many and varied experiences of the many people who fit into any particular sociocultural group, the teacher can make an effort to select work that is relevant to students, relevant to the main concept of the unit, and over the year provides a window to, and mirrors of, different groups' knowledge.

4. *Social action, social reconstructionist, or antiracist.* This curriculum is also organized around a diversity of viewpoints and experiences, but through a lens of social justice and action. Such a curriculum provides students with activities and experiences that will help them improve their life circumstances by changing the status quo for equality and equity. Antiracist education, for example, is "an action-oriented strategy for institutional, systemic change to address racism and the interlocking systems of social oppression" (Dei, 1996, p. 25). A social action curriculum gives tools not only to talk about injustice and oppression, but also to do something about it (Lee, Menkart, & Okazawa-Rey 1998). Although many people view such curricula as "too controversial," well-designed social action curricula can help students understand real issues. Milligan and Bigler (in press) found that curricula which provide information about successful challenges to racism improve racial attitudes of *both* children of color and White children, allowing students to see how racism affects everybody, and offering them the power to change the status quo.

Reflection 6.10
How useful each model appears to you

Contributions	___Not at all ___Somewhat	___ A fair amount	___ A great deal
Single-group studies	___Not at all ___Somewhat	___ A fair amount	___ A great deal
Transformative	___Not at all ___Somewhat	___ A fair amount	___ A great deal
Social action	___Not at all ___Somewhat	___ A fair amount	___ A great deal

Why you think so:

A unit on "wellness" might examine the distribution of health care services. Students could compare statistics on health care needs for different groups, with services they actually receive. Students could look at health care from a variety of perspectives — members of marginalized groups, insurance companies, government — and propose a plan for fair distribution of health care.

Of the four models above, which makes most sense to you? In Reflection 6.10, indicate the extent to which you believe each model would be most helpful to you, and why you think so.

Share your thinking with your classmates. We find it especially helpful when students who take different positions share and debate their reasoning with each other, because this process often deepens their thinking.

Student Dialogue 6.6

Celia: Hold it, this is like a trick question. The chapter has been criticizing the Contributions approach as being too superficial. Why would I mark it as being useful?

Lisa: For me, the Contributions approach is what I'm most comfortable with. And I can see how to use it if I'm teaching young children.

Gilbert: It might be what is the easiest to put into practice, but I'm struck by research that suggests that it isn't actually the most effective. An active approach to learning about and stopping racism actually improved students' attitudes toward each other. That's powerful, and it makes sense to me. Kids see real issues and real differences, so why not work with them seriously?

Lisa: I guess I just haven't seen good multicultural curriculum beyond the Contributions approach, so I'm having trouble visualizing it. But, I guess I could learn to work with it.

Many of you reading this book can empathize with Lisa. We too feel her discomfort. Lisa is on the threshold of a major internal struggle. Much of the challenge to becoming a fantastic teacher is a struggle within the person. Many reasons will abound for maintaining the status quo, but many reasons to disrupt the status quo also exist. Creative teachers recognize that transformative multicultural and social action curricula may not directly follow state curriculum standards or textbooks, but can provide rich contexts in which to teach to curriculum standards, as exemplified by the first-grade teacher mentioned earlier who taught a unit on Monterey County agriculture.

Now it's your turn to work with a concept. Go back to the textbook you analyzed, or a curriculum guide that you might use. Select a concept and one of these models: Single Group Studies, Transformative Multicultural, and Social Action. Sketch out how that concept might be developed, using the guide in Reflection 6.11 on the next page.

You have a start at planning a lesson or unit. Additional considerations typically are also developed, including (1) content standards the lesson plan addresses; (2) teaching procedures; (3) a plan for assessing student learning; (4) resources that will be needed; and (5) estimated time the lesson plan will require. In the next section, we turn to locating multicultural curriculum resources.

Major Concept or Generative Topic:

Subject area(s):

Grade level:

Objectives (What should students be able to do with the main concept by the end of the lesson or unit?)

1.

2.

3.

(From chapter 5): What do students already know about it? What life experiences do they have that relate to this concept?

Using the research process discussed earlier in this chapter, locate information about the concept from the perspective of at least one historically marginalized group. Then suggest how to develop or rework the concept, using either the single-group studies, multicultural, or social action model.

Building Block 14: Locating Multicultural Teaching Resources

Where do teachers locate good multicultural teaching resources? Resources actually abound. However, this section begins with a caveat: Resources cannot substitute for your own thoughtful planning and background knowledge. Resources should be selected to support your teaching goals, not to determine them or to substitute for your own knowledge. Further, there is no "perfect" resource; all resources have biases and limitations as well as strengths. Teachers with a clear sense of what they are teaching can learn to identify and use multiple and varied tools in the classroom, including using very biased textbooks to examine social justice issues. High school teacher Linda Christensen (2002) explained:

> No matter what materials you're given, find a way to create social-justice units out of them. For example, if you're given *To Kill a Mockingbird,* take Charles M. Payne's book *I've Got the Light of Freedom: The Organizing Tradition and the Mississippi Struggle* and talk about the historical background necessary for understanding the context of the book.

Good teachers choose and use resources thoughtfully rather than overrelying on them. In addition, the best teachers are not only ongoing learners themselves, but also inveterate collectors. Over time, their classrooms become well stocked with materials, and usually they have become active in community or professional activities. Also, they seek out other teachers and librarians with whom to share resources, and varied venues where they can locate new resources. They assume that good resources exist and can be found. Below we explore books for children and youth, Internet resources, community resources, and students as resources.

Books for Children and Youth

Very many books for children and youth feature communities and individuals other than the dominant White middle class. They can be located through major publishing houses, small alternative presses (many of which have active websites), catalogs, libraries, and bookstores. For example, several major publishing companies have collections of multicultural children's literature and social studies resources, although one may need to ask specifically about them since teachers may be presented only with basic texts that their school districts can afford.

Electronic book-types of resources also exist. For example, *Patakin: World Tales of Drums and Drummers* (Jaffe, 2001), written by a drummer, explores stories from around the world as it recounts where drums come from and how they are used. The book includes a CD, so that students can hear as well as read.

Books for children and youth need to be examined with the same critical eye as textbooks. Just because a book features African Americans, for example, does not mean that it does not teach stereotypes or provide misinformation. Children's books with Native American characters vary widely in quality; some are excellent and others replicate stereotypes (Slapin & Seale, 1998). Although many collections of women's history resources feature women from a variety of backgrounds, some continue to overrepresent White women. Collections of multicultural resources often ignore disability issues and people with disabilities; characters with disabilities, when featured, may not be realistic.

We encourage teachers not simply to grab whatever looks "multicultural," but also to use guides that evaluate resources, particularly when beginning to develop such collections (see, for example, Gayle-Evans, 2004; Helbig & Perkins, 1994; Muse, 1997; Slapin & Seale, 1998). Journals such as *Multicultural Review* (http://www.mcreview.com) and *Multicultural Perspectives* regularly feature reviews of books, video, and audio materials for children and youth. Websites such as GLSEN (Gay, Lesbian, Straight Education Network) have book recommendations or links to assist teachers and parents in selecting resources (http://www.glsen.org/templates/booklink/index.html). In the long run, you will get better use out of a few well-selected resources than boxes full of poorly selected resources.

Reflection 6.12 involves you in browsing an online library to help select books for children and youth. The Cooperative Children's Book Center at the University of Wisconsin–Madison, established in 1963, has become widely known for its excellent collection of high-quality contemporary and historical books; it also includes recommendations of books for teachers and parents (http://www.soemadison.wisc.edu/ccbc/). Click on the link for K–12 teachers, then the link for original booklist. Select an age level and locate

---

Reflection 6.12
Selecting recommended books

1.

2.

3.

4.

5.

---

three to five books that would be relevant to the lesson plan you began in Reflection 6.11. List them and why you chose them.

Now that you have some book titles and authors, try to locate them in a local school or community library or a local bookstore. You can also order copies from a bookstore if you wish.

Resources on the Internet

Internet tools for locating multicultural resources abound. For example, Multicultural Pavilion (http://www.edchange.org/multicultural) provides a wealth of material, such as songs, poetry, and social justice speeches, as well as links to a wide variety of sources including discussion boards, online bookstores, and so forth. Gorski (2005) compiled an excellent guide to using the Internet for multicultural teaching, in which he emphasizes that Internet resources need to be selected so that they contribute to, rather than distract from, excellent multicultural teaching.

Resources such as the Public Broadcasting Service provide very useful tools for teachers (http://www.pbs.org/teachersource/). For example, on its September 2005 "Concepts across the Curriculum" page, PBS featured plans and resources for teaching about poli-

---

Reflection 6.13
Analyzing a website

Who produced this website?

How is this website intended to be used?

What biases might its developers have? Remember, everyone has biases; biases aren't necessarily good or bad, and identifying them doesn't mean that the website is unusable.

Whose view of the world does it tend to support?

Whose view does it undermine or ignore?

---

tics and art. One of the plans focuses on murals by California muralist Judith Baca; included are links to online resources for teaching this plan. The John F. Kennedy Center for the Performing Arts in Washington, DC offers teachers an excellent online resource of lesson plans and other curriculum resources (http://artsedge.kennedy-center.org/teach/). In addition, a rapidly growing proliferation of multicultural lesson plans is available online. You can find hundreds of them in a few minutes by doing a search for "multicultural lesson plans." But since they range from excellent to superficial and stereotypic, you should select carefully.

When using the Internet to find out about a sociocultural group other than your own, or about recommended teaching resources, it is especially important to pay attention to who created the website and for what purpose. For Reflection 6.13, identify a website that looks to you like it might be useful when you are designing multicultural curriculum, then try to figure out what biases and whose viewpoint it embodies.

Given your analysis, how might you use the website as an educational resource? If you are having difficulty identifying any biases or points of view, show the website and the questions to someone else; often other people can see biases that we may not be able to see. Remember that all resources have biases, and are produced by people with viewpoints — that is not necessarily a problem; the problem is when you don't identify them and adopt the biases of the authors or website creators without being aware of doing so.

Resources in the Community

Communities can offer very rich resources for multicultural teaching. Most communities have local community artists. Cruz and Walker (2001) described a project in Tampa, Florida, in which a high-poverty school serving largely African-American and Latino students developed an eight-week series of trips to local museums, alternating between an African-American art museum and a museum dedicated to the history of Cubans and Spaniards. These trips broke down segregation among the students, and, unexpectedly, to some extent among the parents. Some schools have developed active artists-in-residence programs (e.g., Bressler et al., 2000), or projects connecting students with local muralists (e.g., Conrad, 1994).

Curriculum projects can engage students in community research. Schergen (2005) describes a project in which an elementary school collaborated with the Cabrini Green neighborhood in Chicago to create a "memory museum" of the neighborhood as old buildings were demolished and replaced with newer (and more expensive) buildings. By using the arts, students helped to create an installation documenting the history of Cabrini Green and its neighborhoods that were being displaced in the process of urban renewal. In addition, the cultural knowledge that they developed from living in Cabrini Green was enriched and the cultural capital acquired from a deeper understanding of the role and purpose of museums in society was enhanced.

McIntyre (2000) and several preservice teachers worked with a group of inner-city students to document and find ways to address violence in their neighborhood. The students used cameras to capture "visual stories" of the communities. With guidance, they used their community research to examine issues such as teen pregnancy and welfare. As the students identified problems (such as trash in their neighborhoods), they developed action strategies to address some of them. Throughout the whole project, the teachers connected students' community-based research with academic inquiry. They also used the project as a tool to encourage the students to consider continuing on to higher education.

In chapter 2 we mentioned the Social Justice Education Project in Tucson. There, high school students design and conduct research projects in their community as part of social studies and language arts. A newspaper article about it explains:

> As the result of a process involving dialogue, personal reflection and questionnaires, students and project coordinators chose four topics on which to focus their efforts: media representation of students of color; stereotypes of students within schools; critical thinking vs. passivity in education; and loss of culture for students of color. The class divided itself into four groups, with each taking responsibility for researching one topic…. [In 2005 the class] opted to look at media representation again, but this time by focusing on the negative effects of the media on youth and women of color. Other groups are examining poverty; verbal abuse and racism in the family; and the effects of a negative environment on student motivation. Outside the classroom, the students use college-level techniques to observe, write field notes, interview subjects and draw conclusions. Twice weekly, the high school seniors take on the role of graduate students by bringing the results of their research to class for discussion and critical examination in a seminar-like atmosphere. (Tuttle, 2005)

Engaging students with community resources to investigate real community issues can be a very effective way to link academic knowledge and skills with the "real world."

Reflection 6.14
Broadening your curriculum resources

Topic:

Describe an Internet resource:

Describe a community resource:

Compare and contrast them in terms of strengths and weaknesses.

In projects such as these, students who had been tuned out from school discover ways to appropriate academic knowledge and relevant skills to address issues they care about.

Reflection 6.14 asks you to compare the relative value of different resources you could use to teach the same topic. You can either work with the same topic you used in Reflections 6.11 and 6.12, or select a different topic. Locate an Internet resource and a community resource you could use to teach about this topic from a multicultural perspective. Compare them in terms of their strengths and weaknesses.

Students as Curriculum

Students themselves can be a curriculum resource, particularly through their involvement with youth popular culture. Popular culture includes movies, music, 'zines, video games, fashions, and graffiti that young people consume and produce. As Giroux (2000) pointed out, youth popular culture "is one of the few places where they can speak for themselves, produce alternative public spheres, and represent their own interests" (p. 13).

You can draw on popular culture, for example, by teaching literacy skills through music videos, student-created music, or poetry slams. In chapters 2 and 5 of this book, you have investigated various dimensions of students' worlds. When planning curriculum, try to link that world with academics, and let students help you make those links, since how teachers interpret youth culture often isn't the same as how students interpret it. Teachers often get it wrong, but young people are usually more than happy to share their perspectives with teachers, if the teacher shows genuine interest.

For instance, one of us saw a sixth-grade language arts teacher have her students write a memorial about something in their own lives, after they had studied a poem about a memorial. Students wrote about topics that ranged from a pet dying, to a relative killed in a drive-by shooting, to a national hero killed in a war. Most students volunteered to read what they had written orally, and they listened with interest to each other's memorials. Afterward, an Indonesian girl asked a Bulgarian girl to show her how to read Bulgarian words in a document the Bulgarian girl had brought to share with the class. Through all of this learning from each other, students were learning to hear and engage with diverse viewpoints and perspectives.

Final Thoughts

At this point, we have only begun to open up a much larger issue: the relationship between knowledge and power. On one level, teachers pass on to the next generation what adults "know" and believe is necessary for functioning in adult society. But on another level, teachers also take up a role in political struggles, whether or not they choose to do so or even think about it.

For example, L. T. Smith (1999) points out that a fundamental difference between Western knowledge and indigenous knowledge has to do with assumptions about the earth. Westerners view the earth as nonliving and controllable, but indigenous societies generally view the earth as a living entity of which humans are an integral part. Western societies believe that people can buy and sell land, patent living organisms, rearrange natural phenomena, and live apart from the land, while indigenous societies make opposite assumptions. As a teacher, your curriculum will embody assumptions about the earth as well as many other things you may not have critically examined.

But the most dangerous assumption is that Europeans and Euro-Americans have created the best, most "evolved" system of knowledge and way of life that everyone else should emulate, and that it is based on truth rather than culturally based assumptions. Smith (1999) argues that Western ways of interacting cross-culturally and globally, today as well as in the past, are "designed to destroy every last remnant of alternative ways of knowing and living, to obliterate collective identities and memories and to impose a new order" (p. 69). In school, the dominant society's knowledge is not only taught but also presented as the most evolved and useful system of knowing in human history. It is the latter that is problematic from a multicultural perspective.

At the same time, if children do not learn the dominant group's knowledge and language, they will be locked out of opportunities and access to power. Delpit (1995) argued strongly that "there are codes or rules for participating in power; that is, there is a 'culture of power'" (p. 25). The cultural capital and language of the dominant group has power in part because the dominant group itself has power. Delpit argues that the curriculum for "other people's children" needs to equip them with the conceptual tools to participate in the dominant society. Making curriculum multicultural should not be at the expense of equipping students with academic tools of the culture of power.

Putting It Into Practice

Gilbert was placed in a fifth-grade classroom for his full-time student teaching. His cooperating teacher asked him to implement a unit on North American exploration. She gave him the following unit plan, which she had used in previous years, outlining objectives and procedures:

Unit Focus: Exploration of North America

Objectives:
1. Students will develop research skills to gather information from varied sources such as books, encyclopedias, dictionaries, and the Internet.
2. Students will describe the purpose and explorations of a major early North American explorer, situated in relationship to time and geographic location.
3. Students will write a report using the information found during their research process.

Suggested Procedures:
1. Introduce various resources students can use to gather information. Include nonfiction books, fiction books, magazines, dictionaries, encyclopedias, and computers with Internet access; all resource material should fall within the domain of early North American exploration. Place students in small groups and give each group one type of resource. Give them time to explore their resource; they should list its basic characteristics, including how it is organized, helpful features, what kind of information it provides, and any questions they have about how to use it. Have each group present their findings to the class. As students are presenting, create a list of characteristics for each type of reference.

---

2. Discuss with students the term exploration, both in terms of school and the outside world. Explain that we are going to start a new unit on the early exploration of North America. Create a KWL chart (What do you already know? What do you want to learn? What did you learn?). Fill in the first column by having students brainstorm what they already know about early exploration of North America. Continue the discussion by focusing on the question "What do you want to learn?"

3. Using a question from the KWL chart, model how all the different reference materials could be used to find information. For example, if the question was, "What types of transportation did early explorers use?" a researcher might use the table of contents or index with the key words transportation, boat, or horse.

4. Divide students into three groups. Give each group one of the following names of North American Explorers: Christopher Columbus, Leif Ericsson, and Juan Ponce de Leon. Independently, each student will brainstorm 8 to 10 questions about the group's explorer. Encourage students to ask questions such as: Why did they set off on an expedition? What was their route to North America? What supplies did they take with them? Did they encounter any problems, both during their travels and once they landed in North America? What did they do once they arrived? Did they go back to Europe? If so, did they ever return to North America?

5. Students should then begin their research using all different types of resources. When students have finished taking notes about the explorer, they should prepare a timeline depicting major events of their expedition, a map showing their travel routes, and a written report using the information they collected.

6. Display students' work around the room. Allow time for students to look at each other's work.

Gilbert had many concerns as he read through the unit plan. First, only European perspectives were represented by the explorers chosen for research. He reflected on how curriculum should not only represent multiple perspectives, but also broaden the array of those whose knowledge and voice is being heard. Second, students did not have the opportunity to select whom they were going to research, or how they could present the information they had learned. Third, there was no ongoing plan for assessing what students were learning. Gilbert wanted to change the unit plan to incorporate the building blocks from chapter 6. If you were Gilbert, how would you change the unit objectives and plan in order to do the following:

Organize the unit around a "big idea"?

Develop that idea through multiple cultural groups' perspectives and experiences?

Make sure book and Internet resources are culturally diverse?

```



```

Make more space for students' ideas and perspectives?

```



```

Here is what Gilbert did. He began by thinking about the unit's "big idea," which was "exploration of North America." He realized that led to several questions, such as: What different theories exist as to who came to North America first? How would someone evaluate the theories? What does the concept of "discover" mean? How would North America look from the points of view of different explorers? How do indigenous Americans think about the question of who was here first, and about the Europeans who came? He did some exploring to find out more about these questions.

Then he rewrote some of the objectives and the structure of the unit in order to include multiple perspectives and student voice, while critically questioning the knowledge presented to students by the original unit plan.

Unit Focus: Exploration of North America

Objectives:
1. Students will develop research skills to gather information from varied sources such as books, encyclopedias, dictionaries, and the Internet.
2. Students will critically analyze different perspectives about exploration of North America, and draw conclusions based on that analysis.
3. Students will use research on explorers to analyze the character of an explorer.
4. Students will present information to a group with clarity, appropriate tone and voice, and incorporate visual aids (costumes, props, and maps).

Suggested Procedures:
1. Introduce various resources students can use to gather information. Include nonfiction books, fiction books, magazines, dictionaries, encyclopedias, and computers with Internet access; all resource material should fall within the domain of early North American exploration. Place students in small groups and give each group one type of resource. Give them time to explore their resource; they should list its basic characteristics including how it is organized, helpful features, what kind of information it provides, and any questions they have about how to use it. Have each group present its findings to the class. As students are presenting, create a list of characteristics for each type of reference.

---

2. Discuss with students the term exploration, in terms of both school and the outside world. Explain that we are going to start a new unit on the early exploration of North America. Create a KWL chart (What do you already know? What do you want to learn? What did you learn?). Fill in the first column by having students brainstorm what they already know about early exploration of North America. Continue the discussion by focusing on the question "What do you want to learn?"

3. Ask students who discovered North America first. Present the following list of explorers to students: Hoei-Shin, Brendan the Bold, Bjarni Herjulfsson, Leif Ericsson, Prince Madoc of Wales, Christopher Columbus, Chief Howling Wind. Tell students that each claimed he discovered North America first. In groups, students will research one of the seven explorers. They will plan a presentation trying to convince an audience that their explorer was the first to discover the North America. The presentations will take place as a panel discussion where all seven explorers, in costume, are in front of an audience consisting of other fifth-grade classes and family members. The Master of Ceremonies (MC) will invite each explorer to tell his story of exploration by asking each explorer the same set of questions. The explorer will respond using the information gathered during the research process. Groups will make costumes and props to help convince the audience. At the end of the panel discussion the audience will vote on who they think discovered North America first.

4. Divide students into seven groups and assign two students to be MCs. As a class, devise a method of picking an explorer that will be fair to all groups, such as putting all the explorers' names into a hat and drawing a name, or picking numbers that decide an order for choosing the explorer.

5. Within the groups, each member will help gather factual information about the group's explorer. In addition, group members will fill one of three roles: (1) Writer (responsible for putting the information into script form); (2) Explorer (responsible for costuming and presenting on the panel discussion); and (3) Props Person (responsible for preparing any props needed during the panel discussion, such as maps or diagrams). Students will decide roles by considering how to use the strengths of group members. The two MCs are responsible for facilitating the panel discussion, preparing the stage where it will take place, writing and sending out invitations, and most importantly, checking in with groups on a daily basis. Groups are to seek help from the MCs before going to the teacher.

6. Hand out questions that will be answered by each group:
   • Tell us about yourself. Where are you from?
   • Why did you embark on an expedition? What were you looking for?
   • Tell us about your travel. When did you leave your home, and how long did it take for you to arrive in North America? How did you travel? What did you see during your travels?
   • When you arrived in North America, what did you see?
   • Other than your personal story, is there any other evidence of your travels?
      For Chief Howling Wind only (in addition to the above questions): Why have Native Americans been given so little recognition for the discovery of North America? What is your case against the other men on the panel?

7. Students should decide how to go about answering the questions, using the resources discussed at the beginning of the unit to gather information. Make sure to show how to put information from reference materials into students' own words and how to document findings.

8. As students are moving through the research process, show a format for writing scripts, how to take on the characterization of their explorer, and how to create props. This can be done as a whole group, or within small groups addressing only the members who are responsible for those items.

9. A few days before the performance, conduct a dress rehearsal. Videotape it so students can see themselves from the audience's perspective. Discuss the importance of clarity, expression, and eye contact to the persuasiveness of their performance.

10. On the day of the performance, gather audience members in front of the panel of explorers. At the end of the discussion, take an informal vote of who they thought discovered North America based on the evidence they heard from the panel members. Discuss with the audience how the information they learned today is different from, or the same as, what they had heard before in school. Point out that many Native Americans believe that the origin of human beings was in North America, and that people moved outward from there. In other words, Native Americans did not discover America, but rather were created there and discovered and then populated other parts of the world. See if you and the class can locate information about this perspective on the Internet.

11. As a class, discuss the importance of multiple perspectives when gathering factual information about historical events. Ask students if they had a hard time collecting information, and if they found information while researching that did not represent history form their explorer's perspective. Look at several books (textbooks, encyclopedias, etc.) and evaluate the resources according to all the perspectives they had learned about from the unit performance. Did they find resources that were misleading, false, or didn't tell the whole story? Students should brainstorm why they found what they did.

Assessing student learning

1. Throughout the research phase of the unit, monitor students' ability to gather information from varied sources, and to choose sources appropriate to their research questions.

2. To assess students' critical analysis of different perspectives about exploration of North America, at the end of the unit complete the KWL chart stated at the beginning of the unit. Encourage students to list not only the historical information learned, but also concepts they learned about the recording of history.

3. During the panel discussion, assess students' presentations for clarity, appropriate tone and voice, and incorporation of visual aids (costumes, props, and maps); incorporate audience responses into feedback students get later.

seven
Testing and Assessment

This chapter will help you answer the following questions:

- What forms of assessment have been used most commonly in schools?
- What is high-stakes testing? What is its purpose, and what are some of its limitations?
- What are authentic assessment, portfolio assessment, and exhibition assessment?
- How do authentic forms of assessment contribute to good multicultural teaching?

In chapter 6 we discussed creating or modifying curriculum for good multicultural education. But once teachers teach the curriculum, how do they know what students have learned? How do they know if their teaching strategies were successful, and for which students? In the history of contemporary schooling, a trilogy of tests has been used to assess student achievement: curriculum-based assessment, end-of-unit/sixth-week exam, and standardized achievement or high-stakes tests. For multicultural teaching, the main question is what forms of assessment are most useful and fair, given the diversity among students and the goal of promoting equity in student learning?

Recently, curriculum-based assessment and end-of-unit exams have been deemphasized in favor of standardized achievement or high-stakes tests. But, let us not get ahead of ourselves. First, we will locate curriculum-based assessment and end-of-unit/sixth-week exams in the context in which they were used and respected by many teachers prior to the 1980s. This was a time when teachers' voice and judgment were given greater consideration and professional respect than is currently the case. We acknowledge that the portrait in this chapter will be somewhat idealized, but nevertheless it provides a context for discussing problems and possibilities in assessment. Then, we will consider the standardized achievement test. We will not so much discuss its structure and design, but rather we will consider how standardized testing or high-stakes testing is influencing multicultural education. Following that, we will turn to authentic assessment, including portfolio assessment and exhibition assessment. Authentic forms of assessment have the best potential to capture what diverse students know and have learned, and to guide a teacher's day-to-day teaching. As a teacher candidate, you may employ forms of assessment such as these, once the present high-stakes testing craze mellows out.

The chapter will develop one building block:

Building Block 15: Using Authentic Assessment

Reflections in this chapter ask you to connect new ideas with concepts you have learned in previous chapters, observations you have made, and information gleaned from your interactions with others. For some of the reflections you will need the following:

- Access to one to two classmates (for Reflections 7.1, 7.5)
- Access to a computer (for Reflection 7.4)
- Access to two to three teachers to interview (for Reflections 7.2, 7.3, 7.8)
- Access to one or two students (for Reflection 7.6)
- Access to a student's portfolio (for Reflection 7.7)

The Test Trilogy

We refer to three forms of assessment as "the test trilogy": curriculum-based assessment, the end-of-unit exam, and standardized achievement test/high-stakes testing. Having been students for 15 years or more, you have probably experienced all three forms. But other than studying for tests, taking tests, and worrying about how well you did on them, have you ever thought more deeply about them, let's say from a teacher's perspective? In this section, we introduce you to a teacher's perspective on testing. We will start with curriculum-based assessment.

Curriculum-Based Assessment

The purpose of curriculum-based assessment is to guide daily instruction by monitoring what students are learning relative to what a teacher is teaching. The assessment usually covers the material (e.g., concepts, events in history, grammar rules) taught during the week (or possibly longer). Many teachers spend their weekends correcting students' tests in order to know how and where to start on Monday morning. Through curriculum-based assessment, teachers seek to discover whether they should reteach the entire class or select students in response to identified problem areas, schedule special meetings to address the particular academic needs of one or two students, or go on with the material, clarifying one or two points along the way.

Curriculum-based assessment, whether in spelling, mathematics, social studies, or reading, can create a climate of anxiety on the day of the test. Monday morning, for students, is a "moment of truth" that can quickly turn into a time of celebration and big smiles if the results are good. Or it can be a somber time if the test results are not good. Usually the attitude of those who fall short is that, with the encouragement of the teacher, "I will study harder and I will do better on the next test." With personalized help from the teacher, most students demonstrate improvement and share their successes with classmates and family. For those who continue to have difficulty, a specialized assessment might be required to determine if there are physical, psychological, or emotional impediments to learning. The teacher, family members, and other school staff members meet and plan an instructional program based on that diagnosis.

Student Dialogue 7.1

Celia: I remember that when I got into middle school, there were tests every week, somewhat like we have in some of our college classes. Also teachers were friendly, but they were no-nonsense. They demanded that we do well.

Gilbert: Right, often my mother would ask to see my tests. I can remember when I was very young, wondering how she knew we had a test. At first I thought she was looking through my book bag. She must have known what I was thinking, because one day she said to me, "You know, Gilbert, in South Korea we had the Friday test, too."

Teachers use curriculum-based assessment to monitor students' progress, and to catch little learning problems before they become large learning problems. We find curriculum-based assessment to be quite useful and compatible with other forms of assessment that we will discuss later. From a multicultural point of view, at least two considerations are important. First is the assessment designed to capture what all of the students know and can do? For instance, are students given adequate time to take the test, and are they familiar with the vocabulary that is used in it? Second, does the assessment reflect multicultural content that, following from our discussions in chapter 6, should guide curriculum design?

End-of-Unit Exam

The next act in the test trilogy is the end-of-unit exam. Teachers who wish to make certain that students are retaining what they are learning give a sixth-week or end-of-unit exam. Some of these exams are teacher-made and some come with textbooks. Rather than being used primarily to guide daily instruction, the results from these exams are used to judge how well students learned. These tests often carry a lot of weight come report card time. The end-of-unit exams are usually preceded by one or two days of intense study, and most students in the class strive to help each other get ready.

Ideally, teachers and students want to work in close partnership because the test results affect both, indicating how well the teacher has taught and how well the students have learned. A fantastic teacher establishes an atmosphere where test anxiety and exam phobia are minimized through mutual support of learning. Students are encouraged to work together and support each other to develop a sense of classroom camaraderie that offsets test anxiety. In general, students learn that although excellence is demanded, their self-respect is not trashed if they don't do well on a test. If students understand that they will be supported in working harder and that the possibility for improvement exists, they can learn to be accountable to themselves, teachers, and parents. Parents/caregivers and the teacher serve as valuable resources for students, helping them review material for a big exam. In this context, the exam itself is not seen as a monster, but instead as a challenge, much like the first speech given before an audience or the first piano solo in front of parents and adult friends.

Everyone — students, teachers, parents — knows that the results from the exam, along with the cumulative average from curriculum-based assessments, will be reflected on the report card. Pressure is felt, but for most students, it is pressure in a safe environment, where love and help are demonstrated. However, for students who are not successful on exams, repeated low scores can precipitate a spiral of low self-esteem and failure with life-changing consequences if teachers, other school officials, and parents do not reach out to help them attain success.

Reflection 7.1 asks you to look at your own experience as a student with these two kinds of assessment. Based upon your experience, what are the pros and cons of both? Share your thoughts with a classmate.

Reflection 7.1
Your thoughts about exams

What has been your experience with the curriculum-based assessment exam and the end-of-unit exam?

Curriculum-based assessment exam

Pros

Cons

End of unit exam

Pros

Cons

Since you are a college student in a teacher education program, or a teacher who has completed college, chances are that you have done fairly well with exams in most subject areas all of your life. The difficulties you had, if any, were probably overcome without too much hassle. We bet your grade point average is a "B" or higher. But, how do you think the students who struggle in school academically would answer the questions in Reflection 7.1? Would you consider their experience useful in helping you understand testing and assessment?

Standardized Achievement Test (High-Stakes Test)

The third and final act of the testing trilogy is the standardized achievement test. According to R. Mitchell (1992), standardized tests are "given under the same conditions and asking the same questions across different populations in order to permit comparisons" (p. 5). They are expected to provide answers to questions such as: "Is my child reading at the national level for her age? Is our district doing better than theirs on grade 3 reading? Are this year's students reading at a higher level than last year's?" (p. 5). Over the years, many tests have been developed to survey student achievement in the basic academic skills at the elementary, secondary, and college levels, including the California Achievement Test and the Iowa Test of Basic Skills. Achievement tests are developed in "batteries" to measure students' skills in such areas as reading, mathematics, grammar, social studies, and spelling.

Prior to the mid-1980s, teachers and students approached standardized achievement tests differently from the way they do today. Since they came around only once every two or three years, many students and teachers approached the test as a "challenging project." Teachers did not deliberately teach to the test, but they did prep students in basic skills areas and gave them test-taking tips. Carl recalls that when he was teaching there was friendly competition between classrooms scheduled to take the tests. Students hoped the overall score of their classroom would be higher than that of the room across the hall. Also, much like preparation for the end-of-unit exam, preparation for the standardized test was an active collaboration between teachers, students, and other staff members. In getting his class of eighth graders ready for the Metropolitan Achievement Test, Carl taught his students how to remain focused for 25- and 35-minute blocks of time. He shared strategies with them (e, g, choices that used the word *never* and *always* could probably be discounted), and he taught them that they had the smarts to be successful on the test.

Standardized testing can be a useful gauge for identifying who is being undertaught and needs more help, since standardized tests compare every test taker either with each other or with a target of proficiency. But there has always been a downside to standardized testing as it relates to equity. Intelligence testing, a form of standardized testing, was advocated by members of the eugenics movement as a way of identifying who should reproduce and who shouldn't, and who should be admitted for immigration into the United States versus who should not. Standardized intelligence tests are now used much less than they were in earlier times; most standardized tests today assess students' mastery of content and skills rather than general learning ability. However, generally, these tests have been developed and normed based on dominant cultural assumptions about curriculum and human development. In other words, the tests are devised based upon normative cultural capital — the high-status knowledge that the average White middle-class students knew and understood. As a result, using such tests to place students into gifted programs and special education has generated controversy about racial, cultural, social class, and language biases (Obiakor, Obi, & Algozzine, 2001).

For most students in the past, results of standardized testing did not affect their school placement. That changed with the emphasis put on standardized tests in the context of the present education reform movement that began in the 1980s, after publication of *A Nation At Risk* (National Commission on Excellence in Education, 1983). That report placed a major responsibility for the invasion of foreign technology (e.g., Sony televisions) and automobiles (e.g., Hyundai) on the American education system. The publication states: "If only to keep and improve on the slim competitive edge we still retain in world markets, we must rededicate ourselves to the reform of the educational system for the benefit of all" (p. 7). This kind of discourse became the central focus of educational reform. However, educators were not in control or actively involved in the discussions. Federal, state, and local political leaders and officials took control of it, pushing teachers to the side. Teachers were not invited to high-level summit meetings on the status of education in the United States. The political leaders directed reform toward a return to the basics. "Back to the basics," "excellence and accountability in education," and the "New Basics" became education slogans. Presidential candidates claimed that, if elected, they would be the "education president." Gubernatorial candidates made the same claim.

The education reform started in the 1980s has continued to gain momentum each year. In the early 21st century it is alive and well in the form of accountability and high-stakes testing. As noted in chapter 3, the term *high-stakes testing* means using standardized tests to make important decisions that have direct consequences for students, such as promotion, retention, and graduation. The No Child Left Behind Act of 2001, a reauthorization of the Elementary and Secondary Education Act, requires states to give annual reading and mathematics tests to all students. The tests are "aligned" with a state's content and academic achievement standards, and provide information about how well students are meeting those standards.

The current reform effort, we should note, is not the first of its kind. A brief discussion of two previous education reform movements can provide a context for examining the present one. Like the present reform movement, both came about in times of great societal concern.

The first was a child of the Cold War born in 1957, when the Russians launched the first space vehicle, Sputnik. Many Americans were shocked and dismayed that our space-probing technology was second to that of the Soviet Union. Others feared our very survival was threatened if the Russians moved ahead in the space race. Along with that, our national pride was shattered. Politicians and civic leaders demanded a reexamination of what was being taught in U.S. schools, and how it was being taught. In response to civic outcry, Congress passed the National Defense Education Act of 1958, and schools were ordered to change the curriculum. More attention was given to science, mathematics, and languages. Teachers were told to teach the "new math" (e.g., sets, Venn diagrams), which was, according to Hanna (1983), "characterized primarily by the promotion of a more abstract approach to mathematics in schools" (p. 14). Hanna argues that "the central stress in 'new math' lay in making school mathematics similar in structure, content, and manner of presentation to what was perceived to be the theory and practice of mathematics as an intellectual discipline" (p. 14). Since teachers were not trusted to know subject matter or instructional skills, curriculum materials were developed that required teachers to "follow a script" or rigid procedures as they taught (e.g., the Distar Reading Program). In other words, when teaching, teachers were instructed to use the ideas, and in some case to repeat the actual words, written by subject matter "experts."

The second major education reform effort was in 1964, when President Lyndon Johnson initiated the War on Poverty and ushered through Congress the Economic Opportunity Act (the Anti-Poverty act). This legislation established compensatory education programs such as Project Head Start and provided schools with human and material resources. Initially, Head Start was designed to help preschool children compensate for what was called "cultural deprivation" in the 1960s. Also, in 1965, as part of an effort to use education to eliminate poverty, Congress passed the Elementary and Secondary Education Act (ESEA). Title I of ESEA was written to improve reading and math achievement. Other titles of the Act provided money for libraries, instructional materials, and staff development.

Since the passage of the 1965 Title I of ESEA, program evaluation through large-scale testing has been a major component of federal support for the education of low-achieving students who live in poverty. In the 1970s, some states, such as Florida, begin to rely on tests of basic skills to make certain that students were learning at least the minimum competencies necessary to be productive citizens. These states introduced a testing program that used large-scale, standardized achievement tests to assess whether individual students achieved at a level (minimum competency) necessary to graduate from high school. By the mid-1980s, some 33 states had mandated some form of "minimum competency." However, due to criticisms that "minimum competency" promoted low standards, this idea lost steam.

In 1983, *A Nation At Risk* claimed there was a "rising tide of mediocrity" in American education. Citing poor national test scores, deterioration in school quality, and a cafeteria-style curriculum, the report warned that the United States was rapidly losing its global respectability. By the mid-1990s, following the 1989 summit that established the National Education Goals Panel, 18 states implemented test-based requirements for graduation. In about 25 states, students' test performance had significant ramifications for their schools, determining federal funding, autonomy, accreditation, and even allowing external takeover when scores were persistently low (National Research Council, 1999, p. 15).

At this same time, President Clinton upped the rhetoric on standards. In his 1997 State of the Union address, he challenged the nation to undertake "a national crusade for education standards — not federal government standards, but national standards, representing what all students must know in order to succeed in the knowledge economy of the twenty-first century" (p. 14). The President argued that, "Every state should adopt high national standards, and by 1999, every state should test every fourth-grader in reading and every eighth-grader in math to make sure these standards are met." Clinton declared, "Good tests will show us who needs help, what changes in teaching to make, and which schools need to improve." "Tests," the President declared, "… can help us to end social promotion. For no child should move from grade school to junior high, or junior high to high school until he or she is ready" (National Research Council, 1999, p. 14). With these words, the focus on "standards," discussed in chapter 6, increased tenfold and social promotion was not permitted. School districts in many urban areas implemented promotion test policies.

It is important to realize that high-stakes testing and accountability have become strongly associated with national pride; it rankles the national psyche, and causes a collective anxiety among many U.S. citizens to see that students in the United States are not testing as well as students in some other industrialized countries. Although concern over the status of the United States in relationship to the global economy seems to be driving the push for high-stakes testing, testing has taken on a life of its own, morphing into testing for the sake of raising test scores. Doing good multicultural education demands that a fantastic teacher be concerned with the whole child and not just his or her score on a high-stakes standardized exam.

The value in the current extensive use of these tests is hotly debated. At their best, tests fairly assess what students are actually taught in school, and are useful in identifying areas in which to improve classroom instruction. Some educators, such as Archbald (1997), maintain that standardization and assessment are good tools for improving teacher effectiveness and student achievement, and that it is too soon to write off this model. Archbald contends that without clear standards and good assessment data, the assumption that standards are high, teachers are teaching effectively, and students are achieving at acceptable levels remains unexamined. Instead Archbald argues that, "If a school has neither clear grade level achievement standards nor standards-based assessments of achievement, it is hard to know whether instruction is effective" (p. 157). He claims that without clear standards "conditions are created in which ineffective teachers can be buffered from accountability or pressures to improve, while exemplary teachers go unrecognized, with the outcomes of their efforts remaining invisible within the organization" (p. 159). Similarly, several researchers have worked in schools in which testing has served as a useful lever for improving teaching and learning, especially for students from historically underserved communities (e.g., Palmaffy, 1998; Roderick, Jacob, & Bryk, 2002).

But overreliance on mandated standardized tests for making important decisions about children's education is being protested increasingly in states such as Michigan and

California. Many educators question the validity of using a multiple-choice format to measure learning. Teachers protest they are forced to abandon more comprehensive lessons and simply "teach to the test." Many teachers argue against highly standardized and scripted teaching, saying they are being professionally deskilled (Apple, 1982). As Luke (1998) explains, "The deskilling of teachers' work … occurs when teachers are required to perform specific tasks and pedagogies without having any direct control or say in their conceptualization and evaluation" (p. 307). Rather than being expected to exercise professional judgment and use their professional knowledge and skills, teachers become deskilled when they are expected to follow specific directions created by others.

Reflection 7.2 asks you to locate and interview a teacher who follows a script as part of a curriculum package, or who used to follow a script, in order to find out the teacher's perspective about this practice.

Reflection 7.2
Scripted teaching and deskilling

Interview a teacher who is instructed to follow a "script" provided in the curriculum guide. Ask her or him:

How do you feel about following a script?

Does it help or hinder your teaching?

How do students respond to you teaching this way?

To what extent does the scripted curriculum help you develop new teaching skills?

To what extent does it get in the way of your ability to use what you know?

New teachers, particularly those who have experienced abbreviated teacher education programs, sometimes find scripts useful because they show exactly what the teacher is expected to do. But more experienced teachers often find them frustrating and constraining, treating the teacher as if she or he has little intelligence.

Despite the controversy, tests continue to prosper and proliferate. Actually, they have become a very big business. Mitchell (1992) reported that between "1955 and 1986, the dollar volume of sales of tests at the elementary and secondary level grew by 400 percent and are now about half a billion dollars a year" (p. 172). More recently, Olson (2004) reports that the federal Government Accountability Office has estimated that testing requirements will cause states to spend between $1.9 billion and $5.3 billion over the next six years. Olson goes on to point out that nine companies have accumulated about 87% of the business from state tests. The largest four companies who have state contracts for testing materials are CTB/McGraw-Hill, Harcourt Assessment, Pearson Assessment, and Riverside Publishing.

It is helpful to listen to perspectives about high-stakes testing from people who have varying kinds of responsibilities in education. Reflection 7.3 invites perspectives from classroom teachers.

Reflection 7.3
How high-stakes testing affects teaching and learning

Interview two or three classroom teachers, asking the following kinds of questions:

1. What kinds of assessment information help you most in teaching your students?
2. What kinds of high-stakes standardized tests are you required to administer?
3. To what extent and in what ways does high-stakes testing affect your teaching?
4. How does high-stakes testing affect your students' learning?

To what extent did the teachers share common perspectives? How did their perspectives differ? How do they see the effect of high-stakes testing on what happens in the classroom, and to what extent do they see these effects as either helpful or problematic?

Now let us examine reactions to high-stakes testing of some who have borne the responsibility of providing educational leadership for all students in the United States. Two previous Secretaries of Education reflect their concerns about high-stakes testing. Shirley Hufstedler (2002), the first U. S. Secretary of Education appointed by Democratic President Jimmy Carter, argues: "In recent years 'accountability' has often been used as shorthand for students' scores on standardized tests. Test scores are useful for the same reason that a thermometer is useful: each can detect a symptom. However, neither discloses the causes of symptoms" (p. 686). Lauro F. Cavazos (2002), appointed Secretary of Education under the Republican administration of Ronald Reagan, states:

> Now the federal government is stepping into testing as a means to ensure enhanced education and increased student academic performance. The federal approach will be to use testing as a mechanism of ensuring accountability before funding is given to the states. I see the development and use of any sort of national test as fraught with enormous difficulties and possible negative outcomes. We know too much testing is counterproductive, if valuable class time is used to continuously test students. Many schools already emphasize "test taking," and some "teach to the tests." With the federal government stepping into the testing business, I am concerned that there may be more schools focusing on how to take tests than on what every student should learn. (p. 694)

Professional measurement specialists also voice concern. The American Educational Research Association (AERA), the nation's largest professional organization devoted to the scientific study of education, issued a position statement cautioning against inappropriate use of high-stakes testing in preK–12 education (AERA, 2000). The following are excerpts from the statement:

Decisions that affect individual students' life chances or educational opportunities should not be made on the basis of test scores alone. Other relevant information should be taken into account to enhance the overall validity of such decisions. As a minimum assurance of fairness, when tests are used as part of making high-stakes decisions for individual students such as promotion to the next grade or high school graduation, students should be afforded multiple opportunities to pass the test.

When content standards and associated tests are introduced as a reform to change and thereby improve current practice, opportunities to access appropriate materials and retraining consistent with the intended changes should be provided before schools, teachers, or students are sanctioned for failing to meet the new standards.

When testing is for school accountability or to influence the curriculum, the test should be aligned with the curriculum as set forth in standards documents representing intended goals of instruction.

Examinees who fail a high-stakes test should be provided with meaningful opportunities for remediation, which should focus on the knowledge and skills the test is intended to address, not just the test performance. There should be sufficient time before retaking the test to assure that students have time to remedy any weaknesses discovered.

If a student lacks mastery of the language in which a test is given, then that test becomes, in part, a test of language proficiency. Special accommodations for English language learners may be necessary to obtain valid scores.

There must be explicit policies specifying which students are to be tested and under what circumstances students may be exempted from testing. Such policies must be uniformly enforced to assure the validity of score comparisons. In addition, reporting of test score results should accurately portray the percentage of students exempted.

The governmental body that mandates the test should also provide resources for a continuing program of research and for dissemination of research findings concerning both the positive and the negative effects of the testing program. (p. 2)

Amrein and Berliner (2002) examined high-stakes testing in 18 states to determine how it was affecting student learning. They state flatly, "If the goal of high-stakes testing policy is to increase student learning, then that policy is not working." They go on to observe that, "While states' high-stakes tests may show increased scores, there is little support in these data that such increases are anything but the result of test preparation and/or the exclusion of students from the testing process" (p. 4). Central to Amrein and Berliner's argument is that standardized tests should be indices of general cognitive and academic growth. If performance goes up on one, it should also be correspondingly high on similar tests. But in many states, improvement on state-mandated high-stakes tests actually corresponds with lower scores on other standardized tests like the National Assessment of Educational Progress (NAEP). This suggests that high-stakes testing is forcing schools to become specific test-prep institutions rather than educational institutions. In other words, transfer of learning is not a typical outcome of the state's high-stakes testing policy. In addition, Amrein and Berliner note another disturbing trend: "Tests have often been defended because they can distribute or redistribute resources based on a notion of 'merit.' But often the testing programs become thinly disguised methods to maintain the status quo and insure that funds stay in the hands of those who need them least" (pp. 7–8).

Such concerns have caused many educators to protest that high-stakes tests are unfair, and that they are used to "shame and blame" without taking into account some very important issues. Why is the high-stakes test discourse silent about or focused myopically on the difference in achievement levels between affluent homogenous suburban schools and schools in urban areas? Why are there numerous discussions about teacher quality, but very few about housing segregation, poverty, and the inequities in financial support, as discussed in chapter 3, that keeps poor people isolated in certain neighborhoods? Orfield and Wald (2000), for example, point out that the Civil Rights Project at Harvard University found a persistent negative effect on the education of students of color as a result of high-stakes testing. For reasons embedded in layers of institutional racism, African-American male students were particularly affected. And, why does the No Child Left Behind Act underestimate, or choose to ignore, the range and depth of needs borne by students who fall behind in school?

It seems high-stakes pressure is having a negative effect on many teachers' practice as well. Popham (2002) states that in more and more localities, the relentless pressure to produce higher test scores has driven some teachers to (1) exclude any curricular content not covered by the applicable high-stakes test; (2) drill students so heavily on items akin to those on the test that some students' love of learning is extinguished; and (3) engage in questionable or downright dishonest test-preparation and test-administration practices.

Student Dialogue 7.2

Lisa: What am I hearing? What should I believe? I don't particularly like tests, but should I believe that their major purpose is to get teachers and students?

Gilbert: Are all high-stakes tests bad? This is what Sleeter and Grant seemed to be arguing.

Celia: I'm not sure they're all bad. It is hard to believe that advisors to Presidents Clinton and Bush didn't know what they were doing when they recommended high-stakes testing to these presidents. Some teachers in my schools didn't expect us to learn much, and at least this kind of reform might get them to teach material that's on grade level.

Lisa: Good point, I don't like high-stakes tests myself, but shouldn't we respect the opinion of those who believe in them?

Gilbert, Lisa, and Celia are on to something. Is all high-stakes testing bad? Popham (2002) helps us with this question when he states, "I am not opposed to all high-stakes testing programs. I am however, fiercely opposed to flawed high-stakes testing programs — the kind that end up harming children. Unfortunately, the high-stakes testing programs we now find throughout our nation are so flawed that without delay, they should either be dumped or dramatically overhauled" (p. 2). One reason that Popham contends the tests are flawed is that "Educators assess students so that children's *overt* responses (to tests) will allow educators to draw inferences about children's *covert* knowledge, skill, and affect" (p. 3). In other words, educators cannot see directly into children's heads, but need indicators they *can* see that tell them what children do know. Popham argues, "You can't tell how well a child can spell by observing the child. Even with a magnifying glass or through a one-way mirror. Similarly, children's knowledge of U.S. history, their ability to write narrative essays, or their attitude toward mathematics are *covert*" (p. 20).

Most educators, including most who believe in doing good multicultural education, are not against standards, high achievement, and even some standardized testing. But they are concerned that a flawed high-stakes testing program will become a form of oppression and tyranny. Below we have identified 11 forms of oppression associated with high-stakes testing.

1. Oppression exists when students, teachers, parents, and others are not operating on a level playing field. All students are required to take the tests, but all have not received fair or equitable preparation. For example, students in affluent schools often benefit from small class sizes, well-prepared teachers, a challenging, culturally responsive curriculum, early identification of students who need help, after-school and summer programs — benefits that may be compromised or entirely lacking in schools serving high-poverty areas.

2. Students are in an oppressive learning environment when high-stakes decisions such as tracking, promotion, and graduation are made on the basis of a single test.

3. Offering students in low-tracked classes only basic skills work, the least qualified teachers, and teachers who have low expectations of the students is a form of oppression.

4. When students fail a test, not offering them the opportunity to retake, in an alternate form, the test that is being used to make promotion decisions is a form of oppression.

5. Failing to consider the needs of students with disabilities throughout the test development and administration process results in a form of oppression.

6. Failing to consider the learning needs of English language learners during test development, and making placement decisions based on tests that do not incorporate information about education accomplishments, knowledge, abilities, and particularly literacy skills in the primary language of English language learners is a form of oppression.

7. Oppression operates within the high-stakes testing movement when educational policy and practices neglect the total education of students in order to prepare them to take tests. It also operates when educators neglect the needs and interests of students, especially those who are poor, of color, physically or mentally challenged, or English language learners.

8. Oppression abounds when low-achieving students are pushed out of school or are not included in the test-taking population, and have not received individualized academic attention.

9. When undo pressure is applied to teachers to boost students' test scores on poorly conceived, culturally biased tests, oppression thrives.

10. The failure of educators to educate themselves about the problems and issues of high-stakes testing is self-inflicted oppression.

11. Until the financial investment gap between poor and rich schools closes, oppression abounds.

Student Dialogue 7.3

Lisa: Wow! Those are powerful ideas. Popham's statement is also helpful, because he is pointing out why we should be concerned about high-stakes tests.

Celia: You know, there is a great deal of debate about all of this testing. I read that hundreds of Massachusetts high school students, along with some 4th- and 8th-grade students, refused to take the high-stakes achievement test.

Gilbert: I learned there are websites that provide information about testing. Maybe we should check them out, and locate other material that argues the pros and cons of testing.

Reflection 7.4 invites you to examine several sources that discuss high-stakes testing, in order to develop an essay on your response to it. Some sources should consider

---

Reflection 7.4
Looking further into high-stakes testing

Read at least one source that views testing as useful, and one that views it as problematic. Examples of sources are below. Then prepare a one- to two-page essay about your perspectives on the arguments presented.

Testing as useful	Testing as useless
Education Trust: http://www2.edtrust.org/edtrust	FairTest: http://www.fairtest.org/states/survey.htm ; for example, "Testing Our Children: A Report Card on State Assessment Systems"
U.S. Government, No Child Left Behind: http://www.ed.gov/nclb/landing.jhtml	Rethinking Schools: http://www.rethinkingschools.org, for example, Stan Karp (2003). "Let Them Eat Tests"
Skrla, L., & Scheurich, J. J. (Eds.). (2003). *Educational Equity and Accountability: Paradigms, Policies, and Politics*	Johnson, D., & Johnson, B. (2002). *High stakes: Children, Testing and Failure in American Schools*

---

testing as useful — not necessarily perfect, but still useful; others should view testing as so problematic as to be useless.

Assessment for Doing Good Multicultural Education

What kind of assessment is recommended for doing good multicultural education? What is needed to determine how well students are faring in this tough instruction and assessment climate? How can a teacher tell how well students are learning an academic skill area like reading or understanding a concept like fractions? Actually, as Linn (1990) points out, teachers assess students' learning all the time using class discussions, homework, worksheets, and so forth. Fantastic teachers regularly use informal means of assessment to guide their instruction. Fantastic school leaders use varied evidence of student learning to engage teachers in a cycle of reflection and planning for improved classroom instruction, as illustrated in Box 7.1

The National Council of Teachers of Mathematics (1998) recommends several useful strategies that are consistent with doing good multicultural education. The Council argues there should be a shift:

- away from basing inferences on single-source evidence and toward basing inferences on multiple and balanced sources of evidence;
- away from reliance on comparing students' performance with that of other students and toward reliance on comparing students' performance *with established criteria;*

Box 7.1

Evidence of student learning, including but usually not limited to test data, can be used productively to guide a cycle of reflection and planning for improved instruction. Springboard Schools (2005), for example, helps schools use student learning data to plan for a cycle of inquiry illustrated below. Often the focus is on students who are the most behind, so that improvement efforts will be directed toward improving their achievement.

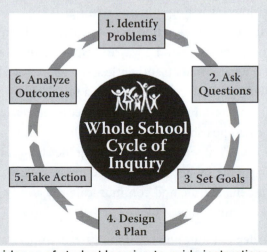

FIGURE 7.1 Using evidence of student learning to guide instructional improvement

- away from relying on outside sources of evidence and toward a balance between these sources and evidence compiled by teachers; and,

- away from a preponderance of assessment items that are short, skill-focused, single-answer, and decontextualized; and toward a greater use of tasks that are context-based, open to multiple approaches, and, in some cases, to multiple solutions, and are complex in the responses they demand. (pp. 1–2)

This direction in assessment is called *performance or authentic assessment*. The building block which follows provides a way to understand and use authentic forms of assessment.

Building Block 15: Using Authentic Assessment

Most teachers describe authentic assessment as judging students' real learning on the basis of the quality of their performance or work on real (authentic) learning tasks. Ryan (1994) explains, "Authentic assessment is the process of gathering evidence and documenting a student's learning and growth in an authentic context" (p. 1). Ryan adds that, unlike traditional assessment, authentic assessment is used to evaluate the individual student. "The student's work is compared to his or her previous work rather than compared to the work of others, in order to measure growth and progress" (p. 1). Authentic assessment is usually curriculum based, but rather than taking the form of paper–pencil tests, it mirrors the form of using a skill or concept in the "real world."

One reason many teachers prefer authentic assessment is because it involves teachers much more in the process than do standardized tests. Authentic assessment is based upon the daily work of teacher and students. In authentic assessment, teachers are regarded as knowledgeable professionals with the best interests of the students at heart. The teacher's professional judgment counts in making a determination about the student. This in no way means that the teacher does not or should not rely on other evaluations to assist her or him in making decisions. But like good doctors, teachers who use authentic assessment rely on discussion with colleagues and numerous diagnostic tools available to make decisions regarding student learning.

Ryan (1994) explains that an authentic assessment of mathematics should include both an inquiry-oriented approach and a way to help students construct meaning and understanding. Also, she states that an authentic assessment task should include the following characteristics: (1) the task can be solved in a number of ways; (2) the task elicits a range of responses; (3) the task requires students to communicate in some way; and (4) the task stimulates the best possible performance of the student (p. 60).

Imagine that Celia is student teaching in a sixth-grade classroom. The math curriculum in the first months of the school year is guided by the following state standards:

- All students will demonstrate and communicate the ability to solve problems, reason, and make connections.

- All students will demonstrate and communicate an understanding of geometry and measurement to solve real-world problems.

Box 7.2

Newman, Secada, and Wehlage (1995, p. 15) suggest that for math and social studies tasks to be authentic, the following seven standards within three areas need to be adhered to:

Construction of Knowledge
1. Organization of Information
2. Consideration of Alternatives

Disciplined Inquiry
3. Disciplinary Content
4. Disciplinary Process
5. Elaborated Written Communication

Value Beyond School
6. Problem Connected to the World
7. Audience Beyond the School

Celia listens to a student in the class, Jenny, explain several ways she could go about figuring out the number of yards of plywood and cloth needed to make the scenery for a play the sixth graders are staging about life in a small U.S. town in the 1920s. Celia and Jenny discuss the math concepts and skills Jenny can use to solve her design and construction problems in making the scenery. Jenny had seen similar scenery in an exhibit at the local museum. She and Celia plan to inquire at the museum to see if the curator could provide books and other materials that would help her design the scenery. Celia sees this as an opportunity to listen to Jenny express her ideas to someone else about applying mathematical concepts to scenery. Jenny also tells Celia that she and a friend have an appointment to talk with the school librarian about additional resource materials. Throughout the project, Celia and Jenny discuss Jenny's knowledge of measurement and review how Jenny can put this mathematical and research knowledge into practice in this project. They also discuss Jenny's mathematical progress since the beginning of the school year. The assessment procedure allows Jenny to see first-hand how well she is progressing, to participate in the assessment process, and to gain a sense of self-efficacy, especially if her results are good.

For Reflection 7.5, determine which of Ryan's (1994) characteristics of authentic assessment are being met, along with the state standards, in the example above. Write a sentence from Celia's work with Jenny that supports or does not support each characteristic.

Compare your written response with those of one or two classmates. Which of Ryan's characteristics of authentic assessment were identified?

Authentic assessment gives attention to the individual growth of the student (Jenny) and not just to how she compares with her classmates. Jenny and her teacher decided that she should write an essay discussing the historical information and math concepts pertinent to her problem, and place the essay in her portfolio (we will discuss portfolios

Reflection 7.5
Using authentic assessment

Write a sentence about Celia's work with Jenny that supports or does not support each of Ryan's (1994) characteristics of authentic assessment.

Task can be solved in number of ways.

Task elicits a range of responses.

Task requires students to communicate.

Task requires best possible performance.

Student's work is compared to her previous work.

---

shortly). Jenny will also include her observations that the commercial and residential streets in the 1920s were smaller than streets today and her theories about why this might be so.

Authentic assessment encourages a close working relationship between teacher and student. Also, it does not privilege some data and marginalize other data. Although Jenny and Celia will closely assess Jenny's mathematics skills (e.g., application of mathematics to making scenery, measurement of commercial and residential streets, and doing mathematical computations on a computer or calculator), they will also pay attention to her knowledge and skills in other discipline areas. For example, the data collected in the interview with the curator, and the information gathered from library research, will be used to assess Jenny's language arts and literacy skills, and the historical data collected from a visit to the office of the city engineers will be used to assess Jenny's social studies skills.

Kronowitz (1999) tells us that authentic assessment addresses the process and continuum of learning and pays attention to the demonstration of knowledge, skills, and attitudes. According to Kronowitz's views, Celia needs to be sensitive to Jenny's attitude about this project. She may wish to discover if Jenny is working on this project for an additional reason, such as a good friend got hurt riding her bike on the street or because of some long-term goal (e.g., interest in becoming a city planner or an engineer). Both reasons are valid and laudable. Nevertheless, with the second reason Celia may need to show more sympathetic understanding as the two of them work on the problem; with the second reason, Celia may wish to serve as career counselor. She may give Jenny advice that will prepare her for the sexism she may encounter as she pursues her career goal, and she may explain to her why it is important for her to take all of the math courses she can.

Authentic assessment is particularly pertinent to good multicultural education because it invites teachers and students to consider students' learning strengths. Students who do not perform well on paper–pencil tests have other ways of showing what they know, as the example above illustrates. Teachers need to clearly communicate what criteria they are using to judge students' learning, and students need a variety of ways to demonstrate their learning according to those criteria.

For Reflection 7.6, select a student, much as Celia did, and work with him or her using authentic assessment and state standards. Have the student identify a project, large or small, in which he or she can use concepts and skills that are in the standards being taught. Try to use as many of Ryan's characteristics of authentic assessment as possible.

Reflection 7.6
Applying the concept of authentic assessment

Describe the project (e.g., subject area, goal)

List the state standard(s):

Check to see which of Ryan's characteristics of authentic assessment are being met.

1. Task can be solved in number of ways.

2. Task elicits a range of responses.

3. Task requires students to communicate.

4. Task requires best possible performance.

5. Student's work is compared to her or his previous work.

Student Dialogue 7.4

Gilbert: I like authentic assessment. I can tell that it seems like more work for teachers, but it will be so much bvetter for students.

Lisa: Yes, they'd be much more engaged, and that in and of itself will serve as motivation for them.

Celia: It will for the teacher, too, because nothing is as sad and difficult for teachers as students who are not motivated.

Portfolio Assessment

Authentic assessment is often associated with the use of "portfolios." Paulson, Paulson, and Meyer (1991) describe a portfolio as "a purposeful collection of student work that exhibits the student's efforts, progress, and achievements in one or more areas" (p. 60). The work in a portfolio is often called "artifacts." Developing the portfolio includes students' participation in establishing the *rubric*: criteria and standards for selecting content and judging the merit of the work, and evidence of student self-reflection. Critical to portfolio assessment is the idea that it should be an act of learning for both teacher and student. Since portfolios may be both paper and electronic, students who have computer knowledge may wish to develop an "e-portfolio." For example, a decision about whether Jenny's portfolio will be electronic or paper may depend on the technological resources available at the school or at Jenny's home, as well as Jenny's and Celia's knowledge and understanding about developing a web-based portfolio.

The portfolio includes a statement of purpose, an outline of the contents, criteria for the selection of work samples, and evaluation of work samples using criteria on a rubric. Jenny's math portfolio would include an overview of the math learning outcomes for the year, and a discussion of how each work sample reflects Jenny's mastery of the math concepts. Jenny could include a photograph of the scenery for the play, with a discussion of mathematical concepts she used to create the scenery, cross-referenced with the math learning outcomes.

Also included in Jenny's portfolio are materials that feature both longitudinal and multidimensional artifacts. Jenny includes work samples from the beginning to the end of the year which show her growth in using mathematical concepts. Some of her work samples might connect math with another discipline, such as social studies. For example, in her research on life in a small town in the 1920s, Jenny found that the streets were narrower in some neighborhoods than others. She wrote an essay describing what she found, and discussing why she thinks this was so. Also included in the portfolio are materials that show how Jenny engages in self-reflection.

Portfolios can be and often are different from one another. They are not from a "cookie cutter" design. However, Barton and Collins (1972, p. 2) believe that the following seven characteristics are important to portfolios:

1. The presentation of the concept or idea should come out of many different sources and teachers should have opportunities to evaluate a variety of specific evidence; for example, artifacts (e.g., student papers); reproductions (e.g., special projects produced outside of the classroom or school); attentions (e.g., observational notes taken during an oral presentation); and productions (e.g., documents students prepare for the portfolio), to determine the student's competency.

2. They are authentic; instruction and evidence in the portfolio are directly linked.

3. They are a dynamic form of assessment. They capture student growth and change over time.

4. They explicitly define the purpose of instruction so students have a clear understanding of requirements before they begin developing evidence for their portfolio.

5. They promote integration. The portfolio evidence the students compile must establish a correspondence between academic course work and their life experience.
6. They are each a unique creation because students determine the evidence to be included and complete a self-evaluation reflection.
7. They are multipurpose in that a teacher can assess his or her instruction using the same evidence used to evaluate the student.

At the University of Wisconsin–Madison, the *Student Teaching Handbook* (Elementary Education Student Teaching Program, 2005) tells teacher candidates their portfolios have several purposes, including helping candidates: (1) to become more thoughtful, articulate, and effective; (2) to document achievement for initial certification. These two ideas are pertinent for K–12 portfolios as well. In addition, the *Handbook* states:

> Everything in the portfolio should be there for a reason that should be clear [to the parent/caregivers and others viewing the portfolio].
>
> The portfolio should show evidence of the student's growth over time, and his/her ability to learn from doing, thinking and performing at different levels of ability.
>
> The portfolio should include samples of student work that demonstrates the student's ability to analyze their work (e.g., the mistakes they make, their growth and development).
>
> The portfolio should show how the student has gone beyond achieving minimum standards required by the state. (p. 24)

Student Dialogue 7.5

Lisa: These are good suggestions for the professional and curriculum portfolio we have to develop to complete our teacher certification program.

Celia: Yes, since last year, when the State Department of Education set performance standards and the School of Education adopted portfolio assessment, I think every student has been experiencing a portfolio nightmare. But, we will be able to use this idea in our teaching. That may make all of the effort worthwhile.

Gilbert: I agree, it's a good idea, and goes well with doing good multicultural education, but it's going to require a lot of time and patience to explain to students and their parents what we are doing and why we are using portfolios.

To get an idea of what Barton and Collins's characteristics look like "in practice," obtain a student's portfolio and assess it for Reflection 7.7 on the next page. It would be most beneficial if you can examine a portfolio of a K–12 student, but if you do not have access to one, you can examine a student teaching portfolio.

    Which characteristics did you see best reflected? In what ways might the portfolio be improved? Overall, to what extent did the portfolio serve as a useful tool for assessing student learning over time?

    Portfolio assessment is pertinent to good multicultural education because it gives students a variety of ways to showcase their learning, and it involves them in the process of self-evaluation. Christine used to be a learning disabilities teacher, focusing on high school language arts. Although she used standardized tests and other published and teacher-made tests for diagnostic purposes, she quickly realized that she needed to broaden the way she assessed students' learning because most of her students simply did not do well with paper–pencil tests. She periodically involved each student in setting individualized learning goals. Her students had folders, and in their folders they kept their learning goals and samples of their best work. These samples included stories students wrote, lists of books they read, worksheets they completed, and other artifacts of their learning. In the years Christine spent as a learning disabilities teacher, she found this kind of assessment helped her to shift her focus from what her students could not do to what they could do; it gave a more holistic portrait of students' learning than paper–pencil tests alone gave.

    To find out more about the uses of portfolio, locate one or two teachers who use portfolios in their teaching. Then complete Reflection 7.8.

Exhibition Assessment

Exhibitions serve as another form of authentic assessment. Exhibitions involve formal presentations of the results of learning in a particular area. Occasions such as science fairs offer an opportunity for students to demonstrate comprehensive and cumulative knowledge and understanding through the use of several different disciplines. Theodore

---

Reflection 7.8
Portfolio assessment

Interview two teachers who include portfolio assessment in their teaching. Ascertain what they think about this method of assessment, and how long it took them to implement the idea. Also, ask them what advice about assessment and testing they would give to a beginning teacher. Write a one- to two-page summation of your findings.

Sizer (1992), chair of the Coalition of Essential Schools, popularized exhibitions as a form of assessment. The sixth "Common Principle" of the Coalition states: "A diploma or certificate is awarded on a successful final demonstration of mastery for graduation — an exhibition. This exhibition by the student should demonstrate his or her knowledge of the school's curriculum. Both faculty members and school district officials may conduct the exhibition" (p. 208). Performance assessment of portfolios, students' essays, science experiments, and classroom debates, according to B. Johnson (1996), are checkpoints that enable students and teachers to assess students' work as it builds toward a culminating activity, the exhibition.

Several students in Celia's class, including Jenny, prepared exhibitions. Jenny's exhibition included the following elements:

- A photo and initial sketches that she made with Celia's help.
- Essays about life in small-town America in the 1920s, the successful struggle of women for voting rights, the treatment of African Americans, Asian Americans, Native Americans, and Mexican Americans in the 1920s, and songs of protest and songs of love from the 1920s.
- Reports containing mathematical information about the widths of residential and commercial streets.

Jenny exhibited her essays, reports, and sketches on poster board with appropriate labels and titles. School officials, parents, and other students invited to the exhibitions were given a scoring rubric to assess Jenny's and the other students' work.

Exhibitions are only one of many kinds of authentic assessment. The movement toward authentic assessment has continued to grow as an increasing number of educators and others recognize that it has academic and social promise for students. Teachers know that testing students with a curriculum-based or an end-of-unit exam does not provide the teacher or the students with a complete picture of learning and teaching. Also, since different curriculum models (e.g., interdisciplinary) are used in some schools, tests that consider only one subject area (e.g., spelling or science) are inadequate.

Authentic assessment has the potential to restore confidence in schools. Parents/caregivers and school officials can examine students' portfolios and attend an exhibition, receiving both a long-range and short-range view of the students' progress. By reading teachers' feedback on essays or examining scoring rubrics, parents and education officials can get an indication of the teacher–pupil rapport and how teachers are preparing students to live in our culturally and socioeconomically diverse world. Also, by examining rubrics, checklists, and anecdotal comments within the portfolio, student exhibitions, and other documents, parents can acquire substantive data about how their children are being judged, the learning opportunities they are receiving at school, and the career goals they are being steered toward.

Finally, how well teachers and education officials actively support authentic assessment will serve as an indicator of their willingness to pursue better and more equitable assessment procedures for all children, regardless of how varied their needs and backgrounds may be. This is especially relevant at this time when politicians and the business community are pushing "quick-fix" standardized paper and pencil tests to assess students and teachers.

Putting It Into Practice

Celia had a student teaching experience in a seventh-grade social studies class. She arrived before the beginning of a world history unit on Islamic civilizations in the Middle Ages. Her student teaching class of 33 students was a fairly average, diverse class: 18 of the students were White, five were African American, five were Latino, four were Asian American, and one was American Indian. English was the second language for three Latino and two Asian students. Socioeconomically, the students varied widely, but they were mainly working class. Their academic skills were also diverse; while three read at about the 10th-grade level, another five struggled with material written at the 4th-grade level.

The teacher's name was Mrs. Harden and her usual approach to assessing student learning was to give a unit test, and also to mark written homework assignments that generally followed the questions in the textbook. However, she invited Celia to help her rethink her approach to assessment. Celia asked to see the standards; Mrs. Harden shared the state standards with her. They were as follows (adapted from California State Board of Education, 2000):

Students will analyze the religious and intellectual foundations of Islam in the Middle Ages.

Trace the origins of Islam and the life and teachings of Muhammad, including Islamic teachings in connection with Judaism and Christianity.

Explain the significance of the Qur'an and the Sunnah as the primary sources of Islamic beliefs, practice, and law, and their influence in Muslims' daily life.

Describe intellectual exchanges among Muslim scholars of Eurasia and Africa and the contributions Muslim scholars made to later civilizations in the areas of science, geography, mathematics, philosophy, medicine, art, and literature.

Celia then asked to see a copy of the unit test used last year. She noticed that most of the items on the test were recall questions; few asked students to analyze, apply information, or evaluate. Mrs. Harden acknowledged that she was not satisfied with this test, and that many of her students (especially those with lower reading levels and those whose first language was not English) did not do very well on it. Celia then asked what "big idea" Mrs. Harden was trying to help students grasp in this unit.

Mrs. Harden replied, "Hmmm. No one has asked me that before. I really want the students to see connections between Islam and other parts of the world. Most of the students have only very hazy, stereotypical ideas of what Islam is, and think of it as removed from the modern world. They have no idea of its rich intellectual history, its strong values, and its relationship to Christianity and Judaism. So I would like them to know some basic information about Islamic history and teachings. But I'd also like them to come away wanting to know more, and respecting Islam as having as much depth and complexity as religions they are more familiar with."

Celia and Mrs. Harden then discussed the fact that assessment and teaching should be interconnected. Redesigning the way student learning is assessed might necessitate rethinking how the unit is taught. As they talked, they both became increasingly excited by the possibilities for igniting student interest in Islam while teaching this unit.

If you were Celia, how would you design an authentic assessment plan? What would you have students do, and what might you have them include in a portfolio, given the learning outcomes and goals for the unit described above? Before reading further, write about the following:

1. What kinds of artifacts would you have students produce as they learn?

2. How would you examine students' growth over time, using artifacts like these?

3. How would you plan for authentic assessment in a way that capture students' ability to think at varying levels of complexity?

Now here is what Celia and Mrs. Harden did. They decided to use the Curriculum Assessment exam to assess learning of basic facts-recall material. They reasoned that students do need to know some basic information about Islam, and that the Curriculum Assessment exam is a useful way of making sure this happens. However, they structured test preparation around the "team games" approach to cooperative learning (discussed in chapter 5), encouraging students to help each other learn the material. As it turned out, this adaptation was successful; students who in previous years might have scored poorly on the unit test did reasonably well.

They also had each student create an individual portfolio on Islamic intellectual history. Each portfolio had five parts:

- A brief paragraph students wrote at the beginning of the unit, describing what the student knew about Islam (most of these turned out to be only a couple of sentences long);
- An interview with someone who is familiar with the Qur'an, in which the person discusses its significance to the person's life;
- An analysis that the student produced in either written or picture form, comparing and contrasting Islam, Christianity, and Judaism (in terms of basic teachings and history);
- A booklet, produced in cooperative groups using the "group investigation model," that chronicles contributions Muslim scholars made in one of the following areas: science, geography, mathematics, philosophy, medicine, art, or literature;
- A one-page self-evaluation, reflecting on learning that each of the items above illustrates.

The projects in the students' portfolio guided the teaching of part of the unit. The textbook was still a useful teaching tool, but the text did not dominate the unit as it had in the past.

At the end of the unit, Celia and Mrs. Harden reflected on this teaching and assessment approach. They were very pleased with most of the work students submitted, and the depth of learning the projects reflected. However, students had not been asked to write self-evaluations before, so these were not done very well. Celia realized that self-evaluation is a skill students need to develop and practice. Mrs. Harden and Celia also struggled with how to assign grades. They realized that next time they would need to work out more specific criteria that would accommodate the variety of work students produced. But they also found that authentic assessment encouraged them to assist and give students corrective feedback as the unit progressed. Since students were working on projects over time rather than completing one-shot tests, the teachers were able to monitor students' learning as it progressed. As a result, by the end of the semester, they felt students had learned quite successfully. They concluded that well-designed authentic assessment takes effort and planning, but at the same time supports complex learning and diverse approaches.

eight

Taking Action in the Classroom and Beyond

This chapter will help you answer the following questions:

- Why should teachers who care about equity and diversity take democracy seriously?
- How do I help my students distinguish between democracy as a social idea and democracy as a system of government?
- What is the difference between critical thinking and critical consciousness, and why does this matter?
- How do I help my students develop the know-how (knowledge, skills, and attitude) to engage in democratic decision making?

We opened this book by asking you to reflect on your vision of a fantastic teacher. As the book progressed, we examined challenges that complicate that vision. Fantastic teaching is much more complex than simply walking into a classroom and doing what you remember worked well for you when you were a student. This is especially true when we consider the diversity of students served by schools, and inequities that persist in our schools and society such as:

- Achievement gaps reflected on tests;
- Student self-actualization and learning;
- Access to fair, high-quality education;
- Access to jobs, adequate income, housing, shelter, food, health care, and other life-sustaining resources;
- Affirmation of home language and culture;
- Community self-determination.

We hope you are clearly seeing connections between what happens in classrooms and schools, and broader cultural and political relationships. The more unequally resources are distributed in the wider community, and the more competitive the wider society is, the more schools take on features of inequality and competition, exacerbating gaps in achievement and access to quality education. Loving and caring for students means respecting the homes and communities they come from and being cognizant of barriers their communities may face. It also means challenging students academically, being willing to go the extra mile to support their learning, and being willing to advocate for them, and act in solidarity with their families and communities. A culturally diverse and just world does not simply happen: it is painstakingly built, and must be constantly guarded.

This chapter moves beyond immediate practicalities of curriculum, instruction, and assessment, and asks you to engage in building connections between schooling, equity, and democracy. In doing so, you will develop the final two building blocks:

Building Block 16: Developing Students' Critical Consciousness
Building Block 17: Building Democratic Participation

Most Reflections in this chapter involve analyzing passages or examining your own experiences and ideas. But for a few of them, you will need access to the following:

- A school or your high school yearbook (for Reflections 8.3 and 8.7)
- The Internet (for Reflections 8.6 and 8.11)

Schooling as a Tool of Freedom and Democracy

As you read the first seven chapters of this book, which equity issues surfaced as most significant to you? Reflection 8.1 asks you to list those that struck you as most important, then to consider how students might learn to act upon one of them.

Reflection 8.1
Equity issues of significance

1. Which equity issues in this book emerged as most important for you?

2. Select one issue, and brainstorm how students might learn to act upon it.

The second question sets the stage for this chapter. Examine what you wrote in response to it. Is this a question you had given much thought to before? To what extent does your response reflect a desire to get students to implement a solution *you* favor? To what extent does it try to prompt young people as citizens to come up with *their own* solutions?

Multicultural education envisions schooling as a tool of freedom and democracy. However, today you may be hearing more about how schools can better prepare young people for work than for democracy. Business organizations repeatedly point out that technological advances and global restructuring have transformed the nature of production and work. They argue that the United States must develop many, many more workers to meet the demands of this new economy and these workers need to master skill sets in technology, abstract reasoning, math, and science.

Although educators certainly cannot ignore the skills that students will need for work, we believe that it is dangerous to reduce education to work preparation. Throughout this book, we have explored various ways in which schools serve as instruments of control when they promulgate a standardized fare of ideas and perspectives, and when they offer a more intellectually rich and demanding curriculum to students from already-advantaged backgrounds than to those most in need of a strong education.

If education is to serve democracy, then it must prepare *all* young people equally well for democratic participation. Parker (2003) argues that schools are particularly well suited for preparing students for democracy in that they are places in which young people who differ from each other congregate and interact:

> When aimed at democratic ends and supported by the proper democratic circumstances, this interaction in schools can help children develop the habits of thinking and caring necessary for public life — the courtesies, tolerance, respect, sense of justice, and knack for forging public policy with others whether one likes them or not. (p. 160)

Once young people leave school, they leave a unique environment that could foster the kind of public interaction and decision making in the context of diversity that democracy entails. But schools usually do not make use of this potential as well as they could.

So, let us begin by examining what democracy means to you. In Reflection 8.2, write your definition of democracy.

Reflection 8.2
What is democracy?

Now let's hear what two other writers have had to say, and then consider whether your definition might need expansion or revision. As you read, reflect on what you wrote above. First, consider the following observation by Paul Woodruff (2005):

> Even educated Americans seem to be confused about democracy, seduced by its doubles, and complacent in their ignorance. When I ask my learned colleagues about democracy, they often say it is "majority rule," or they speak vaguely of putting matters to a vote, as if this made a decision democratic. Sometimes they simply point to the Constitution of the United States, forgetting that this was written by men who feared government by the people and were trying to keep it at bay. (p. 4)

Student Dialogue 8.1

Gilbert: I have a question. Is democracy the same thing as the market? Here's what I mean. When a person chooses to buy some shares of a stock, or even some CDs in the music store, is that the same thing as making decisions democratically? In a market economy, everyone gets to make their own individual choice, as long as they can afford it. But I don't think individual choice is exactly what we are talking about here.

Lisa: Good question. Like, going to the store and buying what you want is different from having all the customers and workers sit down and decide how to run the store or distribute what's in it. If we had to sit down and discuss these things together, then I would have to pay attention not to just what I want, but also to what you want and need as well.

Gilbert: That's what I was getting at. If a teacher lets each student make his or her own individual decision about something, like which assignment to do or which question to answer on a worksheet, the students don't need to pay attention to what someone else needs. It seems like a democracy should require us to hear each other, and work out solutions that work for all of us, rather than thinking only about solutions that just work for me, as an individual.

Celia: I wonder if that's why the United States tends to oppose socialist economies. It would be hard to try to get as much money as you can in a system where you have to pay attention to what everyone needs rather than just being out for yourself. You might not agree, but that is something I'm beginning to wonder about.

Like Woodruff (2005), the students are arguing that democracy as "We the people" rests on faith in governance from the bottom up rather than the top down, belief in the ability of ordinary people to learn to work out differences in order to construct reasonable solutions to problems, and conviction that all citizens should not only have equal rights but also equal power to participate in governance. Woodruff posits seven features that are central to democracy, based on an analysis of ancient Athens. They include: (1)

freedom from tyranny; (2) the rule of law, applied equally to all citizens; (3) harmony (agreement to adhere collectively to the rule of law while simultaneously accepting differences among people); (4) equality among people for purposes of governance; (5) citizen wisdom that is built on human capacity to "perceive, reason, and judge"; (6) active debate for reasoning through uncertainties; and (7) general education designed to equip citizens for such participation (p. 154). He points out that Americans often confuse democracy with three deceptive doubles: voting, majority rule, and elected representation. Voting can be so rigged that it does little more than justify the wishes of tyrants; majority rule negates the rights and interests of minorities; and electing representatives leads to bloc competition for power.

The education philosopher John Dewey anticipated Woodruff's concerns. In "The Public and Its Problems" (1927/1973), Dewey distinguished between "democracy as a social idea and political democracy as a system of government" (p. 621). He explained that the two are connected, but that,

> The idea of democracy is a wider and fuller idea than can be exemplified in the state even at its best. To be realized it must affect all modes of human association, the family, the school, industry, religion. And even as far as political arrangements are concerned, governmental institutions are but a mechanism for securing to an idea channels of effective operation. (p. 621)

In other words, a democratic society should live democracy in the way people make decisions every day, in the various institutions in which they participate. By distinguishing between political systems and broader ideals, Dewey, like Woodruff, challenges us not to be seduced by mechanisms that offer less than the ideal of democracy. Dewey went on to explain:

> The old saying that the cure for the ills of democracy is more democracy is not apt if it means that the evils may be remediated by introducing more machinery of the same kind as that which already exists, or by refining and perfecting that machinery. But the phrase may also indicate the need of returning to the idea itself, of clarifying and deepening our apprehension of it, and of employing our sense of its meaning to criticize and re-make its political manifestations. Confining ourselves, for the moment, to political democracy, we must, in any case, renew our protest against the assumption that the idea itself produced the governmental practices which obtain in democratic states: General suffrage, elected representatives, majority rule, and so on. (p. 621)

Neither Dewey nor Woodruff opposed voting or choosing representatives, but both were concerned that reducing democracy to these elements leaves us with an impoverished view of the ideal of rule by ordinary citizens. As Dewey pointed out,

There is no sanctity in universal suffrage, frequent elections, majority rule, congressional and cabinet government. These things are devices evolved in the direction in which the current was moving, each wave of which involved at the time of its impulsion a minimum of departure from antecedent custom and law. The devices served a purpose: but the purpose was rather that of meeting existing needs which had become too intense to be ignored, than that of forwarding the democratic idea. (pp. 621–622)

Look back, now, at the definition of democracy you wrote in Reflection 8.2. How would you expand on it? Do you see any connections between these discussions of democracy and the issues you identified in Reflection 8.1?

Student Dialogue 8.2

Lisa: Is Dewey saying that in all of our communities, wherever people come together, we need to actually *do* democracy? Is that what would move us toward *democracy for all*?

Celia: Yes, I think he means we have to keep challenging, inquiring, and taking action if our country is to make progress toward fully achieving democracy.

Gilbert: So, when we set up committees "to further investigate" a problem, the setting up of the committee, which seems consistent with democratic principles, may actually be a way to stall taking action on the problem. Dewey calls it "introducing more machinery of the same kind as that which already exists."

Lisa: Good point. And maybe it was the way I learned history, but I never stopped to think that voting, representative government, and features of democracy burst forth when people's needs had become intense. I thought these things were written into the Constitution just because they were good ideas.

Celia: But women, people of color, gays and lesbians, people with disabilities, and the poor have rarely been given anything. They've earned their rights through critical inquiry, dissemination of information, and even civil disobedience like marches and protests.

Gilbert: I think Dewey is right on another point. In many cases, getting voting rights didn't stop other forms of bias. Like you said, Lisa, democracy seems to be something we need to keep working toward. I think he is saying that it is something you *do*, not something you say you are.

As the students are making sense out of Dewey's ideas, they are learning that achieving and maintaining democracy is a never-ending process. In addition, if they don't already know it, they will discover that when ordinary people question how power is used and claim a right to use it for the welfare of people like themselves, they are often seen as "too radical" or "un-American." Yet, everyone having power is exactly the ideal envisioned by ancient Athenians as well as many indigenous Americans. As Grinde and

Johansen (1991) point out, framers of the U.S. Constitution drew some of their ideas about democracy from the Iroquois Great Law.

How might the ideal of democracy become more real than it is at present? Classrooms could be the ideal place in which such preparation and practice can occur. Let's consider this possibility by looking at the decision-making process in a school. Reflection 8.3 asks you to rank various groups or positions in terms of their actual power to determine what happens in a school. Think of a school you are familiar with for this reflection. It might be one you attended as a student; use your yearbook to jog your memory. Or, it could be a school in which you are completing a field placement. In that case, if possible, talk with people in the school to find out how they see various groups' power to make decisions.

Commonly, the principal has the most power and students have the least. Increasingly teachers, too, are told what to teach and sometimes even exactly how to teach it. With the growing stress on school accountability and increased federal regulations, state legislators tell administrators what to do, principals tell teachers what to do, teachers tell students what to do, and schools tell parents what to do, particularly parents who are not well educated or who are economically poor. You may encounter teachers being directed to use curriculum packages that give teachers a script specifying what to say, what questions to ask and when, and sometimes even when to put the book down or show a picture. The extent of teachers' authority varies widely, however. Based on a study of teacher decision making in a context of accountability, T. M. Smith and Rowley (2005) found that schools where teachers are actively involved in helping to shape school reforms get better teacher "buy-in" than schools in which teachers are simply told what to do.

Regardless of whether they occupy the role of teacher, parent, school board member, or administrator, people who are affluent, White, and native English-speaking tend to have power and use it to protect themselves and their children. Rogers and Oakes (2005) argue that the reality of equity in schools lags far behind our knowledge of inequity because those with most power and the greatest vested interest in the status quo work to keep things as they are. For example, although we know that students of color and students from low-income backgrounds are less likely to be placed in college preparatory courses than students from White and affluent backgrounds, parents who are White and affluent tend to support tracking because it benefits their children. Rogers and Oakes observe that, "In many school systems, we have watched low-income African American and Latino communities remain silent or be silenced while powerful White and wealthier parents and policy makers dominate the reform debate" (p. 2189).

So if schools employ democratic decision making to only a limited extent, how are students to learn to become active democratic participants? The two building blocks in this chapter will help you deconstruct patterns of equity and build democracy in a classroom. We begin by exploring the development of students' critical consciousness, and then move to the development of their democratic participation.

Building Block 16: Developing Students' Critical Consciousness

Democracy requires that ordinary people think critically about everyday life, analyzing root causes of problems, and envisioning alternatives. Developing critical consciousness includes but goes beyond critical thinking. Let us consider critical thinking, then critical consciousness.

Critical thinking involves learning to identify the important facts, concepts, and principles of a problem (Gagne, 1985), and to differentiate among facts, opinions, values, and hypotheses in order to evaluate truth claims. Below are some definitions:

- *Fact*: Knowledge that can be verified empirically; does not depend on personal point of view.
- *Opinion*: Personal belief based on personal experience or prejudice that has not necessarily been verified.
- *Value*: Belief or moral principle that is based on faith; cannot be empirically tested.
- *Hypothesis:* Claim about something that might be true and could be, but has not yet been empirically tested.

Reflection 8.4 asks you to distinguish among facts, opinions, values, and hypotheses in relationship to a news event. In 2002, a superior court in California ruled that the phrase "under God" in the pledge of allegiance discriminates against people on the basis of religion. Numerous news articles and broadcasts discussed this issue. For example, in *USA Today*, Johnson and Kiely (2002) wrote:

Attorney General John Ashcroft said Thursday that his department will request a full hearing by the 9th U.S. Circuit Court of Appeals in an attempt to overturn the 2-1 ruling. The ruling from California applied to nine Western states. "At this time when citizens from all backgrounds have come together to express their solidarity as Americans, this Justice Department will spare no effort to preserve the rights of all Americans," Ashcroft said. Senior Judge Alfred T. Goodwin, who wrote that the phrase "under God" violates separation of church and state, stayed his ruling until other 9th Circuit judges decide whether to reconsider the case.

Based on the information above and anything else you know about the issue, identify a fact, an opinion, a value, and a hypothesis related to it.

Compare what you wrote with what some classmates wrote. Were you able to distinguish among these four kinds of statements?

Learning to think critically can be fun for students, and teaching students how to think critically can intrigue teachers because the process coaxes class members out of set patterns. Questions with answers that appear either "this or that" give way to more nuanced meanings and interpretations (Sweaney, 2001), and students are encouraged to think creatively. Learning to think critically does not just happen; it requires opportunities (activities and assignments) and practice, and an environment where teachers relinquish rigid control.

Reflection 8.5 asks you to consider classroom activities that promote critical thinking. Four teaching strategies appear in the left-hand column. For each, identify the extent

---

Reflection 8.5
Promoting critical thinking in the classroom

	How helpful?	Fact	Opinion	Value	Hypothesis
Lecture					
Completing worksheets over reading assignment					
Experiments					
Group problem solving					

---

to which you believe it is generally helpful in promoting critical thinking. Justify your response by providing a fact, an opinion, and a value, and proposing a hypothesis about the statement you made regarding that teaching strategy's helpfulness.

Share responses with your classmates, then discuss the following questions: Do you see the same teaching strategies as being equally helpful for teaching all four kinds of thinking? Or, are some strategies more helpful for some kinds of thinking than others? Which teaching strategies do you see used the most in classrooms? Have you seen these strategies used to help students develop critical thinking (along with other purposes for which they can be used)?

Many assumptions young people take as factual are promulgated through the media, making analysis of media a useful exercise. Children today spend an average of 900 hours per year in school, but 1500 hours per year watching television (Herr, 2001). When we add in movies, magazines, and pop music, this amounts to a huge amount of media consumption. Most media do not invite critical thinking, but rather uncritical acceptance of portrayals of the world.

Student Dialogue 8.3

Celia: Now, I would question the implication that we all just suck up what's in the media. For instance, I know that media show women as thin, and they keep getting thinner. And I know that some people link media portrayal of women as skinny with a rise of anorexia. But I just kind of ignore most of what I see on TV.

Lisa: Is it possible that you, like, ignore it because most of the women on TV are White rather than Mexican? TV is so loaded with people who look like me that it's pathetic. But try to find someone who looks like me, but with about 50 more pounds on her frame.

Gilbert: I think it's important to pay attention not only to what *is* in the media, but also to what *isn't* there. For example, how much insight do you get on Black-Asian relationships through media?

Lisa: Well, there's Tiger Woods.

Gilbert: And that's about it, huh? Consider this. About two-thirds of the people in the world are Asian, and another 13% or so live in Africa. What I wonder is, beyond Tiger Woods, are there any interactions among these huge parts of the world that matter? And I most certainly would like to know more about Black–Asian biracial people, and what our existence says about the whole construction of racial categories. The fact that, beyond Tiger Woods, you never see these kinds of issues or people in the media leaves me feeling like there's a whole world out there that we are totally ignorant of.

Gilbert's point deserves consideration: Critical consciousness means being aware of whose ideas, representations, and points of view are not included in the ongoing discussion, and what the implications are of that situation. Freire (1973) distinguished among three forms of consciousness: naïve, magical, and critical consciousness. Naïve consciousness means believing that those in power have everyone's best interests at heart; and that one's everyday problems have no relationship to one's position in a power hierarchy. Magical consciousness means being aware of injustices, but believing one can do nothing about them. Injustice just happens. Freire argued that both magical and naïve consciousness are fairly common because those in power promulgate these perspectives, which leaves ordinary people accepting being controlled by others. Critical consciousness, on the other hand, entails understanding the relationship between one's everyday problems and larger uses and abuses of power, and seeing oneself as capable of working for change.

Here is an example of how that works. To develop students' critical consciousness, a teacher in a farm worker community encouraged students to inquire into whether pesticides used in the fields were causing health problems for farm workers (including students' family members). Pesticides that are used a lot tend to be presented as fairly safe. But on the basis of their investigation, students recognized a link between health problems they were familiar with and the pesticides. So, they began to speak out about pesticides and farm worker health. Similarly, in an urban area a teacher encouraged students to inquire into why there were a large number of currency exchanges in the community. These outlets charged excess rates for cashing the checks of the minimum wage earners who lived there, in contrast to the large number of banks in middle-class communities which cashed checks for free when the individual had a minimum account balance. On the basis of their investigation, students wrote letters to the newspaper and spoke out about the lack of banks in their community.

Students' lives provide many jump-off points for examining larger issues. For instance, as young people become curious about sex, they also become concerned about diseases such as AIDS. This concern provides an excellent opportunity for students to examine their feelings about AIDS and why some associate AIDS with gay people. Also it is an opportunity to investigate how ignorance about AIDS has translated into inadequate funding for research on cures.

Developing critical consciousness begins by asking questions that arise from everyday living conditions, then probing into prevailing interpretations and explanations. Otoya-Knapp (2004) provides an example of what this process looks like in a high school classroom in Los Angeles. Under the leadership of a White teacher, students from diverse racial backgrounds were encouraged to talk about racism in relationship to barriers students anticipated encountering as they moved into the adult world. In their discussions, rather than immediately seeking solutions to problems, a facilitator encouraged students to probe their experiences with racism in order to get beyond superficial and simplistic understandings. Over the year, as students shared stories, their analysis of racism deepened, as did their ability to articulate its workings. Gradually, too, they began to recognize strategies they could use to challenge racism in their lives, and some began to develop leadership skills that would enable them to do so. Because the students had an opportunity to explore issues deeply, their insights and strategies were better grounded than they would have been had they not been afforded the opportunity to have extensive guided discussions.

Student Dialogue 8.4

Lisa: I keep tripping on this word consciousness. I know what it means to be unconscious, like if someone knocks you on the head, but Freire seems to mean something else.

Gilbert: I'm not so sure it does. If you're conscious, you are awake. I think Freire would like us to be not just awake, but wide awake in the sense that we are really tuning into what goes on around us.

Celia: I think there's an additional meaning. You aren't just wide awake to what is happening now, but you are also awake to how "now" got to be the way it is. I'm thinking back to when I took a Chicano studies class. The professor used to ask us to think hard about how problems of Chicano communities came about historically. The mainstream perspective says that we were always poor, but immigrated to the United States for a better life, so if we work hard, we will pull ourselves up because this is the land of opportunity. Chapter 6 mentioned Acuña's book *Occupied America*, which gives an opposite interpretation. It says that Mexican people were doing OK — or, at least as OK as other people — until the Americans took half of our land and designated us as low-wage workers.

Lisa: Your point? What does this have to do with being conscious?

Gilbert: I think Celia is saying that consciousness also includes tuning into more than the mainstream historical interpretation of today's problems, especially problems ordinary people face. Or at least, being critically conscious means that.

Lisa: So, having naïve consciousness is like being knocked on the head, except you don't know that you're asleep.

Celia: Yeah! And magical consciousness means being awake enough to feel pain, but then waiting for someone else to stop your pain. Being critically conscious means being awake enough to diagnose the cause of your pain and deal with it yourself.

By working together, Lisa, Gilbert, and Celia are better able to develop a critical consciousness about various forms of oppression, and figure out how they can take action. Implicit is the idea that being in a group you trust, where you can raise hard questions, is not only helpful but of major significance in order to expedite your critical awareness. Using issues, problems, and joys that are significant in their lives as data for critical analysis gives students the opportunity to apply their thinking to real-life situations that have personal meaning. Community locations and events, students' personal concerns, and world events can serve as resource materials.

Becoming critically conscious means questioning "truths" one hears every day. Media are especially significant purveyors of "truth." Media may appear to offer a wide range of viewpoints, but the increased concentration of media under a few owners probably limits the range of viewpoints that appear. In 2004, just five huge corporations owned most of the media consumed in the United States and globally: Time Warner, Disney, Murdoch's News Corporation, Bertelsmann of Germany, and Viacom (formerly CBS). This concentration represents a precipitous drop from 50 corporations in the mid-1980s (Bagdikian, 2004). On trips outside the United States, we both have noticed that many world events are not reported on any of our more than 50 television channels. Further, even a story reported on the British Broadcasting Corporation (BBC) in Britain, a country that is very friendly to the United States, is often interpreted quite differently on U.S. national news.

Media are a powerful venue through which the elite persuades us to accept the world as it is by circulating the same messages, images, and points of view over and over. As Stuart Hall (1995) put it, "In modern societies, the different media are especially important sites for the production, reproduction, and transformation of ideologies" (p. 19). Media make some interpretations of the world seem natural, while obscuring others. For example, Baldwin (2001) compared the stereotypes in news stories of similar crimes involving perpetrators of different races. Perpetrators who were youth of color were referred to mainly as "men," while white perpetrators of the same age were referred to as "youth" or "boys." Groups of white youth were "cliques" while groups of youth of color were "gangs." Thus, the language used to report crimes suggest that low-income Black and Latino youth are much more dangerous than White, middle-class youth. If one takes such media-generated images as "fact," then it might seem "sensible" to incarcerate hugely disproportionate numbers of youth of color.

Reflection 8.6 asks you to compare viewpoints about the same issue in two kinds of media: a mainstream media source, and an alternative media source. According to Albert (1997), "A mainstream media institution (public or private) most often aims to maximize profit or sells an elite audience to advertisers for its main source of revenue. It is virtually always structured in accord with and to help reinforce society's defining hierarchical social relationships, and is generally controlled by and controlling of other major social institutions, particularly corporations" (p. 53). A mainstream source is easy to find: just turn on TV or pick up a newspaper. Locating alternative media sources will pose more of a challenge. Alternative media usually don't try to maximize profits or sell advertising. Alternative media, which often operate on low budgets, are venues for distributing information, issue analyses, and sometimes action strategies to specific communities. Historically marginalized communities, for example, often produce local newspapers, radio broadcasts, websites, or other venues. There are several ways you can look into alternative sources:

- Ask people around you if any local community organizations publish newspapers or newsletters about issues.
- Investigate websites of organizations representing historically marginalized groups, such as the National Association for the Advancement of Colored People

(NAACP): http://www.naacp.org), the National Association for Bilingual Education (http://www.nabe.org), the National Association for Women (http://www.now.org), or the Gay Lesbian Straight Education Network (http://www.glsen.org).

- Several publications are widely distributed and also have websites. Examples include *Mother Jones* (http://www.motherjones.com), *Z Magazine* (http://www.zmag.org), *The Nation* (http://www.thenation.com) and (on the radio or TV) Democracy Now http://www.democracynow.org/index.shtml) and Pacifica Radio (http://www.pacifica.org).

- Search the Internet for "alternative media" or "independent media."

After you have located two sources that speak to the same issue, read them. Then compare their perspectives in Reflection 8.6.

Reflection 8.6
Comparing viewpoints in media

1. What issue or news event are you examining?

2. What mainstream source are you using?

3. What alternative source are you using?

Compare their reports in terms of:

What does each define as the central problem or issue?

Who does each define as the perpetrators of the problem?

Who does each see as the most likely solvers of the problem?

How similar or different were the treatments? In each source, what viewpoints were *not* there? If you paid attention only to the mainstream source, what insights would you miss? What insights did the alternative source provide? If you wanted to learn more about the reasoning and experiences behind the alternative media perspective, where might you go for more information? How might using limited sources of information affect what you assume to be true?

Beginning in elementary school, children can learn to identify messages in media. Consider the elementary teacher who asked children to keep track of how many hours per week they watch TV, and to analyze stereotypes in TV shows and advertising (see Bigelow & Peterson, 2002). Or, consider the primary-grade teacher who had children analyze stereotypes and biases in cartoons (Pang, 1991). Such analysis forms the basis for developing critical media literacy and critical thinking about the basis on which information and beliefs rest.

Now let's push our understanding of critical consciousness by moving from something everyday to an analysis of global power. Look at the label on the shirt, sweater, or pants you are wearing; where were these items made? To find out more about who made them, use an Internet search engine: Type in the words *textile workers*, and the country where the clothing was made. You can also add the brand name to your search. Below, the three students engage in a chain of critical inquiry.

Student Dialogue 8.5

Lisa: I found this website called "Labour Experiences in Hong Kong." Hmmm, it says that as companies have been moving to Southeast Asia in search of cheap labor, women workers in Hong Kong have been laid off by the thousands. Those who still have jobs are paid less, on a piecework basis.

Celia: Who is saying that?

Lisa: The International Labour Organization sponsored the website (http://www.ilo.org), and the person giving the information is a member of the Hong Kong Women Workers Association. In the store where I bought these jeans, they only showed me how stylish the jeans are so I'd be willing to pay $60 for them. But it looks like some Asian women made them for me to wear, and they didn't get anywhere near the $60 I paid.

Gilbert: Your sweatshirt was made in the United States. I wonder how much the person who sewed it was paid. Do the same search, but put in "United States" where you have "Hong Kong."

Lisa: Here's a website: "Abbreviations of Unions Affiliated with the AFL-CIO." (http://www.unionlabel.org). If the label on my sweatshirt said ILGWU (Garment Workers' Union, International Ladies), then the workers were probably paid OK. But my label doesn't say that, so I don't know who made the sweatshirt, or whether they were employed fairly.

Celia: It could have been made in a sweatshop. Immigrant women end up working in them in the United States. Where I grew up in Los Angeles, we knew quite a few women who worked in those places. They didn't get paid much, didn't have health insurance, and worked in pretty terrible conditions, but were afraid to say anything or else they would lose their jobs.

Lisa: Here's an article about that, by the Americans for Democratic Action (retrieved June 20, 2002, from http://www.adaction.org/pubs/slavelabor323.html). It describes Thai immigrants in Los Angeles sewing clothing in harsh conditions. It says that many large retailers don't buy clothing through clothing companies any more, but instead, have developed their own global network of low-paid workers. That should be illegal! The Union of Needletrades, Industrial and Textile Employees is trying to address this problem. It's funny, where I grew up, people look at unions like they are troublemakers.

Gilbert: I know a lot of people who think that, too. Hey, look at what this website says! According to the Bureau of Labor Statistics, in 1983, 20% of all workers were in unions, and now it's only 13.5%. And, union workers get paid better than nonunion workers (http://www.bls.gov). It's in the interest of ordinary people to unionize, but unions aren't in the interest of big employers who would have to pay more. So in a lot of the news, you generally hear about how unions cause problems.

Celia: You know all the publicity about how great NAFTA was supposed to be? Large transnational corporations set up sweatshops on the Mexican border where they didn't have to pay workers as much as in the United States. As I understand it, they pressure workers against unionizing for better wages, but then some of the corporations have up and moved from Mexico to Asia where they pay workers even less, leaving Mexican wages not only very low, but thousands of workers laid off.

Gilbert: There's a lot of rhetoric about closing gaps, and we need to look behind that rhetoric to see who is actually benefiting and who isn't.

In the above exchange, the students used critical questioning to guide their search for information and develop a critical consciousness. They asked about the sources of information, who it is that benefits from looking at an issue from a given point of view, and located supporting evidence. In questioning, they discovered examples of oppression, saw how mainstream media often hide that oppression, and discovered organizations working for social justice.

To summarize, one who sees the world naively assumes cause–effect relationships without investigating them, assuming that other people's interpretations are fact. Lisa assumed that workers around the world, who produce goods for export, choose their line of work, and are treated and paid fairly. A person with magic consciousness assumes that someone else will simply take care of the problem. A person with critical consciousness wants to know how the problem actually works, and is willing to analyze things carefully for him- or herself. Critical consciousness also means situating events within political relationships, and analyzing how power flows and works. Celia, Gilbert, and Lisa did some investigating, and found a very different picture from the naïve assumption that global free trade means that everyone is treated fairly, and everyone is free to choose from among desirable work alternatives.

Building Block 17: Building Democratic Participation

Critically analyzing problems can become depressing, and if students lack action strategies for addressing them, may lead to the naïve or magical consciousness that Freire discussed. For example, as a teacher, you may find your school short on resources while other schools are resource wealthy. But figuring how to increase the flow of resources into low-income schools probably seems way too large for you to take on, at least by yourself.

You and your future students may also feel like some social problems are really other people's problems, not yours, so why worry about them? For example, while public hospitals are more likely to serve uninsured people than are private hospitals, between 1975 and 1999, the United States lost one third of its public hospitals (Prokosch & Dolan, 2001). Insured readers who believe that we are only addressing "other people" will be surprised to discover that they too may become the "other." Walter Mosley (2000), in *Workin' on the Chain Gang,* speaks eloquently about this:

> Black American history is American history. There is an echo of Jim Crow in HMO: people shunted aside, denied access, and allowed to suffer with no real democratic recourse. Downsizing is an excellent way of robbing a worker of her accrued wealth. The widening gap between rich and poor is a way of demonizing the latter, because poverty is a sin in the richest country in the world. These new systems of injustices wear the trappings of freedom, but they are just as unacceptable as their forebears. The only difference is that under these systems we all suffer. This time everyone is a potential victim. (p. 49)

But again, shifting the flow of resources into public hospitals may seem "too large" to take on, even if one sees this as pertaining to one's own life. Where does one begin?

For students, the most logical place to begin is with their own education — not just studying and doing schoolwork, but thinking critically about the extent to which the education they experience serves their own needs as well as the needs of other students, and taking action to address ways in which it does not. Young people have an active history of using democratic participation strategies to claim education. For example, in 1968, Chicano students in Los Angeles organized a walk-out to protest inadequate conditions in their schools, including crumbling buildings, too few Mexican-American teachers, and too little attention to Mexican Americans in the curriculum, low teacher expectations, and a vocationally oriented curriculum rather than a college-oriented curriculum. By using sit-ins and demonstrations, students were able to convince the district to make some positive changes in the education program, such as adding courses in Mexican-American studies (Rosales, 1996).

Now consider a school you are familiar with, and ask: To what extent do all of its students have access to curriculum and quality teaching to prepare them for college? This question often prompts objections to its assumption that everyone should or wants to attend college. It is true that college is not the only worthwhile post-K–12 option. But to what extent are all students prepared to make that choice themselves when they graduate from high school? Usually the choice is already made; students are prepared differently depending on what school they attend, whether they were tracked into college preparatory courses, whether they were placed in gifted programs, whether they were assigned to the strongest teachers, and whether they were offered sufficient information about college and other postgraduation options. These are issues that young people can gather information about and take action to address or to persuade others to address.

Student Dialogue 8.6

Celia: Hmm, the way these paragraphs are written, you'd think that student activism in the 1960s actually solved things! But I see the exact same problems plaguing schools in low-income and minority areas now. The Williams v.

State of California lawsuit was settled over inequitable access to basics like textbooks, functional school buildings, and certified teachers. It could have been the 1960s all over again, as far as conditions in schools went.

Lisa: We can't be complacent. Maybe your example speaks to the importance of critical consciousness! Chicano student activism in the 1960s helped up to a point, but it sounds like it was only up to a point. If you know that, then you know to keep on the lookout for past problems that recur.

Gilbert: I'm thinking about children who were displaced by the hurricanes of 2005, especially Katrina. Most of the children affected by Katrina are African American. In New Orleans, most of their schools were closed, but so many of the neighborhoods were destroyed that parents couldn't move back there anyway. What kind of education are the low-income African-American kids of displaced families getting now, especially those families who can't afford to just buy a house somewhere else, or even pay rent on a new apartment? I've read that many of them are ending up in schools that already have too few resources — sort of re-creating conditions that the Williams lawsuit was all about.

Celia: Reinforcing the need for us to be vigilant about equity in our own backyards, not to take it for granted, and to be willing to take action on behalf of equity!

Reflection 8.7 asks you to take an inventory of the extent to which students have equal access to various resources within a specific school. For this reflection, you will need to identify a school you can visit. (If you don't have access to a school to visit, use the yearbook from your high school to help you analyze its patterns.) Rather than asking whether you believe access to resources and opportunities is equal, however, we ask you to find out to what extent student participation actually reflects the racial, ethnic,

---

Reflection 8.7
Who participates most/least in the following?

College preparatory coursework

Computer labs or computer instruction

Gifted/talented class work

Instrumental music

Vocal music

Student government

After-school clubs

"Prime time" athletics

---

language, gender, and social class demographics of the school. Although students of similar backgrounds may choose to cluster together to some extent, patterns of clustering often indicate patterns of inequitable access.

The eight items in Reflection 8.7 are somewhat general in order to accommodate a variety of schools. The first three items ask about academic instruction that is likely to lead to college preparation, or to other forms of advanced academic learning later on. Items 4 and 5 examine participation in music programming. If music instruction is available, who participates in what? Instrumental music is more expensive than vocal music; does being able to purchase a music instrument affect participation? Does the kind of music offered reflect students' cultural music tastes? Items 6 and 7 get at extracurricular student activities, since school clubs and activities have potential to build cross-group friendships and provide leadership opportunities to a wide variety of students. Finally, although all schools are supposed to offer athletics equally to both sexes, there can still be various inequalities. Asking which sports are played when audiences are most likely to attend is one way to find out about equity in athletics. You can also look at who has access to the best facilities, the best coaches, or the most and best equipment.

Identifying who is over- or underrepresented does not tell you *why* this is the case. Students themselves can often give you good answers, if you are able to ask them. For example, although computers may be open to everyone, we have talked with girls who get tired of being harassed by boys who dominate the computers — these girls sometimes decide that working on computers at school isn't worth the aggravation. Students from low-income homes often assume they will not attend college because it is too expensive (and they are not told otherwise by teachers or counselors), so they do not try to get into college preparatory work. School clubs and extracurricular activities may be theoretically open to everyone, but students who rely on public transportation to get home may be unable to stay after school to participate. Often students from affluent communities dominate school government, a pattern that is simply taken for granted. On the other hand, in culturally diverse schools, clubs of one ethnic group or gender can serve as a "safe space" for students from historically marginalized groups, where they can focus on shared interests and concerns, without having to explain themselves or justify their viewpoint to others. For example, Chicano students often join Movimiento Estudiantil Chicano de Aztlán (MEChA), which is a Chicano club that supports Chicano academic learning.

Having gathered information broadly, zero in on one equity issue for further consideration. It may seem large (such as students of color being disproportionately tracked into remedial classes while White students are disproportionately tracked into college preparatory classes); or small (such as girls not having full access to some of the playground equipment), although exclusion is never small for the people who are being excluded. Reflection 8.8 involves asking more questions about the issue, as a prelude to figuring out how it can be addressed democratically. By observing or talking with people, see if you can figure out exactly who seems to be excluded, how the exclusion process works, and who is benefiting from things as they are.

This exercise has involved you in the beginnings of the kind of research that young people can learn to do to investigate issues of concern to them. Not only did the exercise involve you in gathering information about equity matters to identify where problems may exist, but it also engaged you in thinking about who might want to join you, and why, and who might oppose you and why. The more broadly you can involve various people and groups in coming up with solutions to equity issues, the more likely you are to experience success in addressing them.

Students can begin to learn democratic participation with everyday decisions in the classroom. To explore ways in which students can be involved in such decision making, for Reflection 8.9, list decisions you are aware of that directly affect the operation of a classroom on any given day.

Now, circle those decisions you have seen students help to make. Then draw a square around those decisions that students could help to make, if they were taught democratic processes for doing so.

Teaching democratic decision-making processes does not mean simply turning decisions over to students and then walking away. Rather, it means gradually sharing authority with students, offering them increased decision-making power as they learn to handle it responsibly. Class meetings, discussed in chapter 4, are a venue through which democratic decision making in a classroom can be developed. As Shor (1992) points out, "Democratic problem-posing repositions the teacher in the learning process, but the teacher does not become irrelevant or unnecessary. Her or his participation and expertise are still needed, but in a different way.... As this process evolves, the teacher's profile changes so that he or she supervises less while relating his or her knowledge more and more to student initiatives" (pp. 184–185).

To imagine how this might work, look again at the items you wrote in Reflection 8.9, particularly those you drew a square around (those decisions that you believe students could help to make). In what order might you involve students in making these decisions? In other words, rather than opening them up to students all at once, you might involve students, one decision at a time, in collaboratively determining classroom policy decisions with you. As students and teachers get the hang of it, more and more complicated decisions can be taken on.

Now let's consider what it means to engage in democratic decision making. Reflection 8.10 asks you to brainstorm as many skills as you can that citizens of a democracy might need in order to participate.

Reflection 8.10
Democratic participation skills

1.   4.

2.   5.

3.   6.

How long is your list? Often when we ask our teacher candidates to write such a list, they list voting, knowing how to read, and being informed on issues; then they quickly run out of ideas. Did your list also include skills such as these:

- Analyzing how power is actually used
- Negotiating, knowing how and when to compromise, and when not to compromise
- Persuading
- Organizing people
- Examining issues from multiple perspectives
- Writing petitions and letters
- Organizing boycotts and rallies
- Accessing media and funding for publicity

Student involvement in social action can take many forms, including writing letters, engaging in community service, and producing and distributing information about a community problem. The teacher must investigate the suitability of various forms of action in the local community. In addition, the teacher must be careful not to pressure students into doing or saying anything that is contrary to their beliefs. Rather, the teacher should show students how they can act constructively on issues and needs that exist within the community.

There is more to learning to engage in democratic decision making than just learning to vote. Democratic decision making is complicated because it requires unpacking differences of opinion for discussion. Participation means learning to listen to other points of view including those one might have been taught "don't count." Decision making also means learning to negotiate rather than simply acquiescing to or dictating majority rule. People who actually make decisions for the public know how to use skills such as those above. Leaders in powerful organizations use them quite effectively. Ordinary people, however, usually do not learn how to use them, although most communities have community activists equipped with those skills.

In chapter 4, we discussed conflict resolution as a way of involving students in problem solving. By itself, conflict resolution is not necessarily the same as social action, but when it is combined with critical consciousness it can lead to social action. Let us give an example. A school experiences student fighting and implements a conflict resolution program. In that program, students are taught to express their feelings using "I" statements, to actively listen to feelings that other students express, and to cooperatively develop solutions for conflicts in which no student loses. Peer mediators may be trained to assist in this process.

When we examine them more deeply, we find that many of the conflicts erupting within the school stem from community conflicts or issues related to powerlessness in the community. For example, students who lack access to after-school or summer jobs and meaningful recreational opportunities often "hang out" on the streets and become involved in gang activities. Going beyond conflict resolution may mean examining issues in the community that affect students' lives and figuring out how to do something constructive to meet students' needs. If recreation activities are lacking, students can organize to get the city to provide more recreation opportunities. One of our former colleagues spent years organizing urban gang youth to produce murals articulating their concerns publicly. In doing so, she helped students work through conflicts they had with each other, learn to identify the larger social origins of their frustrations and conflicts, and learn to collaborate to voice their needs and concerns to larger audiences. She was able to channel the energy of conflict into social advocacy and action.

History teaches us that, when people organize and coalesce with other existing advocacy groups, they can make a significant difference. However, to do so successfully requires the ability to identify manageable aspects of social problems, which takes practice and commitment. Consider, for example the United Farm Workers, who collectively pressed for and in many cases achieved better working conditions and wages. Consider disability rights organizations that pressed for access to public transportation and buildings. Or, consider community action groups such as renters' organizations, which have won rent controls so that people will not be forced out of their homes. We should remember Dewey's question: "Why should the public and its officers, even if the latter are termed statesmen, be wiser and more effective?" (1927/1973, p. 633). He went on to argue that what is needed to have a democracy "is freedom of social inquiry and [the] distribution of its conclusion" (p. 634).

If we are to participate democratically, we need to recognize that we have the most power when we work with others. Very few people change the world alone. There are many youth organizations that already exist, and students can learn about them and join. Some are small and local, others are large and national. Some have their own websites and newsletters, making them accessible to a wide potential membership. For example, the Youth in Action Network (http://www.teaching.com/act) features an online venue for young people to learn more about and discuss issues such as energy, indigenous rights, education, or forests, and take action. The Youth Empowerment Center (http://www.youthec.org/index2.html) is a California-based organization that involves young activists and artists in political action to address community needs.

For Reflection 8.11, identify a youth organization that involves young people in political action. It can be either a local community organization, or one you find on the Internet. To locate such an organization on the Internet, search using a descriptor such as "youth activism." Find out as much as you can about the organization. Questions in Reflection 8.11 will help you get started.

Reflection 8.11
Youth activist organization

What is the purpose of the organization?

Who sponsors the organization?

What kinds of issues does it work on?

How are children and youth involved?

A junior high social studies teacher built into his curriculum opportunities for student decision making and student exercise of power, in order to enable his working-class and racially diverse students to practice having an effect on an institution. After teaching students about various forms of government, he had the class select a form to use to govern the class (the usual selection being representative democracy). Under his guidance, the class then practiced that form for a period of time. He provided opportunities for them to select topics to research in small groups and to plan their research strategies, guiding their thinking so that their decisions were usually workable. When their decisions were not workable, he helped them understand why, and what might work better next time. He also had the class run schoolwide elections: students organized balloting, made campaign posters, planned campaign strategies, and so forth.

A middle school teacher worked with one of her classes to investigate relationships among people in the school. Concerned that students expected unequal treatment and name calling

within the peer group, she wanted to bring this problem into the open. So, she worked with
students in one of her classes to investigate how students treat (and mistreat) each other,
and to generate solutions. The students designed and administered a survey, analyzed data,
and proposed solutions to the problem, which the teacher then brought to the faculty. She
believed that only by becoming involved in identifying a problem, studying it, debating it,
and proposing solutions to it, would students learn to use democratic processes.

Now take one of the classroom decisions you listed in Reflection 8.9 that students
could help to make. Reflection 8.12 asks you to sketch a process you could use to teach
students some of the collective decision-making skills discussed above, so they would be
able to participate productively in making that decision.

Discuss your ideas with classmates. How can you make the plan above as "workable"
as possible?

Student Dialogue 8.7

Gilbert: Well, you two, how do you take what this chapter says about "Taking Action"
and apply it to closing the achievement gap?

Lisa: I think that teachers, parents, and students need to be more active in questioning the purpose of tests, how they are constructed, and why and how tests
are being sold to the general public. I mean, we should know who benefits
from all of the money that will be made from test production and scoring.

Celia: Good point. I want to know who is writing the test items, and what criteria
they are using to be fair to the many different groups of students who are
required to take the tests. In order to gather this information, people need
to develop strategies, including collaborating with one another. I also want
to know why tests are being used to rank-order schools and students. That
makes it impossible to strive for everyone's success.

Gilbert: Do I hear you saying that you plan to have your class boycott the tests?

Celia: Not necessarily, but to take Dewey's idea, the general public needs to know,
especially teachers. By knowing, we can better help our students, and we can
stand up together for what is right or against what is wrong.

It is important to clarify that democracy does not mean that students agree with us, or with the teacher, or with anyone else in particular. What we are advocating is that students investigate their world, and the belief systems about that world, for themselves, then come to their own conclusions. The main question is how things should operate in ways that maximize fairness to everyone, given than none of us lives in isolation from everyone else.

Putting It Into Practice

by Keffrelyn Brown , University Wisconsin–Madison

We have asked you to consider the importance of teaching students the skills necessary to live and participate within a multicultural, democratic society. The ultimate goal of this type of work is to help students envision new alternatives for the future, including life inside and outside of the school environment. See if, like Lisa, you are up for the challenge!

While student teaching seventh-grade literature, Lisa decided to write a unit focused on genre studies. Lisa loved to read fantasy literature as an adolescent, and thought that it might be fun to expose the students to a genre that is considered both creative and capable of helping students imagine a world different from the one in which they currently live. Before writing the unit, Lisa examined the content standards and realized that students in seventh grade were expected to read several texts that would fall in the fantasy genre. Lisa's cooperating teacher thought this was a wonderful idea because the school district designated literacy as one of the focus areas for the academic year, and was offering numerous professional development opportunities for teachers and student teachers.

Lisa's cooperating teacher suggested that Lisa attend a district-wide literacy workshop. Here, the workshop leader discussed the merits of helping students develop their literacy skills through the examination of genre elements. Like Lisa, the workshop leader enjoyed fantasy and passed along the following unit plan he had used in his own classroom the previous year:

Unit focus: Exploring the genre of fantasy (genre studies)

State/National Standards — Taken from Didax, which integrates the International Reading Association/National Council for Teachers of English (IRA/NCTE) standards for the English Language Arts.
1. Students read a wide range of literature from many periods in many genres to build an understanding of the many dimensions (e.g., philosophical, ethical, aesthetic) of human experience.
2. Students apply a wide range of strategies to comprehend, interpret, evaluate, and appreciate texts.

Objectives:
1. Students will read and comprehend a variety of texts.
2. Students will compare and contrast literature from various genres.
3. Students will identify the components generally found in fantasy literature.

Suggested Procedures:
1. Begin by sharing the unit objectives with the students, then orally review elements of a story, including setting, plot, character development, and theme.
2. Tell students that they will be responsible for thinking about what makes stories similar and different. Show two different books drawn from two different literary genres (e.g., nonfiction and realistic fiction; or biography and science fiction). If needed, read a summary of each book for the students.
3. Then ask students to think about how the books are similar or different. Possible questions: Do you think the books focus on the same topic? What evidence did you use to come up with your decision? Do you think the stories are told in the same manner? What evidence did you use to come up with your decision? The point of this exercise is to get students thinking about the similarities and differences between stories that are written in various genres, as well as the information used to help make these distinctions.
4. Ask students if they are familiar with the word *genre*, which is a category of literature. Most students will probably have some familiarity with the term. Ask for examples of different genres. Make a list of these genres. (Some examples might be: historical fiction, realistic fiction, poetry, ballads, sonnets, science fiction, fantasy, folk tales, fairy tales, tall tales, myths, legends, biography, autobiography, etc.)
5. Tell students that they will be examining a specific genre — fantasy; and that rather than the teacher simply telling the students what elements make up the genre of fantasy, the students will come up with an initial list in groups.
6. Divide students into partner groups. Each group will have three children's books to read. One book will meet the literary elements found within the fantasy genre, another will meet the literary elements of realistic fiction, and the last book will meet the literary elements of folktales. (Students will read children's books because they are shorter and easier to read within a classroom setting than a chapter book. Chapter excerpts may not offer enough of a context to fully understand the element of fantasy writing.)
7. The groups will decide how they will read each book and fill out a genre study worksheet, provided by the teacher, which asks guiding questions about setting, plot, characters, perspective, and other questions that will require the students to think about the differences found in the different genre categories (e.g., Are human characters allowed to do things that nonhuman characters cannot do in "real" life?). Each group will have about five minutes to decide.
8. When finished, the groups will propose a list of four to six bulleted elements found in fantasy literature. Each group will share their list of elements found in fantasy literature with the class, and together the class will compose a master list.

Initially, Lisa believed this unit was just what she was looking for. She liked how it encouraged students to construct their own understanding of fantasy literature first, before the teacher tells them what the genre of fantasy was supposed to include. She also liked that the students were expected to work in groups together, rather than independently.

Since Lisa was not as familiar with children's books as she was with chapter books, she did an Internet search for specific titles she might use. She also sought suggestions from the librarian at the local library, as well as booksellers at the large chain bookstore in her neighborhood. Lisa wanted to make sure she selected books that considered a variety of cultural and ethnic backgrounds, but was disappointed when she realized the difficulty in finding stories in each genre that reflected people and cultures from diverse contexts. Some of the books were excellent, but others were not. Lisa wondered if she might use the uneven quality of books she was finding as a teaching tool.

If you were Lisa, how would you rework the unit to incorporate the two building blocks from chapter 8? In particular, how would you do the following?

1. Help students develop critical consciousness about images in children's books?
2. Help students practice critical thinking?
3. Involve students in democratic participation throughout the unit?
4. Involve students in taking action on an issue?

Here is what Lisa did. She wanted to keep the original unit plan, but decided to extend it to incorporate the building blocks from chapter 8. Although the original plan involved students in making decisions within their groups about how they would work, their direct involvement ended as soon as they proposed a list of characteristics of genres. Lisa wanted students to be able to analyze and speak to limitations in the books themselves. To extend the unit to do that, she made sure that she was also addressing some additional standards. The revised unit is longer, but it also is linked with more standards in order not to take time away from standards students will be held accountable for.

Revised Plan

State/National Standards (Taken from Didax, which integrates the International Reading Association/National Council for Teachers of English (IRA/NCTE) standards for the English Language Arts)

1. Students read a wide range of literature from many periods in many genres to build an understanding of the many dimensions (e.g., philosophical, ethical, aesthetic) of human experience.
2. Students apply a wide range of strategies to comprehend, interpret, evaluate, and appreciate texts.
3. Students adjust their use of spoken written and visual language (e.g., conventions, style, vocabulary) to communicate effectively with a variety of audiences and for different purposes.
4. Students conduct research by generating ideas and questions, and by posing problems. They gather, evaluate, and synthesize data from a variety of sources to communicate their discoveries in ways that suit their purpose and audience.
5. Students use a variety of technological and informational resources together to synthesize information and to create and communicate knowledge.

Objectives:
1. Students will read and comprehend a variety of texts.
2. Students will compare and contrast literature from various genres.
3. Students will identify the components generally found in fantasy literature.
4. Students will analyze the themes and character representations found in selected fantasy literature housed in local school and neighborhood libraries and retail bookstores.
5. Students will write their research findings in informative reports and persuasive letters to book publishers, libraries, and retail bookstores.

Suggested Procedures:
(Steps 1–8 are the same as the earlier lesson unit, and are not repeated here.)

9. Involve students in a process of finding out what kind of children's fantasy literature is to be found in local libraries, local elementary schools, and local retail stores. This might include a field trip; students might also decide to each investigate one venue and then compile their findings.

10. Working in groups, have students examine a variety of fantasy texts, using a data recording instrument devised with the entire class that helps to identify representation according to race, gender, and other social markers. The instrument should attend to: illustrations, the roles and relationships of characters, story line, and the portrayal of heroes and heroines. Each group will be responsible for keeping accurate and full data on the books used for the project.

11. With students, organize a process for finding out some background on the genre of fantasy, including the origins of the genre, its popularity with publishing houses, and its uses in K–12 settings. Encourage students to explore why the patterns they found in their analysis continue to appear. Students might consider the effects media has on the production of fantasy literature, particularly within the large media corporations that simultaneously own publishing houses, movie production companies, and large, retail chain bookstores.

12. After all of the data have been collected, each group will analyze its findings, and write up a report that explains their findings.

13. Students will locate several key institutions, organizations, or businesses in which to distribute the findings from their research. Students will draft and distribute informational reports to each of the selected locations.

References

Abrams, L. M., Pedulla, J. J., & Madaus, G. F. (2003). Views from the classroom: Teachers' opinion of state-wide testing programs. *Theory into Practice, 42*(1), 1–20.

Acuña, R. (2003). *Occupied America: The Chicano's struggle toward liberation* (5th ed.). New York: Longman. (Original work published 1972)

Aiello, B. (1979). Hey, what's it like to be handicapped? Practical ideas for regular class students and their teachers. *Education Unlimited, 1*(2), 28–31.

Albert, M. (1997). What makes alternative media alternative. *Z Magazine, 10*(10), 52–55.

Alder, N. (2002). Interpretations of the meaning of care: Creating caring relationships in urban middle school classrooms. *Urban Education, 37*(2), 241–266.

American Educational Research Association (AERA). (2000, July). AERA position statement concerning high-stakes testing in preK-12 education. Retrieved July 1, 2002 from http://www.aera.net.

Amrein, A. L., & Berliner, D. C. (2002). High-stakes testing, uncertainty, and student learning. *Education Policy Analysis Archives, 10*(18). Retrieved January 15, 2003, from http://epaa.asu.edu/epaa/v10n18/

Apple, M. W. (1982). *Education and power.* Boston: Routledge & Kegan Paul.

Archbald, D. (1997). Curriculum control policies and curriculum standardization: Teachers' reports of policy effects. *International Journal of Educational Reform, 6*(2), 155–173.

Asimov, N. (2005, July 15). Latino and black kids narrow the test gap: Educational survey shows higher scores in reading, math. *San Francisco Chronicle.* Retrieved July 27, 2005, from http:// www.sfgate.com/cgi-bin/article.cgi?f=/c/a/2005/07/15/MNGE3DOH3L1.DTL&hw=achievement&sn=008&sc=545

Bagdikian, B. H. (2004). *The new media monopoly.* Boston: Beacon Press.

Baker, C. (2001). *Foundations of bilingual education and bilingualism.* Clevedon, UK: Multilingual Matters.

Baldwin, C. (2001). The development of rhetorical privilege in the news reporting of violent crime. *Race, Gender & Class, 8*(4), 8–19.

Banks, J. (1975). *Teaching strategies for ethnic studies.* Boston: Allyn & Bacon.

Banks, J. A. (1989). Integrating curriculum with ethnic content: Approaches and guidelines. In J. A. Banks & C. A. M. Banks (Eds.), *Multicultural education: Issues and perspectives* (pp. 189–209). Boston: Allyn & Bacon.

Banks, J. A. (1993). The canon debate, knowledge construction, and multicultural education. *Educational Researcher, 22*(5), 4–14.

Banks, J. A. (1995). Multicultural education: Its effects on students' racial and gender role attitudes. In J. A. Banks & C. M. Banks (Eds.), *Handbook of research on multicultural education* (pp. 617–627). New York: Macmillan.

Baron, R. M., Tom, D. Y. H., & Cooper, H. M. (1985). Social class, race and teacher expectations. In J. B. Dusek (Ed.), *Teacher expectancies* (pp. 251–269). Hillsdale, NJ: Erlbaum.

Barrett, J. (1984). *Culture and conduct: An excursion in anthropology.* Belmont, CA: Wadsworth.

Barton, J., & Collins, A. (Eds.). (1972). Starting out: Designing your portfolio. In *Portfolio assessment: A handbook for educators.* Menlo Park, CA: Addison-Wesley.

Batchelor, K., Beel, E. R., & Freeman, A. (2006). *Community based assessment: A guide for HIV prevention workers.* Retrieved May 20, 2006, from http://www8.utsouthwestern.edu/vgn/images/portal/cit_56417/20/1/205382Community_Based_Assessment_Guide.pdf

Bell, L. I. (2002–2003, December/January). Strategies that close the gap. *Educational Leadership, 60*(4), 32–34.

Berger, R. (2001). *An ethic of excellence.* Portsmouth, NH: Heinemann.

Beyer, L. E., & Liston, D. P. (1996). *Curriculum in conflict.* New York: Teachers College Press.

Bigelow, B. (2002). The lives behind the labels. In B. Bigelow & B. Peterson (Eds.), *Rethinking globalization* (pp. 128–132). Milwaukee, WI: Rethinking Schools.

Bigelow, B., & Peterson, B. Eds. (2002). *Rethinking globalization.* Milwaukee, WI: Rethinking Schools.

Black, J. (2002). Tips for conducting "in person" (face-to-face) interviews. Retrieved July 15, 2006, from http://talewins.com/interviews.htm

Bowen, C. W. (2000). A quantitative literature review of cooperative learning effects on high school and college chemistry achievement. *Journal of Chemical Education 77*(1), 116–119.

Boyd, D., Hamilton, L., Loeb, S., & Wyckoff, J. (2004). The preparation and recruitment of teachers: A labor-market framework. In F. M. Hess, A. J. Rotherham, & K. Walsh (Eds.), *A qualified teacher in every classroom? Appraising old answers and new ideas* (pp.149–172). Cambridge, MA: Harvard University Press.

Bread for the World (2002). *Hunger basics.* Retrieved June 18, 2002, from http://www.bread.org/hunger-basics/domestic.html

Bressler, L., DeStefano, L., Feldman, R., & Garg, S. (2000). Artists-in-residence in public schools: Issues in curriculum, integration, impact. *Visual Arts Research, 26*(1), 13–29.

Brophy, J., & VanSledright, B. (1997). *Teaching and learning history in elementary schools.* New York: Teachers College Press.

Buce, J., & Obolensky, N. (1990). Runaway and homeless youth. In M. J. Bradley & N. Obolensky (Eds.), *Planning to live: Evaluating and treating suicidal teens in community settings* (pp. 25–33). Tulsa: University of Oklahoma Press.

Burt, M. R., Aron, L. Y., Douglas, T., Valente, J., Lee, E., & Iwen, B. (1999). *Homelessness: Programs and the people they serve.* Washington, D.C.: U.S. Department of Housing and Human Services.

Business Roundtable. (1997). *A business leader's guide to setting academic standards.* Retrieved July 7, 2004, from http://www.brtable.org/TaskForces/TaskForce/

Butterfield, R., Demos, E. S., Grant, G., Moy, P. S., & Perez, A. L. (1979). A multicultural analysis of a popular basal reading series in the international year of the child. *Journal of Negro Education, 48*(3), 382–389.

California State Board of Education. (2000). *History-social science content standards for California public schools kindergarten through grade twelve.* Sacramento: California State Board of Education.

Campbell, J. R., Hombo, C. M., & Mazzeo, J. (2000). *NAEP 1999 Trends in academic progress: Three decades of student performance.* Washington D.C.: U.S. Department of Education.

Carrasquillo, A. L., & Rodriguez, V. (2002). *Language minority students in the mainstream classroom* (2nd ed.). Clevedon, UK: Multilingual Matters.

Cavanagh, S., & Robelen E. (2004, December 7). U.S. Students fare poorly in international math comparison. *Education Week,* V.4

Cavazos, L. F. (2002). Emphasizing performance goals and high-quality education for all students. *Phi Delta Kappan, 83*(9), 690–697.

Christensen, L. (2002). Teach the kind of skills they will need to overcome injustice themselves. *Rethinking Schools Online, 17*(1). Retrieved November 20, 2003, from http://www.rethinkingschools.org/archive/17_01/Advi171.shtml

Cirillo, K. J., Pruitt, B. E., Colwell, B., Kingery, P. M., Hurley, R. S., & Ballard, D. (1998). School violence: Prevalence and intervention strategies for at-risk adolescents. *Adolescence, 33*(130), 319–330.

Clinton, W. J. (1997). *Democratic caucus: State of the Union address.* Retrieved July 10, 2006, from http://www.dems.gov/index.asp?Type=B_BASIC&sec=%B4E5

Codjoe, H. M. (2001). Fighting a "public enemy" of Black academic achievement — The persistence of racism and the schooling experiences of Black students in Canada. *Race Ethnicity and Education, 4*(4), 343–375.

Cohen, E., & Lotan, R. (Eds.). (1997). *Working for equity in heterogeneous classrooms.* New York: Teachers College Press.

Computer software industry turns focus to girls. (1997, November 3). *Monterey County Herald*, p. A4.

Conrad, D. R. (1994). Educating with community murals. *Multicultural Education, 2*(1), 7–9.

Cooper, H., & Moore, C. J. (1995). Teenage motherhood, mother-only households, and teacher expectations. *Journal of Experimental Education, 63*(3), 231–248.

Corcoran, T. B., Walker, L. J., & White, J. L. (1988). *Working in urban schools.* Washington, D.C.: Institute for Educational Leadership.

Cruz, B. C., & Walker, P. C. (2001). Fostering positive ethnic relations between African American and Latino children: A collaborative urban program using art and history. *Multicultural Perspectives, 3*(1), 9–14.

Cuban, L. (1994). *How teachers taught* (2nd ed.). New York: Longman.

Cummins, J. (1996). *Negotiating identities: Education for empowerment in a diverse society.* Ontario, CA: California Association for Bilingual Education.

Cummins, J. (2000). *Language, power and pedagogy.* Clevedon, UK: Multilingual Matters.

D'Ambra, S. (2004). From conflict to a sustainable dialogue and peace. *International Journal of Curriculum and Instruction, 6*(1), 113–121.

Darling-Hammond, L., Wise, A. E., & Klein, S. P. (1997). *A license to teach: Building a profession for the 21st-century schooling.* Boulder, CO: Westview.

Dei, G. J. S. (1996). *Anti-racism education.* Halifax, Nova Scotia: Fernwood.

Delpit, L. (1995). *Other people's children.* New York: New Press.

Delpit, L. (1997). Ebonics and culturally responsive instruction. *Rethinking Schools Online.* Retrieved September 20, 2006 from http://www.rethinkingschools.org/archive/12_01/ebdelpit.shtml

Derman-Sparks, L. (1989). *Anti-bias curriculum: Tools for empowering young children.* Washington, D.C.: National Association for the Education of Young Children.

Dewey, J. (1973). The public and its problems. In J. J. McDermott (Ed.), *The philosophy of John Dewey.* Chicago: University of Chicago Press. (Original work published 1927)

Drake, J. A., Price, J. H., & Telljohann, S. K. (2003). The nature and extent of bullying in school. *Journal of School Health, 73*(5), 173–180.

Driscoll, M. J., & Bryant, D. (Eds.). (1998). *Learning about assessment, learning through assessment.* Washington, D.C.: National Academy Press.

Duck, L. (1981). *Teaching with charisma.* Boston: Allyn & Bacon.

Duffy, J. A. (1998, October 21). Poll says Americans satisfied. *Monterey County Herald*, p. A5.

Earthman, G. I., & Lemaster, L. (1996). *Review of research on the relationship between school buildings, student achievement, and student behavior* (Report No. EF005023). Scottsdale, AZ: Council of Educational Facility Planners, International (ERIC No. ED 416 666).

Eck, D. (2001). *A new religious America.* San Francisco: HarperCollins.

Eckholm, Erick (March 20, 2006). Plight deepens for black men, studies warn. *New York Times*, p. 2.

Economic Policy Institute. (2000). *Income inequalities among families in the United States has increased since the 1970's.* Washington, D.C.: Center on Budget and Policy Priorities.

Eisler, R. (2000). *Tomorrow's children.* Boulder, CO: Westview.

Elementary Education Student Teaching Program. (2005). *Student teaching handbook.* Madison, WI: University Wisconsin–Madison.

Fantini, M. D. (1986). *Regaining excellence in education.* Columbus, OH: Merrill.

Farrell, E. F. (2005). Among freshmen, a growing digital divide. *Chronicle of Higher Education, 51*(22), A32.

Feshbach, N. D. (1975). Empathy in children: Some theoretical and empirical considerations. *Counseling Psychologist, 5*, 25–30.

Feshbach, N. D., & Feshbach, S. (1987). Affective processes and academic achievement. *Child Development, 58,* 1335–1347.

Finzi, R., Ram, A., Har-Even, D., Shnit, D., & Weizman, A. (2001). Attachment styles and aggression in physically abused and neglected children. *Journal of Youth and Adolescence, 30*(6), 769–786.

Freire, P. (1973). *Education for critical consciousness.* New York: Seabury Press.

Freire, P. (1998). *Teachers as cultural workers.* Boulder, CO: Westview Press.

Fuller, M. L. (2001). Multicultural concerns and classroom management. In C. A. Grant & M. L. Gomez (Eds.), *Campus and classroom: Making school multicultural* (2nd ed., pp. 109–133). Upper Saddle River, NJ: Merrill Prentice-Hall.

Fuller, M. L., & Olsen G. (1998). *Home-school relations: Working successfully with parents and families.* Boston: Allyn & Bacon.

Gagne, R. M. (1985). *Condition of learning* (4th ed.). New York: Holt, Rinehart & Winston.

Gallas, K. (1998). *Sometimes I can be anything.* New York: Teachers College Press.

Gallimore, R., & Tharp, R. (1990). Teaching mind in society: Teaching, schooling, and literate discourse. In L. C. Moll (Ed.), *Vygotsky and education* (pp. 175–205). New York: Cambridge University Press.

Garcia, E. (1999). *Student cultural diversity* (2nd ed.). Boston: Houghton Mifflin.

Gardner, H. (1995). Reflections on multiple intelligences. *Phi Delta Kappan, 77*(3), 200–203, 206–209.

Gardner, H. (2000). *Intelligence reframed: Multiple intelligences for the 21st century.* New York: Basic Books.

Garforth, F. W. (1964). *John Locke: Some thoughts concerning education.* Woodbury, NY: Barron's Educational Series.

Gathercoal, F. (1993). *Judicious discipline* (3rd ed.). San Francisco: Caddo Gap Press.

Gay, G. (2000). *Culturally responsive teaching: Theory, research, and practice.* New York: Teachers College Press.

Gayle-Evans, G. (2004). *An annotated bibliography of multi-cultural literature and related activities for children three to ten years.* Lewiston, NY: Edwin Mellen.

Giddens, A. (1984). *The constitution of society: Outline of the theory of structuration.* Berkeley: University of California Press.

Gifford-Smith, M. E., & Brownell, C. A. (2003). Childhood peer relationships: Social acceptance, friendships, and peer networks. *Journal of School Psychology, 41,* 235–284.

Gillies, R. M., & Ashman, A. F. (2000). The effects of cooperative learning on students with learning difficulties in the lower elementary school. *Journal of Special Education, 34*(1), 19–27.

Girard, K., & Koch, S. (1996). *Conflict resolution in the schools: A manual for educators.* San Francisco: Jossey-Bass.

Giroux, H. (1981). *Ideology, culture, and process of schooling.* Lewes, UK: Falmer Press.

Giroux, H. A. (2000). *Stealing innocence.* New York: St. Martin's Press.

Gonzalez, N., Moll, L., & Amanti, C. (Eds.) (2005). *Funds of knowledge.* Mahwah, NJ: Erlbaum.

Goodenough, W. H. (1976). Multiculturalism as the normal human experience. *Anthropology & Education Quarterly, 7*(4), 4–7.

Gordon, B. (1997). Cultural knowledge. In C. A. Grant & G. Ladson-Billings (Eds.), *Dictionary of multicultural education* (pp 57–59). Phoenix, AZ: Oryx.

Gorski, P. (2005). *Multicultural education and the internet* (2nd ed.). Boston: McGraw-Hill.

Gorski, P., & Clark, C. (2002). Multicultural education and the digital divide: Focus on the disability. *Multicultural Perspectives, 4*(4), 28–36

Gough, P. (1991). Tapping parent power. *Phi Delta Kappan, 72*(5), 339.

Grant, C. A. & Brown, A. L. (2006). Listening to African American males' conceptions of high stakes tests. In V. Pang (Ed.), *Multicultural education: principles and practices* (103–126). Westport, CT: Praeger.

Grant, C. A., & Sleeter, C. E. (1996). *After the school bell rings* (2nd ed.). New York: Falmer Press.

Grant, C. A., & Sleeter, C. E. (2007). *Turning on learning* (4th ed.). New York: Wiley.

Graue, E., Walsh, D. J., & Ceglowski, D. (1998). *Studying children in context: Theories, methods, and ethics.* Thousand Oaks, CA: Sage.

Grinde, D. A., Jr., & Johansen, B. E. (1991). *Exemplar of liberty: Native America and the evolution of democracy.* Los Angeles: UCLA American Indian Studies Center.

Haberman, M. (1995). *Star teachers of children in poverty.* West LaFayette, IN: Kappa Delta Pi.

Habitat for Humanity. (2005). *Affordable housing statistics.* Retrieved December 13, 2005, from http://www.habitat.org/how/stats.aspx

Hall, E. (1977). *Beyond culture.* Garden City, NY: Anchor Books.

Hall, S. (1995). The whites of their eyes: Racist ideologies and the media. In G. Dines & J. M. Humez (Eds.), *Gender, race and class in media* (pp. 18–22). Thousand Oaks, CA: Sage.

Hamer, J. F., & Blanc, M. (1989). *Bilinguality and bilingualism*. New York: Cambridge University Press.

Hanna, G. (1983). *Rigorous proof in mathematics education*. The Ontario Institute for Studies in Education. Curriculum Series/48. Toronto, Canada: OISE Press.

Hauser-Cram, P., Sirin, S. R., & Stipek, D. (2003). When teachers' and parents' values differ: Teachers' ratings of academic competence in children from low-income families. *Journal of Educational Psychology, 95*(4), 813–820.

Haycock, K. (2001, March). Closing the achievement gap. *Educational Leadership 58*(6), 6–11.

Headley, J., & Lowe, E. (2000). *Mayors' 16th annual survey on "Hunger and homelessness in America's cities" finds increased levels of hunger, increased capacity to meet demand.* Retrieved June 3, 2005, from http://www.usmayors.org/uscm/news/pree_releases/documents/hunger_release.htm

Helbig, A., & Perkins, A. (1994). *This land is our land: A guide to multicultural literature for children and young adults.* Westport, CT: Greenwood Press.

Henning-Stout, M., James, S., & MacIntosh, S. (2000). Reducing harassment of lesbian, gay, bisexual, transgender, and questioning youth in schools. *School Psychology Review, 29*(2), 180–191.

Herr, N. (2001). *The sourcebook for teaching science.* Retrieved November 20, 2005, from http://www.csun.edu/~vceed002/health/docs/tv&health.html

Howard, J., Rhodes, T., Fitch, C., & Stimson, G. V. (1998). *The rapid assessment and response guide on psychoactive substance use and especially vulnerable young people (EVYP-RAR).* Geneva: World Health Organization. Unpublished manuscript.

Hufstedler, S. M. (2002). The once and future K–12. *Phi Delta Kappan, 83*(9), 684–689.

Igoa, C. (1995). *The inner world of the immigrant child.* New York: St. Martin's Press.

Infoplease. (2006). *Homeownership rates by race and ethnicity of householder.* Pearson Education, Inc. Retrieved April 5, 2006, from http://www.infoplease.com

Ingersoll, R. (January 2001). A different approach to solving teacher shortage problem. In *Teaching Quality Policy Briefs.* Seattle, WA: Center for the Study of Teaching and Policy.

Ingersoll, R. M., & Smith, T. M. (2003). The wrong solution to the teacher shortage. *Educational Leadership, 60*(8), 30–33.

Institute for Education in Transformation. (1992). *Voices from the inside.* Claremont, CA: The Claremont Graduate School.

Irvine, J. J. (2003). *Educating for diversity: Seeing with a cultural eye.* New York: Teachers College Press.

Irvine, J. J., & York, D. E. (1993). Teacher perspectives: Why do African American, Hispanic, and Vietnamese students fail? In S. E. Rothstein (Ed.), *Handbook of schooling in urban America* (pp. 161–173). Westport, CT: Greenwood Press.

Jaffe, N. (2001). *Patakin: World tales of drums and drummers.* Peru, IL: Cricket Books.

Johnson, B. (1996). *Performance assessment handbook: Performance and exhibitions.* Princeton, NJ: Eye on Education.

Johnson, D., & Johnson, B. (2002). *High stakes: Children, testing and failure in American schools.* Lanham, MD: Rowman & Littlefield.

Johnson, D. W., & Johnson, R. T. (1999). *Learning together and alone: Cooperative, competitive, and individualistic learning* (5th ed.). Boston: Allyn & Bacon.

Johnson, D. W., Johnson, R., & Maruyama, G. (1983). Interdependence and interpersonal attraction among heterogeneous and homogeneous individuals: A theoretical formulation and meta-analysis of the research. *Review of Educational Research, 53,* 51–54.

Johnson, K., & Kiely, K. (2002, June 27). Pledge decision may be reversed. *USA Today.* Retrieved July 28, 2002, from http://www.usatoday.com/news/nation/2002/06/27/pledge-hold.htm

Jones, E. (1990). *Interpersonal perception.* New York. W. H. Freeman.

Jordan, C. (1985). Translating culture: From ethnographic information to educational program. *Anthropology & Education Quarterly, 16,* 105–123.

Juvonen, J. (2001). School violence: Prevalence, fears, and prevention. *Rand.* Retrieved August 16, 2005, from http://www.rand.org/publications/IP/IP219/

Kane, M. B. (1970). *The treatment of minorities in secondary school textbooks.* Chicago: Quadrangle Books and the Anti-Defamation League of B'nai Brith.

Karp, S. (2003). "Let them eat tests." *Rethinking Schools, 16*(4), 1–3.

Kennickell, A. B. (2003, November). *A rolling tide: Changes in the distribution of wealth in the U.S., 1989–2001.* Annandale-on-Hudson, NY: Levy Economics Institute.

Kleinfeld, J. (1975). Effective teachers of Eskimo and Indian students. *School Review, 83,* 301–344.

Kliebard, H. M. (1982). Education at the turn of the century: A crucible for curriculum change. *Educational Researcher, 11,* 16–24.

Klineberg, O. (1963, February). Life is fun in a smiling fair-skinned world. *The Saturday Review,* 75–77.

Kozol, J. (2005). The shame of the nation: The restoration of apartheid schooling in America. *Rethinking Schools, 20*(1) 22–30.

Kravetz, N. (1983). The United States of America: The languages of education: New ethnicity and the drive to power. In R. M. Thomas (Ed.), *Politics and education: Cases from eleven nations.* Oxford, UK: Pergamon Press.

Kronowitz, E. L. (1999). *Your first year of teaching and beyond* (3rd ed.). New York: Longman.

Krucks, G. (1991). Gay and lesbian homeless youth. *Journal of Adolescent Health, 12*(7), 515–518.

Kumashiro, K. K. (2004). *Against commonsense.* New York: RoutledgeFalmer.

Labov, W. (1969). The logic of non-standard English. *Monograph Series on Languages and Linguistics,* 22. Washington, D.C.: Georgetown University School of Languages and Linguistics.

Lee, E., Menkart, D., & Okazawa-Rey, M. (Eds.). (1998). *Beyond heroes and holidays: A practical guide to K–12 anti-racist, multicultural education and staff development.* Washington, D.C.: Network of Educators on the Americas.

Lei, J. (1997). Cultural capital. In C. A. Grant & G. Ladson-Billings (Eds.), *Dictionary of multicultural education* (pp 55–56). Phoenix, AZ: Oryx.

Lemlech, J. K. (1991). *Classroom management: Methods and techniques for elementary and secondary teachers.* Waveland, IL.: Waveland Press.

Leondar-Wright, B. (2004). "Executive excess" report. *United for a fair economy.* Retrieved December 13, 2005, from http://www.faireconomy.org/press/2004/EE2004_pr.html

Lewis, A. (2000). *Figuring it out: Standards-based reforms in urban middle grades.* New York: McConnell Clark Foundation.

Lewis, A. E. (2003). *Race in the schoolyard.* New Brunswick, NJ: Rutgers University Press.

Lezotte, L. (2003). *Effective schools.* Retrieved November 15, 2003, from http://www.effectiveschools.org

Linn, R. L. (1990). Essentials of student assessment: From accountability to instructional aid. *Teachers College Record, 91*(3), 422–436.

Linton, S. (1998). *Claiming disability.* New York: New York University Press.

Lucas, L. (1992). Does ability grouping do more harm than good? Don't ignore the potential of talented students. *On Campus, 11*(6), 6.

Lucas, S. R. (1999). *Tracking inequality.* New York: Teachers College Press.

Luke, A. (1998). Getting over method: Literacy teaching as work in "new times." *Language Arts, 75*(4), 305–313.

Madhere, S. (1991). Self-esteem of African American adolescents: Theoretical and practical considerations. *Journal of Negro Education, 60*(1), 47–61.

Marx, S., & Pennington, J. (2003). Pedagogies of critical race theory: Experimentations with European-American pre-service teachers. *Qualitative Studies in Education, 16*(1), 91–110.

McCombs, B. L. (2003). A framework for the redesign of K–12 education in the context of current educational reform. *Theory into Practice, 42*(2), 93–101.

McIntyre, A. (2000). *Inner-city kids.* New York: New York University Press.

Meier, D. (2002). *In schools we trust.* Boston: Beacon Press.

Michigan Department of Public Instruction. (1963). *The treatment of minority groups in textbooks.* Lansing: Michigan Department of Public Instruction.

Milligan, J. K., & Bigler, R. S. (in press). Addressing race and racism in the classroom. In G. Orfield & E. Frankenburg (Eds.), *Lessons in integration: Realizing the promise of racial diversity in America's schools.* Charlottesville: University of Virginia Press.

Mitchell, B. L. (1992). Does ability grouping do more harm than good? It creates labels that last a lifetime. *On Campus, 11*(6), 6–9.

Mitchell, R. (1992). *Testing and learning: How new approaches to evaluation can improve American schools.* New York: Free Press.

Moll, L. C. (Ed.). (1990). *Vygotsky and education.* New York: Cambridge University Press.

Moses, R. P., & Cobb, C. E., Jr. (2001). *Radical equations.* Boston: Beacon Press.

Mosley, W. (2000). *Workin' on the chain gang: Shaking off the dead hand of history.* New York: Ballantine.

Muse, D. (1997). *The New Press guide to multicultural resources for young readers.* New York: New Press.

National Center for Education Statistics. (2005). *The condition of education 2000–2005*. Retrieved July 29, 2005, from http://nces.ed.gov/programs/coe

National Commission on Excellence in Education. (1983). *A nation at risk*. Washington, D.C.: U.S. Government Printing Office.

National Commission on Teaching and America's Future. (1996). *What matters most: Teaching for America's future*. New York: Author.

National Research Council. (1999). *High stakes: Testing for tracking, promotion, and graduation*. Washington, D.C.: National Academy Press.

National Women's Studies Association. (2005). NWSA mission. Retrieved May 11, 2005, from http://www.nwsa.org/about.html

Newman, F. M., Secada, W. G., & Wehlage. G. G. (1995). *Authentic instruction and assessment: Vision, standards, and scoring guide*. Madison: Wisconsin Center for Education Research, University of Wisconsin–Madison.

Nieto, S. M. (2003). What keeps teachers going? *Educational Leadership*, 60(8), 14–18,

Noddings, N. (1995). Teaching themes of care. *Phi Delta Kappan*, 76(9), 675–679.

Noddings, N. (2005) Caring in education. *The encyclopedia of informal education*. Retrieved August 9, 2005, from http://www.infed.org/biblio/noddings_caring_in_education.htm.

Noguera, P. (2003). *City schools and the American dream: Reclaiming the promise of public education*. New York: Teachers College Press.

Nussbaum, M. C. (1997). *Cultivating humanity*. Cambridge, MA: Harvard University Press.

Oakes, J. (2005). Keeping track (2nd ed.). New Haven, CT: Yale University Press. (Original work published 1985)

Obiakor, F. E., Obi, S. O., & Algozzine, B. (2001). Shifting assessment and intervention paradigms for urban learners. *The Western Journal of Black Studies, 25*(1), 61–71.

Okpala, C. O. (1996). Gender-related differences in classroom interaction. *Journal of Instructional Psychology, 23*(4), 275–285.

Olson, L. (2003). The great divide. *Education Week, 22*(17), 9–18.

Olson, L. (2004, December). NCLB law bestows bounty on test industry. *Education Week, 1*(1), 18–19.

Orfield, G., & Wald, J. (2000). Testing, testing: The high-stakes testing mania hurts poor and minority students the most. Retrieved September 19, 2006 from http://www.thenation.com/doc/20000605/orfield

Organization for Economic Cooperation and Development. (2004). *Principles of corporate governance*. Paris, France: OECD Publications.

Otoya-Knapp, K. (2004). When central city high school students speak: Doing critical inquiry for democracy. *Urban Education, 39*(2), 149–171.

Palmaffy, T. (1998). The gold star state: How Texas jumped to the head of the class in elementary-school achievement. *Policy Review, 88*, 30–38.

Palmer, P. (1998). *The courage to teach*. San Francisco: Jossey-Bass.

Pang, V. O. (1991). Teaching children about social issues: Kidpower. In C. E. Sleeter (Ed.), *Empowerment through multicultural education* (pp. 179–198). Albany: SUNY Press.

Pang, V. O., & Sablan, V. A. (1998). Teacher efficacy. In M. E. Dilworth (Ed.), *Being responsive to cultural differences* (pp. 39–58). Washington, D.C.: Corwin Press.

Parkay, F. (1983). *White teacher, black school: The professional growth of a ghetto teacher*. New York: Praeger.

Parker, W. C. (2003). *Teaching democracy*. New York: Teachers College Press.

Paulson, F., Paulson, L., & Meyer, C. (1991). What makes a portfolio, a portfolio? *Educational Leadership, 48*(5), 60–63.

Phelan, P., Davidson, A. L., & Cao, H. T. (1991). Students' multiple worlds: Negotiating the boundaries of family, peer, and school cultures. *Anthropology and Education Quarterly, 22*(3), 224–250.

Ploski, H. A., & Williams J. (Eds.). (1989). *The Negro almanac: A reference work on the African American* (5th ed.). Detroit: Gale Research.

Popham, J. W. (2002). *Educational mismeasurement: How high-stakes testing can harm children (And what we might do about it)*. Washington, D.C.: National Education Association. Retrieved July 1, 2002 from http://www.new.org/issues/high-stakes/popham.html

Prokosch, M., & Dolan, K. (Eds.). (2001). *Our communities are not for sale!* Boston: United for a Fair Economy.

Pugh, T. (2002, March 21). Study shows minorities get lower-quality health care. *The Monterey County Herald*, A3.

Raider, E., & Coleman, S. (1992). *School change by agreement*. New York: Ellen Raider International.

Robinson, D., & Groves, J. (1999). *Introducing philosophy.* Lanham: MD: National Book Network.

Roderick, M., Jacob, B. A., & Bryk, A. S. (2002). The impact of high-stakes testing in Chicago on student achievement in promotional gate grades. *Educational Evaluation and Policy Analysis, 24*(4), 333–357.

Rogers, C. (1961). *On becoming a person.* Boston: Houghton Mifflin.

Rogers, J., & Oakes, J. (2005). John Dewey speaks to Brown: Research, democratic social movement strategies, and the struggle for education on equal terms. *Teachers College Record, 107*(6), 2178–2203.

Roper-Huilman, B. (1998). Conceptualizing truth in teaching and learning implications of truth seeing for feminist practice. In B. Bar & A. Fergunson (Eds.), *Daring to be good: Essays in feminist ethico-politics.* New York: Routledge.

Rosales, F. A. (1996). *Chicano! History of the Mexican American civil rights movement.* Houston, TX: Arte Publico Press.

Rosenthal, R., & Jacobson, L. (1968). *Pygmalion in the classroom: Teacher expectation and pupils' intellectual development.* New York: Holt, Rinehart & Winston.

Russell, S. T., & Joyner, K. (2001). Adolescent sexual orientation and suicide risk: Evidence from a national study. *American Journal of Public Health, 91*(8), 1276–1281.

Ryan, D. C. (1994). *Authentic assessment.* Westminster, CA: Teacher Created Materials.

Safren, S. A., & Heimberg, R. G. (1999). Depression, hopelessness, suicidality and related factors in sexual minority and heterosexual youth. *Journal of Consulting and Clinical Psychology, 67,* 859–866.

Sall, N., & Mar, H. H. (1999). In the community of a classroom: Inclusive education of a student with deaf-blindness. *Journal of Visual Impairment and Blindness, 93*(4), 197–110.

Schergen, M. J. (2005). Art: An educational link between school and community. In L. Johnson, M. E. Finn, & R. Lewis (Eds.), *Urban education with an attitude* (pp. 79–86). New York: SUNY Press.

Schultz, K. (2003). *Listening: A framework for teaching across differences.* New York: Teachers College Press.

Sears, J. T. (1993). Responding to the sexual diversity of faculty and students: Sexual praxis and the critically reflective administrator. In C. Capper (Ed.), *Educational administration in a pluralistic society* (pp. 110-172). Albany: SUNY Press.

Secada, W. (2003). *Conceptions of equity in the teaching of science.* Retrieved July 6, 2002 from http://www.wcer.wisc.edu/dime/manuscript/secadamanuscriptpsf

Secada, W. G. (1989). Educational equity versus equality of education: An alternative conception. In W. G. Secada, (Ed.), *Equity in education* (pp. 68–88). New York: Falmer Press.

Shade, B. J. R. (1989). *Culture, style and the educative process.* Springfield, IL: Charles Thomas.

Sherman, W. L., & Theobald, P. (2001). Progressive Era rural reform: Creating standard schools in the Midwest. *Journal of Research in Rural Education, 17*(2), 84–91.

Shields, C. B., Bishop, R., & Mazawi, A. E. (2005). *The impact of deficit thinking on education.* New York: Peter Lang.

Shipler, D. K. (1997). *A country of strangers: Blacks and Whites in America.* New York: Alfred A. Knopf.

Shor, I. (1992). *Empowering education: Critical teaching for social change.* Chicago: University of Chicago Press.

Siegel, D. L., Coffey T. J., & Livingston, G. (2001). *The great tween buying machine: Marketing to today's tweens.* Ithaca, NY: Paramount Marketing.

Silberman, C. E. (1970). *Crisis in the classroom: The remaking of American education.* New York: Random House.

Sizer, T. (1992). *Horace's compromise: The dilemma of American high schools.* New York: Houghton Mifflin.

Sklar, H. (1995). *Chaos or community?* Boston: South End Press.

Skrla, L., & Scheurich, J. J. (Eds.). (2003). *Educational equity and accountability: Paradigms, policies, and politics.* New York: RoutledgeFalmer.

Slapin, B., & Seale, D. (1998). *Through Indian eyes: The native experience in books for children.* Los Angeles: American Indian Studies Center, University of California.

Slavin, R. E. (1986). *Using student team learning.* Baltimore: The Johns Hopkins Team Learning Project.

Slavin, R. E. (1995). Cooperative learning and intergroup relations. In J. A. Banks & C. M. Banks (Eds.), *Handbook of research on multicultural education* (pp. 628–634). New York: Macmillan.

Sleeter, C., & Grant, C. (1991). Race, class gender, and disability in current textbooks. In M. W. Apple & L. K. Christian-Smith (Eds.), *The politics of the textbook* (pp. 78–110). New York: Routledge.

Sleeter, C., & Grant, C. (2007). *Making choices for multicultural education* (5th ed.). New York: Wiley.

Sleeter, C. E. (2001). *Culture, difference and power.* New York: Teachers College Press.

Sleeter, C. E. (2005). *Un-standardizing curriculum: Multicultural teaching in the standards-based classroom*. New York: Teachers College Press.

Smith, L. T. (1999). *Decolonizing methodologies*. London: Zed Books.

Smith, T. M., & Rowley, K. J. (2005). Enhancing commitment or tightening control: The function of teacher professional development in an era of accountability. *Educational Policy, 19*(1), 126–154.

Smitherman, G. (1981). What go round come round: King in perspective. *Harvard Educational Review, 51*(1), 40–56.

Spender, D. (1982). *Invisible women*. London: Writers & Readers.

Spindler, G. B. (1982). General introduction. In G. D. Spindler (Ed.), *Doing ethnography of schooling: Educational anthropology in action* (pp. 1–13). New York: Holt, Rinehart, & Winston.

Springboard Schools. (2005). *Tools and resources: Cycle of inquiry*. Retrieved May 9, 2006, from http://www.springboardschools.org/about/index.html

Steele, C. M., & Aronson, J. (1995). Stereotype threat and the intellectual test performance of African Americans. *Journal of Personality and Social Psychology, 69*(5), 797–811.

Stigler, J., Gonzales, P. A., Kawanaka, T., Knoll, S., & Serrano, A. (1999). *The TIMMS videotape classroom study: Methods and findings from an exploratory research project on eighth-grade mathematics instruction in Germany, Japan, and the United States*. Washington, D.C.: National Center for Education Statistics.

Style, E. (1996). *Curriculum as window and mirror. The S.E.E.D. project on inclusive curriculum*. Retrieved November 20, 2003, from http://www.wcwonline.org/seed/curriculum.html

Sunburst Communication. (1994). *Student workshop: Conflict resolution skills*. New York: Houghton Mifflin.

Suzuki, B. H. (1980). *An Asian-American perspective on multicultural education: Implications for practice and policy*. Paper presented at the Second Annual Conference of the National Association for Asian and Pacific American Education, Washington, D.C.

Sweaney, A. L. (2001). Fostering critical thinking: Making learning fun. In F. Stephenson (Ed.), *Extraordinary teachers: The essence of excellent teaching*. Kansas City, MO: Andrews McMeel.

Tatum, B. D. (1997). *Why are all the black kids sitting together in the cafeteria?* New York: HarperCollins.

Tetreault, M. K. T. (1989). Integrating content about women and gender into the curriculum. In J. A. Banks & C. A. M. Banks (Eds.), *Multicultural education: Issues and perspectives* (pp. 124–144). Boston: Allyn & Bacon.

Tettegah, S. (1996). The racial consciousness attitudes of White prospective teachers and their perceptions of the teachability of students from different racial/ethnic backgrounds: Findings from a California study. *Journal of Negro Education, 65*(2), 151–163.

Thomas, J. P. (2000). Influences on mathematics learning and attitudes among African American high school students. *Journal of Negro Education, 69*(3), 165–183.

Thompson, A. (1998). Not the color purple: Black feminist lessons for educational caring. *Harvard Educational Review, 68*(4), 522–554.

Tobin, J. (2000). *"Good guys don't wear hats": Children's talk about the media*. New York: Teachers College Press.

Turner, J. H. (1996). A curriculum dominated by the teaching of history, classics and humanity. In J. H. Turner (Ed.), *Education: An encyclopedia*. New York: Garland.

Tuttle, C. (2005, March 31). Addressing inequality: A Cholla High class uses scientific methods to learn about the social environment they live in. *Tucson Weekly*. Retrieved May 15, 2005 from http://www.tucsonweekly.com/gbase/currents/Content?oid=oid:67205

Tyack, D., & Cuban, L. (1995). *Tinkering toward utopia*. Cambridge, MA: Harvard University Press.

Uribe, V., & Harbeck, K. M. (1991). Addressing the needs of lesbian, gay, and bisexual youth: The origins of PROJECT 10 and school-based intervention. In K. M. Harbeck (Ed.), *Coming out of the classroom closet* (pp. 9–28). New York: Harrington Park Press.

U. S. Bureau of the Census. (2000). *Statistical abstracts of the United States* (120th ed.). Washington, D.C.: U.S. Government Printing Office.

U.S. Bureau of the Census. (2001). Housing and Household Economic Statistics Division. Retrieved July 17, 2002, from http://www.census.gov/hhes/hlthins/hlthin00/hlt00asc.html

U.S. Bureau of the Census. (2005). Current population survey, 2005. *Annual Social & Economic Supplement*. Retrieved April 5, 2006, from http://pubdb3.census.gov

U.S. Bureau of the Census. (2006). Income stable, poverty race increases, percentage of Americans without health insurance unchanged. Retrieved April 5, 2006, from http://www.census.gov/Press-Release

U. S. Department of Education. (1998). *Status of educational equity for girls and women in the nation* (Vol. 2). Washington, D.C.: U. S. Government Printing Office.

U. S. Department of Education. (2000). *Fall 1998 elementary and secondary school civil rights compliance report: Projections.* Washington, D.C.: Office of Civil Rights.

U.S. Department of Education. (2001). *No child left behind.* Retrieved February 14, 2006, from http://www.ed.gov/nclb/landing.jhtml?src=ln

U. S. Department of Health and Human Services. (2001). *Health and heritage.* Indian Health Service. Retrieved October 15, 2003, from http://info.ihs.gov/HeritageHealth.pdf

U.S. Department of Labor. (1998). *Monthly labor review online.* Washington, D.C.: U.S. Government Printing Office.

U.S. Department of Labor. (2002). *Report 960: Highlights of women's earnings in 2001.* Washington, D.C.: U.S. Government Printing Office.

U.S. Department of Labor. (2004). Displaced workers summary. Retrieved June 3, 2005, from http://www.bls.gov/news.release/disp.nr0.htm

U.S. Department of Labor. (2005). Adjustments to household survey population estimates in January 2005. Retrieved March 25, 2005, from http://www.bls.gov/cps/

U. S. General Accounting Offices, Health, Education, and Human Services Division, United States Senate, Moseley-Braun, C., Kennedy, E., Kerry, J., Pell, C., Simon, P., & Wellstone, P. (1996). *School facilities: America's schools report differing conditions.* (No. AO/HEHS-96-103). Washington, D.C.: General Accounting Office.

Valentine, C. A. (1971). Deficit, differences, and bicultural models of Afro-American behavior. *Harvard Educational Review, 41,* 137–157.

Valentine, G. (1997). Ode to a geography teacher: Sexuality and the classroom. *Journal of Geography in Higher Education, 21*(3), 417–424.

Valenzuela, A. (1999). *Subtractive schooling: U.S.-Mexican youth and the politics of caring.* Albany: State University of New York Press.

Van Ausdale, D., & Feagin, J. R. (2001). *The first R: How children learn race and racism.* Lanham, MD: Rowman & Littlefield.

VisionMark. (2005). Students speak out on educational inequalities. Retrieved July 28, 2005, from http://www.visionmark.org/feature.php

Vygotsky, L. S. (1978). *Mind and society.* Cambridge, MA: Harvard University Press.

Wan, G. (2001). The learning experience of Chinese students in American universities: Cross-cultural perspective. *The College Student Journal, 35* (1), 28–44.

Wang, F. (2002). A "textbook solution" to curing our country's education woes: How textbooks and the considerable economic resources of textbook publishers can be used to improve student achievement. Retrieved April 6, 2004, from http://www.educationnews.org

Warren, S. R. (2002). Stories from the classroom: How expectations and efficacy of diverse teachers affect the academic performance of children in poor urban schools. *Educational Horizons, 80*(3), 109–116.

Webster's Dictionary. (1989). *The new lexicon Webster's dictionary of the English language.* New York: Lexicon.

Wharton-McDonald, R., Pressley, M., & Hampston, J. M. (1998). Literacy instruction in nine first-grade classrooms: Teacher characteristics and student achievement. *The Elementary School Journal 99* (2), 101–128.

Wiggins, G., & McTighe, J. (2005). *Understanding by design* (2nd ed.). Alexandria, VA: Association for Supervision and Curriculum Development.

Wirt, J., Choy, S., Gerald, D., Provasnik, S., Rooney, S., Watanabe, S., et al. (2001). *The condition of education: 2001* (No. NCES 2001072). Washington, D.C.: U.S. Department of Education, Institute of Education Sciences, National Center for Education Statistics.

Wiske, M. S. (1998). *Teaching for understanding: Linking research with practice.* San Francisco: Jossey-Bass.

Women on Words and Images. (1975). *Dick and Jane as victims: Sex stereotyping in children's readers.* Princeton, NJ: Women on Words and Images.

Woodruff, P. (2005). *First democracy: The challenge of an ancient idea.* New York: Oxford University Press.

Young, A. A., Jr. (2004). *The minds of marginalized black men.* Princeton, NJ: Princeton University Press.

Young, M. F. D. (1977). An approach to the study of curriculum as socially organized knowledge. In H. M. Kliebard & A. A. Bellack (Eds.), *Curriculum and evaluation* (pp. 274–275). Berkeley, CA: McCutchan.

Zimmerman, J. (2002). *Whose America? Culture wars in the public schools.* Cambridge, MA: Harvard University Press.

Zirkel, P. A. (2003). Bullying: A matter of law? *Phi Delta Kappan, 85*(1), 90–91.

Zollo, P. (1999). *Wise up to teens: Insights into the marketing and advertising to teenagers* (2nd ed.). Ithaca, NY: New YorkNew Strategist Publications.

Index